"Reading and writing at the sentence level is all too often overlooked in today's classrooms. Enter Geraldine Woods' *Sentence*. In addition to providing several strategies for reading closely and writing analytically, Woods also provides literally hundreds of sentences (categorized for thematic unit use) as examples with teaching ideas for immediate classroom use. This book will be one that I reach to again and again for ideas and inspiration."

—**Susan Barber**, AP Literature Teacher and
Consultant, Atlanta, GA

"As we all spend more time online power-browsing and skimming text at warp speed, it's more important than ever that we also slow down and read carefully. *Sentence: A Period-to-Period Guide to Building Better Readers and Writers* is chock full of classroom-ready activities that support teachers as they guide their students in becoming better writers and thinkers. As a writing teacher for over 30 years, I appreciate Woods's diverse set of examples and insightful analysis. Whether you're looking for a way to fill a few minutes at the end of class or build an entire session around one sentence, this book has you covered."

—**Chris Sloan, Ph.D.**, English Department Chair, Judge Memorial
Catholic High School, Salt Lake City, UT

"Geraldine Woods does teachers a great service by offering this book. She not only serves up an instructional guide for how to help students understand the importance of sentence crafting, she also gives numerous practical examples and lesson suggestions. Of particular note is her 'interdisciplinary' section, which should help writing teachers venture beyond their own disciplines to help students realize that a well-wrought sentence is a powerhouse in any field."

—**David G. Miller**, Professor, Department of English and
Philosophy Honors Faculty, Mississippi College

"As a high school English teacher, I'm always looking for new ways to engage students. For years, I've been thinking about the 'big picture' and how my lessons and units can connect to the larger narrative in society. In her engrossing new book, *Sentence.*, Geraldine Woods argues that we should be going small. By focusing on a single sentence, teachers can change the 'lens' through which we view a text and find a new way to reach students. Woods's book provides concrete and engaging examples that any teacher can use tomorrow in their classroom."

—**Kabby Hong**, English Teacher, Verona Area High School

"With clarity her cause and passion her method, Geraldine Woods clarifies the workings of one of our most significant and old-time technologies: the sentence. Her latest offering promises to engage teachers new and old seeking to shape lessons toward close reading and writing. That she curates from vivid contemporary sources will spark the stellar writer in her readers."

—**Edie Meidav**, Novelist and Associate Professor of
English at University of Massachusetts Amherst

"In 'Song of Myself,' Walt Whitman writes: 'I believe a leaf of grass is no less than the journey-work of the stars.' In a related spirit, Geraldine Woods's phenomenal book *Sentence.: A Period-To-Period Guide to Building Better Readers and Writers* encourages students, teachers, readers, and writers to think at the level of the sentence. Rather than beginning with big ideas and then attending to the granular, Woods locates big ideas in the granular. Grammar, rhetoric, philosophy, and history come alive in the alchemy of a string of words. Woods's unique method for teaching literary composition and criticism is flexible enough to accommodate everyone from adults learning to read for the first time to advanced graduate students of literature. And perhaps most important of all, the book makes an implicit case for how an understanding of the sentence 'strengthens students' ability to participate in civic life and elevates the level of public discourse.' In an age of tweets and declining readership, Woods makes a compelling case for the relationship between the sentence and how we speak, write, and listen to one another. Never before has the teaching of grammar, syntax, diction, and the literary imagination felt closer to pure poetry than in this beautifully crafted book!"

—**Andrew McCarron**, Chair of the Religion, Philosophy & Ethics Department at Trinity School in Manhattan, New York, Faculty Associate at
Bard College's Institute of Writing and Thinking, and author of
The Ballad of Sara and Thor: a novella (Station Hill Press, 2017)

SENTENCE.

Norton Books in Education

SENTENCE.

A Period-to-Period
GUIDE TO BUILDING
BETTER READERS AND WRITERS

GERALDINE WOODS

W. W. NORTON & COMPANY

Independent Publishers Since 1923

Note to Readers: Models and/or techniques described in this volume are illustrative or are included for general informational purposes only; neither the publisher nor the author(s) can guarantee the efficacy or appropriateness of any particular recommendation in every circumstance. As of press time, the URLs displayed in this book link or refer to existing sites. The publisher and author are not responsible for any content that appears on third-party websites.

For information about permission to reproduce selections from this book, write to Permissions, W. W. Norton & Company, Inc., 500 Fifth Avenue, New York, NY 10110

For information about special discounts for bulk purchases, please contact W. W. Norton Special Sales at specialsales@wwnorton.com or 800-233-4830

Manufacturing by Sheridan Books
Production manager: Katelyn MacKenzie

Library of Congress Cataloging-in-Publication Data

Names: Woods, Geraldine, author.
Title: Sentence : a period-to-period guide to building better readers and writers / Geraldine Woods.
Description: First edition. | New York, NY : W.W. Norton & Company, 2021. | Series: Norton books in education | Includes bibliographical references and index.
Identifiers: LCCN 2020023934 | ISBN 9780393714814 (paperback) | ISBN 9780393714821 (epub)
Subjects: LCSH: English language—Sentences—Study and teaching (Secondary) | English language—Sentences—Study and teaching (Higher) | English language—Composition and exercises—Study and teaching (Secondary) | English language—Composition and exercises—Study and teaching (Higher)
Classification: LCC PE1441 .W673 2021 | DDC 428.0071—dc23
LC record available at https://lccn.loc.gov/2020023934

W. W. Norton & Company, Inc., 500 Fifth Avenue, New York, N.Y. 10110
www.wwnorton.com

W. W. Norton & Company Ltd., 15 Carlisle Street, London W1D 3BS

1 2 3 4 5 6 7 8 9 0

In honor of teachers, chronically overworked and underfunded, who accomplish the impossible every single day. Because you care, students learn.

CONTENTS

ACKNOWLEDGMENTS

I've learned from colleagues and mentors at every stage of my teaching career, especially Harry Bauld, Catherine Conley, Pilar Enright, Karen Johnson, Deborah Kassel, Sharon Kunde, David Schiller, Wendy Steiner, and Don Yates. I'm fortunate to have an all-star team working with me on this book: Carol Collins, Jamie Vincent, Mariah Eppes, Nancy Palmquist, and Sophia Seidner. And of course, I bow to the creative people on whose sentences my teaching rests.

INTRODUCTION

I WAS NEVER SO GOOD OR SO BAD A TEACHER AS I WAS DURING MY first year on the job. Having no idea what would work, I was willing to try almost anything to get my point across. Like many new teachers, I began each literature or writing class with a Big Idea: most often a universal theme or the implications of an argument. Some days were spectacular; I still remember a student's gasp when she realized what William Golding was saying about human nature in *Lord of the Flies*. I also recall the blank stares in response to my request to write "your own design for an ideal society." Sad fact: most students wrote fewer than ten sentences, all statements like "everyone will be happy."

At some point I had a Big Idea of my own. Instead of leading with a Big Question ("How does the title character in *The Great Gatsby* relate to the American dream?"), I zeroed in on a single sentence from F. Scott Fitzgerald's novel ("There was a small picture of Gatsby, also in yachting costume, on the bureau—Gatsby with his head thrown back defiantly—taken apparently when he was about eighteen"). I discovered that examining those few words in depth led students to ponder the effect of personal appearance on perception, the rewards and pitfalls of ambition, and the significance of socioeconomic class. To my delight, students traveled seamlessly from Little Ideas—one sentence— to Big Ideas. In the process, they saw the synergy that arises when form and content align. I've never abandoned the Big-to-Little approach, because sometimes the material or my goals require it. But I often work in the opposite direction, too.

Sentence. A Period-to-Period Guide to Building Better Readers and Writers presents my most effective Little-to-Big strategies. As I describe in the *Gatsby* example, I start with a significant sentence and expand the discussion to the themes, characters, or purpose of the work as a whole. I also give students sentences from works they haven't read, in which case the "Little" is an element of the sentence's style and the "Big" an exploration of how that element shapes reader reaction.

I've refined this approach over many years of teaching students from the fifth grade through adulthood, with varied skill levels and an array of interests. Rest assured that *Sentence. A Period-to-Period Guide to Building Better Readers and Writers* isn't the straw that will break the back of your already overstuffed curriculum. Nor is it intended as a replacement for what you're doing now. It's a small shift in focus, an occasional change of lens to reach students in a different way.

THE WHY OF TEACHING SENTENCES

This book presents a flexible approach to directing students' attention to language, thereby improving skills useful on standardized tests and in other, more important life situations. Knowing how to write a great sentence gives students the power to express their ideas and to persuade others to accept or at least consider another point of view. Understanding how a great sentence influences their own reactions confers a kind of power also: once students perceive the techniques at work in a sentence, they can look beyond style and evaluate the content more objectively. Plus, I firmly believe that developing writing and close reading skills strengthens students' ability to participate in civic life and elevates the level of public discourse.

An additional benefit of great-sentence study is that it exposes students to artistry, even beauty, in language. All accomplished musicians started by learning scales, but none stay on that level. The study of English must always begin with the basics, but it should never end there. No one ever yearned to curl up with a skill-builder card on a rainy day! Wouldn't it be lovely if students spotted a sentence that led them to a paragraph and then to a novel or an article or a poem or . . . well, to anything fashioned skillfully and creatively from words?

A lesson based on a great sentence has other advantages, too. It eases the anxiety of struggling students: they don't have to absorb, or write, an entire piece. Analyzing or fashioning a single sentence is a much less intimidating task, a nibble instead of a gulp. Mastering a sentence builds students' confidence to take on larger reading and writing assignments. Another advantage: with sentence-based lessons you can nimbly adjust the difficulty level, first matching and then gradually stretching your students' skills.

Great-sentence lessons may also serve as bait for the reluctant reader, the sort who dismembers a book and chucks it in the trash as soon as class discussion of it has concluded. Don't like Jane Austen? Check out a sentence from Red Smith. Or J. K. Rowling. Or Winston Churchill. You see where I'm going with this. By the way, one student really did demolish *Pride and Prejudice*, chapter by chapter, right in front of me. When the class finished Austen's masterpiece, I presented a sentence from Neil Gaiman's *Anansi Boys*. I was thrilled to see him seek out Gaiman's novel and devour it. I couldn't have torn him away from that book if I'd tried, and of course I didn't want to. He'd made his point (he never did appreciate Austen), but I'd also made mine: there's a good book for everyone.

Perhaps the most important advantage of great-sentence lessons is one we educators often don't acknowledge: they're as short as we want them to be. I imagine that your students' lives, not to mention your own, are as pressured as mine. Writing or analyzing a single sentence is much more manageable than a weeks-long project, though you can, if you wish, build a course around great sentences. To be clear: I'm not advocating sentence work as a substitute for full-length reading and writing assignments. Those are indispensable. But on a Friday afternoon or the first morning following vacation, a sentence lesson slides easily into everyone's mind—and the kids actually learn something. And did I mention that the sentences they write and you collect can be read and commented on quickly, and that they work as well online as they do in a physical classroom? A fair number of teachers report that they spend the same amount of time on schoolwork after the school day ends as they do when they're officially on duty. It's no wonder so many of us burn out! Saving a few minutes can also sometimes save a life, in the sense of giving you time to have a personal one.

THE HOW OF TEACHING SENTENCES

Before I go any further, I should say that my teaching rests on two general principles. The first is that writing and close reading are skills that can be taught. People sometimes tell me that I'm "lucky to be a writer," as if writing were an innate quality. It's not. Nor is close reading. I learned both from excellent teachers when I was growing up, and I continue to learn from my colleagues and editors. The second principle is that all students can hone their skills, regardless of their starting point—whether they're learning English or have already demonstrated a high level of competence.

Now to particulars. Here's the great-sentence method in brief:

- Select a great sentence from the work students are reading, from the sentences in Part II of this book, or from any other source.
- Present it to your students with some context, either brief or extensive.
- If necessary, help students decode the sentence.
- Direct their attention to one element of its style—a vivid verb, an unusual structure, an interesting comparison, and the like.
- Discuss what that element of style adds to the sentence.
- In a writing lesson, or as an addition to a reading lesson, have students craft an original sentence modeled on the one you presented.

WHAT'S WHERE

Part I of *Sentence. A Period-to-Period Guide to Building Better Readers and Writers* discusses classroom-tested, general strategies for teaching writing and close reading, as well as methods for related work, such as research or mixed-media projects. One chapter explains how great sentences can serve as the foundation for interdisciplinary study—combining history, science, art, media literacy, or psychology with English. Another chapter addresses timing and explains how to design lessons that fit your goals and schedule.

Part II comprises twenty-five short sections across five chapters. Each section focuses on a different element of style and features sentences that employ that element effectively. In addition to a general guide to teaching the element, there are ready-to-go lesson plans based on two or three sentences in the section, plus seven or eight other sentences with enough information to help you design your own lesson plans.

The grouping of style elements in Part II is somewhat arbitrary, as many overlap and interweave:

- *Structure*: Every sentence has an organizing pattern that influences audience reaction. Sections in this chapter examine effective and unusual structures: crossed, parallel, pocket, reversed, U-turn, lists, and visual presentation.
- *Diction*: Authors carefully select or create words to suit their purpose. Section topics in this chapter include expressive verbs, effective nouns and descriptions, tone, word shifts, and coinage.
- *Sound*: Nothing's more basic to language than sound, even when it's a silent, inner voice. In this chapter are sections on onomatopoeia, rhyme, repetition, and the rhythm created by varied sentence lengths.
- *Connections*: Writers and speakers require readers or listeners. Sections in this chapter consider techniques for connecting with the audience: first- and second-person point of view and strategic placement of questions, rhetorical or otherwise.
- *Comparisons*: The tendency to compare is so strong that it's probably hardwired into human DNA. It's certainly a thread that runs through great writing! This chapter shines a spotlight on sentences that contrast, contradict, and describe. Other sections address negative statements, synesthesia, and time markers.

Each model lesson plan includes:

- an optional activity to introduce the element of style
- "brief context" for the sentence (just enough to help students decode) and "extended context" (for more comprehensive study)
- questions to guide students in analyzing the sentence, sorted into two groups: those that work with "brief context" and those you can add if you've opted for "extended context"
- suggested answers to analysis questions
- a section with additional information—grammatical elements of the sentence and their relationship to content, relevant rhetorical terms, and ideas for activities and research

- At the end of each section are writing prompts to spark your students' imagination.

It might sound like a lot, but think of Part II as a buffet rather than a five-course meal; *Sentence. A Period-to-Period Guide to Building Better Readers and Writers* offers an array of choices so you can select just what your class needs and your schedule permits.

The Appendices speed the planning process with charts that group sentences by theme and genre and identifies sentences that work well with younger or less proficient students.

A note on sources: I've included sentences from varied authors, time periods, and genres. Some sources are staples of English classes: novels, plays, poems, and nonfiction articles or books. Others are less traditional: song lyrics, speeches, films, television shows, and popular sayings. Language is language, wherever it's found, and great sentences can appear in all sorts of places.

So can great teaching. With this book, I hope you'll find support for the crucial job you do. I also hope you perceive the admiration I have for all who undertake this work. As educators, we function in two time periods, giving students what they need now and planting seeds that we hope will grow to robust maturity in the future. Bravo for making that effort, and may it be successful!

PART I

INSTRUCTIONAL OVERVIEW

CHAPTER 1
CLOSE READING

FOR SOME YEARS I VOLUNTEERED AT A LITERACY CENTER, WHERE I was assigned to tutor an adult who'd had little opportunity to attend school while growing up. She could read few words, and those only with difficulty. One aspect of our work together stood out from the very beginning: Once she heard a sentence aloud, she was nearly always able to grasp its nuances. She was a good close reader before she was even a reader.

I mention this because close reading—the examination of such elements as syntax, diction, and figurative language in relation to overall meaning—isn't a practice limited to those who decode easily. Nor is it solely the province of a particular age group. There's no doubt that life experience improves the ability to infer meaning, but all readers bring something to the text, naturally engaging in dialogue with the words on a page or screen. To teach close reading, then, is to build on a foundation already present.

DESIGNING A CLOSE-READING SENTENCE LESSON

How you structure a close-reading sentence lesson depends on your goal. You can look at every noteworthy element of a sentence or concentrate on only one aspect of style. This general design works for either approach.

Denotation

Check that students know the definition of every word in the sentence. You don't have to explain all the words: simply ask whether there are any unfamiliar words and provide definitions as needed. Students may also consult a dictionary (more on dictionaries below). Once the parts are taken care of, move on to the whole: ask students to restate the sentence in their own words.

Connotation

Now things get tricky, because the attitudes and emotions attached to a word—its connotation—are partly cultural and partly individual. To Americans, *scheme* suggests illegality or disobedience; to the British, it's a neutral term for "plan." An artwork reviewed as *edgy* attracts those who connect the word with originality but repels those who associate it with mindless innovation. To check students' understanding of connotation, have them jot down what comes to mind in relation to significant words in the sentence. Expand or correct as needed.

Analysis

Now students become detectives, seeking clues to the ways an author has extended, subverted, or emphasized an idea. Start with the connotation notes they just compiled. Which connotations relate to the sentence? What do they add? Here's an example, based on a sentence from Edwidge Danticat's story "Nineteen Thirty-Seven":

My Madonna cried.

The *Madonna* of this simple statement is a plaster statue of Mary, venerated by Christians as the mother of Jesus. That's all I told my students when I asked them to free-associate about *Madonna*. Students mentioned "mother," "child care," "love," "family," and the pop star of that name. We discarded the singer, who wasn't alive in 1937, the time period of the story.

Next I added more context. *My* refers to the narrator, a girl whose mother has been imprisoned for witchcraft because an ailing child died in her presence. The statue "cries" when bits of wax hidden near the statue's eyes melt. The narrator brings the statue to the jail every time she visits her mother. During their final visit, the mother tells her daughter to keep the Madonna.

I asked students which words from their free association apply to Danticat's sentence. All of them, they replied, grasping immediately that the *Madonna* represents what the dying mother can no longer give her daughter—

love, care, and so forth. With such a loss, it's easy to understand why the narrator says, *My Madonna cried.*

Another analysis technique relies on "alternate reality" questions. In a lesson on diction, for example, ask students to plug in a synonym. What if the statue *shed tears* or *sobbed* instead of *cried*? How would the meaning change? What happens if they delete the word *My*? Suppose your focus is on sentence structure. Does reader reaction change if they rearrange the order of ideas or break a single sentence into two or more? Danticat's sentence is too short for this sort of exercise, but you can easily imagine how much students can learn by manipulating a longer sentence. For figurative language study: what shades of meaning would be lost from the first sentence of William Wordsworth's "Surprised by Joy" if *impatient as the Wind* were replaced by *restless* or *eager*? Answering alternate-reality questions shines a light on the author's choices and their effect on the reader or listener.

As they analyze sentences, students sometimes offer vague answers untethered to the text. In response to another sentence from Danticat's story ("In the prison yard, I held the Madonna tightly against my chest, so close that I could smell my mother's scent on the statue"), a student may remark that the narrator sounds sad. A response like that is a gift-wrapped, teachable moment: "How do you know she's sad? Which words reveal her feelings?" By requiring evidence (in this case, *held . . . tightly, close, smell my mother's scent*), you force students to examine the text carefully—the very definition of close reading and a habit that carries over to full-length works and to other life arenas.

Writing

This part's optional, but in my experience a writing assignment based on a great sentence reinforces what students learn from a close-reading lesson. Practicing a technique clarifies its function—much as teaching it does! I conclude a sentence-reading lesson with writing whenever time permits. (See Chapter 2 for suggestions on crafting writing assignments based on great-sentence study.)

Research

This is another optional activity, but a valuable one that also strengthens reading skills. To build on whatever context you've given for the sentence, ask students to research related topics: the era in which the sentence was written or the work it comes from, its intended audience, and the like. Perhaps most importantly, require that they cite—and evaluate—their sources. Media literacy is a crucial skill, and every research project serves up at least one teachable moment.

Research requires time, so you may opt to assign it for homework with a few days' lead time, with students reporting their findings in a paper or a presentation. Occasionally you may want them to respond to the sentence by expressing its content in a different genre: a painting, dramatic portrayal, or musical interpretation. These, too, are homework tasks that can be shared with the class as you wish.

In Part II of this book, I apply this general close-reading design to specific sentences, providing step-by-step instructions for lessons on various elements of style. You can "plug and play" these lessons or adapt them to match your preferred teaching methods.

THE DICTIONARY ISSUE

Some people love the heft of language on paper. To them, hauling two—or twenty!—pounds of pages devoted to definitions isn't a chore but a badge of honor, the sign of a proud word lover. Others (like me, I admit) happily jettisoned our magnifying glasses when the *Oxford English Dictionary* went online. Many (again, like me) see nothing wrong in permitting students to ask a knowledgeable person for a definition, if such a person is available and if students have no need for extensive information. Whatever your decision on the dictionary issue—and I've attended some education conferences where passions ran so high I feared a fistfight—remember the goal: you want students to know what the sentence means and, if possible, enjoy reading it. While I'm guiding students to close reading, I tend to offer quick answers for denotation and conduct a class discussion of connotation. I ask them to consult a dictionary (either on the internet or on the shelf) when etymology matters or when I want them to work independently. Your class, your choice.

TO CONTEXT OR NOT TO CONTEXT?

With apologies to Hamlet, that is indeed the question. When you're presenting a sentence and not an entire work, how much will your students understand? Quite a lot about most sentences, in my experience, with the bare minimum of context: who's speaking, about what. At times, though, students need a longer explanation in order to grasp the meaning of a sentence. You can supply that information or send them off to find it themselves. The first method is faster but the second builds research skills.

The discussion in the previous section about a sentence from Edwidge Danticat's "Nineteen Thirty-Seven" shows one way to weave both brief and extended context into a sentence lesson. Here are two additional examples, to illustrate how to decide what's needed. Take a look at this sentence:

> So, first of all, let me assert my firm belief that the only thing we have to fear is fear itself—nameless, unreasoning, unjustified terror which paralyzes needed efforts to convert retreat into advance.

This sentence is from President Franklin Delano Roosevelt's first inaugural address, which he gave in 1933. That's all you need to say, because even if your students don't know that the nation was mired in the Great Depression when Roosevelt was elected, they'll likely understand that he was attempting to quell panic. Some points they can glean from this sentence with a brief introduction, or with no introduction at all:

- The core of the sentence—*the only thing we have to fear is fear itself*—defines the problem as emotion arising from the situation, not the situation per se.
- Repeating *fear* and adding *terror* intensifies the emotion.
- *Unreasoning* and *unjustified* imply that this sentence is a plea for logical analysis; the fact that the plea must be made shows that the speaker believes his audience has retreated from rationality.
- This sentence asks for the courage to act, because *terror . . . paralyzes needed efforts*.

- There's optimism in this sentence, because those *efforts* will *convert retreat into advance.*

Of course, with extended context they'll glean more from the sentence and the reasons underpinning Roosevelt's choice of words. If they know, for example, that the fear of bank failure actually led to bank failure, they'll understand why Roosevelt said *fear* twice and then escalated to *terror.* Nevertheless, you can present the sentence with minimal context and expect a fairly accurate analysis.

Not so with this sentence:

A boy enters.

Decoding isn't a problem, but what on earth can students get from these three words without additional information? Nothing! But everything changes when they learn that this sentence comes from a play in which characters narrate their own stage directions. The audience hears "A boy enters" as an actor steps on stage in full combat gear. The play, *Elliot, A Soldier's Fugue* by Quiara Alegría Hudes, describes the experiences of three generations of one military family. Grandpop, the character who says this line, served in the Korean War. With perspective attained over the years, he understands that when he marched off to battle he was really just *a boy.* His grandson is only eighteen when he enlists. His entry line is "A man enters," reflecting the tendency of inexperienced soldiers to idealize war as a rite of passage and of eighteen-year-olds to see themselves as adults. With that context, students immediately grasp the irony the playwright intends.

Back to the main question: to context or not, and how much? In most cases, one sentence is enough of an introduction, but additional context never fails to deepen students' understanding of content and appreciation of style. In every model lesson plan (and there are two or three for every section in Part II), I provide both brief and extended context, pegging some questions to the first approach and providing others that you can add if you've opted for extended context. As always, select what meets your needs.

One last comment about context: traditionally, educators have untangled the threads of knowledge to isolate the one corresponding to their area of interest. In the real world, though, knowledge is a seamless cloth, interdisciplinary by nature. If your curriculum and the authorities in charge of it allow a history/English study (just to name one combination), your students will benefit from the expanded perspective.

HOW CLOSE IS TOO CLOSE?

One issue arising from close reading is what I call the eye-roll objection: "Aren't you reading too much into it?" I must confess that the answer, sometimes, is yes. By definition, close reading *is* reading into the sentence, and it's possible to go too far. That's exactly where I've traveled at times, such as when a visiting poet told my class that the detail we'd been minutely examining was nothing more than a typo. In the sample sentences and lesson plans of Part II, you'll see my interpretation of the significance of various elements of a sentence. Skip the ones that make *your* eyes roll, and use what you deem justified. And if your students hit you with "you're stretching it," ask them to defend that judgment. Both they and you may learn something from the ensuing discussion.

CHAPTER 2
WRITING

WRITING SENTENCES: WHAT COULD BE MORE BASIC—TO EXPRESSION and to an English class? I've devoted more hours than I can count to teaching every aspect of sentence writing, so I know it's a challenge to help students grasp even the basics of standard English. Consider, for example, the traditional rule that a sentence must express a complete thought. It's tough to explain the concept of completeness to students who think *ttyl* (text language for "talk to you later") is all they have to write.

Hard though the work may be, I don't recommend that you skip the basic elements of sentence writing: the conventions of punctuation, grammar, and so forth. Nor do I think you should stop at the sentence level; every student must know how to write a full-length piece. I do, however, recommend that you occasionally employ great-sentence lessons to strengthen the writing skills you're already working on with the class.

Suppose you're examining powerful verbs. Present a sentence like this one from Robert Caro's biography of Lyndon Johnson, *The Passage of Power*, in which he describes how Johnson reacted when he learned of efforts to overturn legislation he supported:

> "I hope that [bill] gets *murdered*," he snarled, and, sitting in the Oval Office, he kept telephoning senator after senator, cajoling, bullying, threatening, charming, long after he had the majority, to make the vote overwhelming enough to ensure the lesson was clear.

The verb forms Caro employs—*murdered, snarled, cajoling, bullying, threatening, charming*—paint a vivid picture of anger, pride, and ruthless determination. How much better they are then *tried to persuade*! Once they've looked at Caro's sentence, ask students to select vivid verbs to incorporate into a sentence of their own.

Another example: Let's say your focus is on tone. Have them read a sentence from J. D. Salinger's *The Catcher in the Rye*, such as this one:

> If you really want to hear about it, the first thing you'll probably want to know is where I was born, and what my lousy childhood was like, and how my parents were occupied and all before they had me, and all that David Copperfield kind of crap, but I don't feel like going into it, if you want to know the truth.

Or this sentence from Shirley Jackson's short story "The Lottery":

> The people of the village began to gather in the square, between the post office and the bank, around ten o'clock; in some towns there were so many people that the lottery took two days and had to be started on June 26th, but in this village, where there were only about three hundred people, the whole lottery took less than two hours, so it could begin at ten o'clock in the morning and still be through in time to allow the villagers to get home for noon dinner.

What tone do they detect in Holden Caulfield's first-person narrative or in Jackson's dry, third-person account? Have them determine which words in the text create that tone. They might mention *lousy* and *crap* in the Salinger sentence, or the defiance and fear of rejection in *If you really want to hear about it*. In Jackson's sentence, they may cite neutral words such as *gather*, everyday details such as location (*between the post office and the bank*), time (*ten o'clock in the morning*), and a sense of normalcy (*through in time . . . for noon dinner*).

Now ask them to write a sentence from a rebel or one from a detached observer. As they read their sentences, have other students identify the words or expressions that create the desired tone. Also note any expressions that break the tone.

These lessons are examples of modeling. They can be challenging, because in a single sentence there's no room to ramble. But they can also encourage reluctant or anxious students: how hard can one sentence be? The key point is that students learn much from master writers by attempting to employ those writers' techniques. Imitation leads to appreciation, which builds to incorporation of the techniques they've practiced, which facilitates the formation of their own unique style.

That last point *is* the point of modeling lessons. No one but J. D. Salinger could be J. D. Salinger, and why would anyone else want to be? I often ask students what they like and what they hate in an array of sentences. I don't challenge their taste, but I do ask them to explain their choices. The results can be surprising. For example, I nearly always have a couple of students whose writing is sprinkled with obscure words they've memorized for the SAT exam. While reading *Great Expectations,* these students frequently declare that Charles Dickens's style is "too fancy" and would be better "in plain words." My response is to suggest that they select one sentence from an old paper and "de-Dickens" it. "Why not write what you'd like to read?" I ask. Little by little, in subsequent assignments, their prose becomes more natural, their "fancy" words fewer but more effective. This approach also works in the opposite direction. I encourage students who love Li-Young Lee's figurative language to select a single sentence from a paper ready for submission and replace an adjective with a metaphor or simile. A "delicious" salad may acquire the taste of "the sun shining on the first day of spring break" or something equally vivid.

Some tips on structuring a modeling assignment:

• *Focused tasks are easier than general assignments.* You probably noticed that my instructions to students tend to be very specific. There's a good reason for that approach. If I say, "Write a sentence like the one you just read," a fair number of students will sit there, perplexed. One tactic that's worked well for me is to underline something in the original and ask students to create a sentence with a similar feature. Here's an example based on a sentence from Renée Watson's short story "Half a Moon":

The dining hall is a symphony of <u>mouths</u> chewing, <u>mouths</u> talking, <u>mouths</u> laughing, <u>mouths</u> yelling across the room.

You can, if you wish, discuss the effect of Watson's repetition, which reduces people to body parts and shows how overwhelmed the narrator feels. But that analysis isn't necessary. Instead, you can simply ask for a sentence ending with a chain of repeated and parallel elements. A typical student's response might resemble this:

> **Swim practice is torture by free-style laps, butterfly laps, backstroke laps, sidestroke laps.**

A swimming coach would not be pleased with this sentence, but an English teacher would.

- *Share the results.* If you can spare the time, read some student sentences aloud in class. You can also copy and distribute the sentences or post them on the class website or a shared document. By examining others' responses, students see how others' choices affect audience reaction. They also pick up techniques to incorporate into their own writing. Plus, you're more likely to get their best efforts if they know their friends will read their sentences.

I must insert a note of caution here. Kids can be cruel, and their sentences may contain coded messages that sail over adult heads. Forestall bad behavior by establishing guidelines for a respectful atmosphere before you share any writing. I find it helpful to ask my students how they want their work to be discussed. Starting from that point, it's easy to arrive at a general rule that everyone deserves respect and honesty. You can't stop there, unfortunately, because once you establish a limit, someone will feel the need to test it. That's just human nature! Resolve to ask about anything your students have written or said that you don't understand. Pose the question immediately, in public, or privately after class. Investigate every smirk, and don't let infractions slide. Check your school's policy on bullying to see what resources are available to help you through any potentially difficult situation.

- *Ask why.* What was the rationale for writing this or that or whatever? Answering such a question sometimes pries students away from old habits, their "automatic pilot" writing mode. This question also moves them toward an understanding of the writing process as a series of conscious choices.

- *Let them play.* Nothing bottles up creativity as quickly as a calculating mind busily averaging a course grade. Instead of placing a number or a letter on a sentence, make a comment about it. If you must give a grade, ask for revision and evaluate whether the second attempt shows improvement.

- *Revise, sometimes.* No one produces a masterpiece on the first try. In fact, trying to do so is close to a guarantee of failure. Don't insist on revision for every modeling assignment, but do request it from time to time. I like to send students back to something they wrote weeks before. The literal meaning of "revision" is "to see again," and fresh eyes help. Plus, revising one sentence sometimes results in their seeing the entire piece in a new way. They may detect a pattern (too wordy or repetitive, too short or vague). When they begin a new piece of writing, they can be alert to their default pattern and improve their style by applying what they've learned.

- *Stress process.* It may be a cliché, but it's true: to produce a good result, writers must engage in a process. One more advantage of great-sentence work comes in here, because each step—gathering ideas, writing a sentence, revising it—is short and manageable.

Though modeling is my go-to writing assignment based on great sentences, it's not the only one. In every chapter of Part II, I offer suggestions for other exercises geared to the element of style the section explores. Most call for a single-sentence response, but I also include prompts for longer works.

A word about comments: It's hard to swim in a sea of red ink, and if you mention every aspect of a sentence that needs improvement, students may give up and drown. Instead, suggest improvements only for the element they're practicing or zero in on one spot, even a single word, that's especially apt. Explain why it works. Then ask the writer to revise a different sentence, employing the same technique you praised.

CHAPTER 3
GRAMMAR AND RHETORIC

WHETHER YOU'RE USING GREAT SENTENCES AS THE BASIS FOR A writing or close-reading lesson—or both—the question of grammar arises, swiftly followed by the issue of rhetoric. Grammar first: many of the great sentences I include in this book—or that students find in their own reading—break traditional grammar rules. As someone who's written a number of books about those rules, any infraction should horrify me, right? Wrong.

Let me backtrack for a moment. I firmly believe that we must teach our students the conventions of Standard English and demand that they adhere to those conventions in formal writing. Not to do so is to limit their employment and academic opportunities; a resume declaring that the applicant took a course because of "it's strong curriculum" will not open the door to a good job or advanced study. Granted, linking Standard English to learning and earning potential isn't fair, but it is the way the world works.

That said, students should know not only how to conform to the rules but also when to break them. Great writers shake things up for a reason, consciously or not. Student writers need to understand that in some circumstances they also can deviate from the rules they've learned. In practice, this means that breaking the conventions of Standard English should have a purpose and, in the case of student writers, one that they can identify. Perhaps they've written a sentence fragment as a punch line emphasizing a point. Maybe they've strung a series of fragments together because they're discussing an incomplete process or describing a disorganized character. The goal is to align form and content, even if writers break a few rules along the way.

While I'm on the subject of rules and standards, I should talk about how to talk about them—during both writing and close-reading lessons. When

I was in elementary school, my teachers ensured that I could distinguish a *predicate nominative* from a *predicate adjective* and identify a *copulative verb*. By the time I was in high school, my teachers spoke about *subject complements* (a term comprising both *predicate nominatives* and *predicate adjectives*) and *linking verbs* (née *copulatives*). The grammar hadn't changed, but the terminology had. Perhaps that's one reason why I tend to shy away from the technical language of grammar now that I'm on the other side of the desk.

Don't misunderstand: I have great respect for those who study and label units of expression. To my mind, they've built a beautiful intellectual house that I love to visit. However, any house constructed from specialized terminology shelters those who understand the vocabulary and leaves everyone else out in the cold. Grammar terms are useful when they're the simplest way to explain why or how something is expressed.

It's surprisingly easy to discuss grammar without the "Naming of Parts." The words in quotation marks, by the way, are the title of a poem by Henry Reed that contrasts the technical terms for weaponry with the simple pleasures of everyday life that a soldier must forgo. That's not a bad metaphor for sentence lessons that rely heavily on grammatical terminology, because in my experience the "naming of parts" is a surefire way to drain enthusiasm from the class and life from great writing.

A grammar-less grammar lesson begins with decoding. What does the sentence say? Which words form each unit of thought? Are all the ideas equally important? If not, where does each rank? Can any portion of the sentence be deleted without changing the main idea? These questions arise from meaning, which, after all, is why people read and write.

Here's an imaginary exchange between a teacher and some students. I've lumped into one slot comments that would typically come from several different students. I've also left out remarks that take the class off topic; as every teacher knows, in this respect the exchange is somewhat implausible. However, this imagined class discussion accurately reflects the content of many conversations I've had with my students. The sentence is from Samuel Beckett's novel *Murphy*.

Sentence:

The sun shone, having no alternative, on the nothing new.

Class Discussion:

TEACHER: Are there any unfamiliar words here?

STUDENTS: *Alternative.*

TEACHER: An *alternative* is "another choice." Okay, now tell me what Beckett is saying in this sentence.

STUDENTS: It was sunny. The sun came up. It was daytime.

TEACHER: Which words tell you that?

STUDENTS: *The sun shone.*

TEACHER: Okay, you know *the sun shone.* Why say that?

STUDENTS: To tell you that's it's daytime. It's dawn. No, it could be any time of day. It doesn't say that "the sun came up." It says that *the sun shone.*

TEACHER: What else does the sentence say?

STUDENTS: Nothing was going on. It was a typical boring day. There was nothing special happening.

TEACHER: Which words give you that idea?

STUDENTS: There was *nothing new.* It says *on the nothing new.*

TEACHER: Why *the nothing* instead of just *nothing?* Does *the* change the meaning?

STUDENTS: *The* makes it special. You're not looking at *nothing.* You're looking at *the nothing.* It sounds like a thing. A big thing! Something you could see. Maybe it's the world. There isn't anything new in the world.

TEACHER: Think about those two ideas: that *the sun shone* and that it shone on *the nothing new.* How do they relate to each other?

STUDENTS: The sun has to come up. But it doesn't have to shine! It could be cloudy. Yes, but on a cloudy day, the sun is still shining. You just can't see it through the clouds. Even in bad weather, you have daytime because the sun comes up. So that's *nothing new.*

TEACHER: Any other ideas in the sentence? What words have we skipped?

STUDENTS: *Having no alternative.* That means there isn't any choice. It has to happen. So the sun has to shine and that's *nothing new* because it can't do anything else.

TEACHER: Which idea do you think is most important?
STUDENTS: That the sun came up. No, that's not important. That's just how nature works. How nature works is important!

TEACHER: So the first thing in this sentence is the most important?
STUDENTS: Maybe the real idea here is that life just keeps going the way it always does. Like the sun, it's natural. There's *nothing new.*

TEACHER: That's the order of ideas in the sentence. If you shifted the sentence around a little, saying that "there was nothing new and the sun shone," would you get the same impression?
STUDENTS: Not really. Now it sounds like a weather report. It sounds like a boring day. A boring life!

TEACHER: So what meaning or impression does Beckett want you to walk away with?
STUDENTS: Days keep coming, the sun keeps shining, nothing is new, but it keeps on happening.

TEACHER: Can you take any words out and still have the same meaning?
STUDENTS: You could probably skip *having no alternative* because *the nothing new* gets that idea in.

TEACHER: Why do you think he put those words into the sentence?
STUDENTS: Saying the same idea twice hammers it into your head. It emphasizes that you have no choice.

TEACHER: How is *having no alternative* different from the rest of the sentence?
STUDENTS: There are commas around it.

TEACHER: So Beckett makes sure that it stands out. Why?
STUDENTS: Because you can take it out. Because it says the same thing. He says it twice, so you know he's emphasizing the point.

I could continue, but you see the direction. The meaning comes first. The teacher pushes everyone away from generalizations and into the specific words in the text. No labels required! If you want them to learn a rule or a grammar term, you can introduce it *after* they've already identified the concept. For example, in the last exchange about *having no alternative*, you could note that nonessential information is often surrounded by commas, which they can imagine as little handles that lift words out of the sentence. You can reinforce that principle organically, whenever a nonessential phrase or clause appears in their reading or writing.

One last comment on the specialized language of grammar: If you like those terms and want your students to appreciate them also, go right ahead. In the sample lessons in Part II, I include and define them, so you can employ grammar terminology whenever you wish.

RHETORIC, TOO

Not only grammar, but rhetoric, too, has its own set of specialized labels. As with grammar, the way my teachers spoke about rhetorical devices changed as I grew. My ninth-grade teacher, for instance, called attention to the *repetition* and *wordplay* in this exchange between Viola and the Clown in *Twelfth Night*:

> **Viola: . . . dost thou live by thy tabour?**
> **Clown: No, sir, I live by the church.**

In college, the professor cited the lines as an example of *antanaclasis*, repeating a word but shifting its meaning, in this case from "earn a wage" to "reside." I didn't need technical terms to understand the comedy, but discussing the lines helped me see Shakespeare's real point: Viola, a noblewoman disguised as a man, questions the Clown's place in the social hierarchy; the Clown answers with location—a signal that rank doesn't matter to him.

Giving names to the interplay between form and content is fine, though not strictly necessary, in my view. (For those who enjoy rhetorical terminology, I provide labels and explanations in the chapters of Part II.) I do acknowledge one benefit of such terms: the link they forge between us and the distant past. Students often tell their elders that "everything is different now." Isn't it wonderful to show them that language has been important in every era and to every society? The techniques of persuasive writing have a long history.

Another point: The *Oxford English Dictionary* defines *rhetoric* as "the art of using language effectively so as to persuade or influence others." That's a fairly neutral statement. However, type *rhetoric* into a search engine, and auto-fill suggests "empty rhetoric" or, more disturbingly, "bombast" and "hot air." Somehow we've come to expect that those who use language skillfully have nothing to say. I can only imagine the reaction of the ancient Greeks, who considered mastery of rhetoric an essential aspect of education, to this development. Perhaps that's another reason to teach students the proper terminology: they'll see that rhetoric doesn't have to be empty and that persuasive speech and writing can be used to effect real change.

CHAPTER 4
INTERDISCIPLINARY STUDY

IT'S NO SECRET THAT MY FAVORITE SUBJECT IS ENGLISH, BUT EVEN people who walk around in a cloud of words must acknowledge that the real world exists. Sentences come with context: they're products of a specific time, place, and author. Digging into the circumstances that shape an author's viewpoint not only helps students appreciate the sentence they're reading but also pushes them to understand how personal experiences and common assumptions of the era infiltrate content. A logical extension of this point, which they may not grasp for years, is that they too are influenced by events and assumptions, consciously or not. Also, however different their creations, performances, or findings may appear, the same impulse gives rise to visual arts, music, and scientific inquiry. Guiding students to see these connections reunites what educators have artificially divided into distinct disciplines.

I should note that interdisciplinary study does not necessarily extend the time you devote to a sentence. One minute of commentary may be all that's needed, or you may want to make the sentence the core of an extended study. Either way, interdisciplinary study is well suited to the virtual classroom many of us must teach in these days, as so much research takes place online. Of course, students may turn to traditional, paper-and-ink sources, too. In every way, great-sentence work is flexible.

I've taught interdisciplinary units alone, and I've also partnered with colleagues. It's fun—both for me and for my students—to peer through a different lens and see how a great sentence relates to history, the arts, psychology, science, and other subjects. Below are several pairings, with suggestions for teaching approaches and assignments.

NOTE: All the lessons can easily be adapted to focus on writing or reading.

HISTORY

There's been much debate about the merits of the New Criticism versus Reader-Response approach to a text: the former viewing the work as having a self-contained identity and the latter emphasizing the reader's role in constructing meaning. To my mind, the text matters, but so do the time, place, and person it comes from, as well as the knowledge and experience of those who read it. With this in mind, English and history are a natural match for interdisciplinary study. You can start students off with information about the beliefs or important events of the era in which the sentence was written. You can also ask them to cite equivalent issues or events of the current day.

Questions for a history/English lesson may include any of the following:

- Who is the author?
- What work does the sentence come from?
- When was it written?
- Who was the intended audience?
- What was the author's goal?
- What was the reaction to the work?
- What events, if any, does the sentence allude to?
- Does the style of the sentence relate to any aspect of history?
- Does the sentence relate to any current issues or events?

Take a look at these questions applied to this famous sentence:

> **Ask not what your country can do for you; ask what you can do for your country.**

Some answers: this sentence is from John F. Kennedy's 1961 inaugural address, broadcast around the world to great acclaim. Like every such speech, the goal was to set the tone for the new administration. There are many allusions to contemporary events in Kennedy's speech (the Cold War and nuclear disarmament, for example), but they don't appear in this sentence.

Now, style: Kennedy's sentence resembles an X in structure. Its two arms employ the same words, arranged to signal opposing directions. (In rhetorical terms, it's an example of *chiasmus*.) The content mirrors the structure by presenting opposing views of the role of government, two paths that lead to different outcomes.

Furthermore, the sentence structure matches the opposing platforms of Democrats and Republicans during the 1960 presidential race. Kennedy urged activism, while Nixon stressed continuity. The sentence lends itself to an extended English/history project relating syntax to politics as well as to other arenas of change: the increasing intensity of the civil rights movement and the coming of age of the baby-boom generation, to name just two. Moving on to the last questions: the proper role of government is debated as much now as it was in 1961. We stand at a crossroads in relation to many issues, just as the nation did on Kennedy's inauguration day.

If you're concentrating on writing, have students fashion a sentence with Kennedy's X structure or report their research in a paper or online presentation about one of today's "crossroad" issues. Have them compare their creations with Kennedy's sentence or with the entire inaugural address.

THE ARTS

As anyone who's been to Bloomsbury or Brooklyn knows, creative people tend to hang out together, perhaps because music, the visual arts, and writing feed off each other in unpredictable ways. Nurture your students by consciously entwining other arts with language arts:

• Compare the sentence you're discussing to a work in a different artistic genre. Consider all possibilities—painting, sculpture, photography, music, theater, film, architecture, and so on—and select something that reflects an element of the sentence's style. For example, "Only connect" is a minimalist sentence from E. M. Forster's novel *Howards End*. It suggests far more than it states. Have students look for similarities between Forster's sentence and the sleek arc of Constantin Brancusi's sculpture *Bird in Space*.

• Select several works from different genres, all created in the same era, and discuss them in relation to a great sentence. Along with a sentence from a Harlem Renaissance work, for example, you might show students a painting by Aaron Douglas or a photo by James Van Der Zee. Then, students can listen to one of Eubie Blake's or Ethel Waters's songs. What common themes do they notice? Any similar techniques? How are those themes and/or techniques reflected in the sentence?

• Present a sentence and ask students to interpret it in another artistic medium. For example, they might paint or photograph a scene inspired by this sentence from Anita Brookner's *Hotel du Lac*:

> **An autumn sun, soft as honey, gilded the lake; tiny waves whispered onto the shore; a white steamer passed noiselessly off in the direction of Ouchy; and at her feet, on the sandy path, she saw the green hedgehog shape of a chestnut, split open to reveal the brown gleam of its fruit.**

NOTE: Prepare for giggles when they see the word *Ouchy*, which isn't a response to a boo-boo but rather a resort on Lake Geneva in Switzerland.

• Take the cross-medium interpretation in the opposite direction. Show a work of visual art or a film clip. Play a song or distribute an advertisement or a meme. If they find a great sentence in the work, they can analyze it. Alternatively, they can search for a sentence that matches the style seen in the other medium.

• Pair a painting with a sentence from a poem describing it (Breughel's painting *Landscape with the Fall of Icarus* and W. H. Auden's "Musée des Beaux-Arts," perhaps). Which conveys the idea more forcefully? Does the response of a viewer differ from that of a reader or listener?

• Show a photo or a few seconds from a film. Ask students to write a sentence that captures a detail highlighted in the visual medium. Can they find a great sentence in something they're currently reading that captures detail in the same way?

PSYCHOLOGY

In my experience students are far too willing to put an author or character on the couch, examining and diagnosing all sorts of psychological conditions on the flimsiest of evidence. That said, considering the psychological element of some sentences can be valuable, if only because you can teach your students the limits of their interpretative skills. A few suggestions:

• Have students read a first-person sentence. What can they deduce about the narrator's personality or mood? For example, you might give them this sentence from Mark Haddon's *The Curious Incident of the Dog in the Night-Time*:

> **I know all the countries of the world and their capital cities and every prime number up to 7,057.**

What are their impressions of Christopher, who says this to introduce himself? Can they write an original sentence that fits what they've perceived in Christopher's character?

NOTE: Haddon never names Christopher's condition, but experts have noted that the character has some qualities associated with autism.

• Developmental psychology is a good fit for other sentences, such as this one about being fifteen from Amy Silverberg's "Suburbia!":

> **The age is a diving board, a box half-opened.**

How accurate is that description? Students can answer from their own experience (or speculation), but you can also have them do some research to support their beliefs. A multitude of scientists have investigated the adolescent mind, perhaps because that age group can be so perplexing. In a writing-focused lesson, ask students to sum up a stage of growth with their own sentences.

• Select a sentence that describes motivation, such as this one from Kekla Magoon's story "Out of the Silence," which describes classmates when one of their number has been killed in a car accident:

> **To be close to her, to be one of the dear friends feeling the pain most deeply, that was a coveted position.**

What psychological state does the sentence embody? How universal is the impulse described? Can the students capture another reaction to an event, either joyful or tragic, in a sentence of their own?

MEDIA LITERACY

Bombarded by information from more media—and types of media—than ever before, students need a way to sort the wheat from the chaff. Investigating and evaluating sources is a long-range project, and it should be part of every extended research assignment. Even on the sentence level, though, much can be taught. A few suggestions:

• Note the diction. What do the words an author has chosen tell you about the author's point of view and possible bias? Here's an example, based on a *New York Times* article by John Leland on the "oldest old" in which he discusses society's attitude toward mortal illness:

> **Instead, there is language suited to war: the *battle* against illness or *refusal to quit*, the *heroic struggle* whose linguistic alternative is failure or giving up.** (italics appear in the original)

Just before this sentence the author notes that no one has trouble being eloquent after a loved one has died, but the period prior to death is trickier. What does the author accomplish by presenting *failure* as an alternative to *battle*? What does the author believe is the superior attitude? How do you know?

• Examine a sentence that quotes a source. How is the source identified? Does a quotation seem more trustworthy than a paraphrased statement?

Here's an example from Dashka Slater's article "How to Get Out of Prison," which focuses on the parole hearing of James Morgan, who was incarcerated for twenty-two years:

> "That boardroom," says Lawrence Strauss, the state-appointed lawyer who represented Morgan at his hearing, "is a house of pain."

Does knowing that Lawrence Strauss advocates for a potential parolee affect readers' reaction to his statement? Whose pain is he talking about when he says the parole *boardroom is a house of pain*? Does his identity give the statement more credibility, or less?

• Analyze the effect of audio and visual context in multimedia platforms. First, ask students to read the sentence and jot down some reactions. Then play an audio version of the same sentence. Do their reactions change? Alternative: divide the class in half. Some read; others listen. Have them compare notes. Similarly, present a sentence alone and then with its visual context, perhaps in a film. Any reaction changes?

• You can follow up on these interpretive lessons with media assignments: have them select a great, or at least a good, sentence from an internet site or a broadcast show. (You may have to explain to parents that watching television or surfing the internet is, in fact, homework. I guarantee the kids will be delighted.) Have students note the context and analyze its effect on the sentence. Encourage skepticism, but not knee-jerk doubt. One leads to informed citizenry, the other to paranoia.

• Have students track the changes over time in one or more sentences on the same topic. Ask them to look at vocabulary (when global warming gave way to climate change, for example). Or, have them consider the relative importance of a person or idea within the sentence or as part of an extended research project. An example of this last task: my students were working on a research project based on a sentence from "Oh Freedom," a protest song recorded by many folk singers and an anthem of the modern civil rights movement. I showed them a video clip of Joan Baez singing "Oh Freedom" during the 1963 March on Washington. Students who typed her name into their internet browsers found that the links on the first two or three screens tended to identify Baez as a former girlfriend of Bob Dylan. Only when they read newspaper articles from 1963 did they discover that Baez was not only a star in her own right but also a tireless activist. The study of that sentence yielded insight into the way perspective can shift over time. They learned a little about sexism, too.

SCIENCE

Great sentences abound in science, as they do in every discipline. Interweaving science and language arts builds students' powers of observation and their ability to render complex ideas clearly. Some suggestions for interdisciplinary lessons:

• Metaphors and other forms of creative comparisons are especially plentiful in science writing, such as this sentence describing the human biome from "The Teeming Metropolis of You" by Brendan Buhler:

Think of your body as a big city apartment building.

Buhler goes on to say that most of the normal biota are good "tenants" who "keep up the maintenance, take out the trash, and pay their rent." As valuable residents, he writes, the normal biota promote "healthy tissue growth" and aid digestion. With Buhler's work as a model, assign a scientific concept and ask students to create a metaphor or simile to express it. Or, ask them to look in science publications for well-written comparisons.

• Sentence structure may also emphasize scientific concepts. Here's another sentence from Buhler's article:

Viewed from the perspective of most of its inhabitants, your body is not so much the temple and vessel of the human soul as it is a complex ambulatory feeding mechanism for a methane reactor in your small intestine.

By beginning the sentence with a reference to microbes, which are *most of* [the body's] *inhabitants*, and reporting from their *perspective*, Buhler elevates the importance of the biome. How would the effect of this sentence change if Buhler had begun with *your body is a complex ambulatory feeding mechanism*?

• Science/language arts sentence lessons can also stress the importance of detail. In this sentence from *Underground* by Will Hunt, the author describes a site far below the surface of the earth:

> **Moe pointed out that we were in a place that had been perfectly dark and exactly 57 degrees Fahrenheit since it was created, a space untouched by all natural rhythms.**

Ask students to substitute general expressions for the specifics Hunt provides ("cold" instead of *57 degrees*, for example). Would the rewritten sentence be as effective?

• Sources are particularly important in science writing. After they read a sentence that quotes an expert, have students check the credentials not only of the expert but also of the sentence writer. Discuss how to assess their reliability.

• A good writing assignment, best given after they've analyzed the techniques employed in a few great science sentences, is to have students select a poorly written sentence from their science textbook and rewrite it. (Apologies to any science writers now reading this book. I'm sure no mediocre sentences appear in your work!)

For all interdisciplinary units, consider assigning student presentations. Yes, they can be time-consuming, but no one ever understands the material as well as the person who must explain it to others. This we know as teachers! Students can present what they've learned to their history, science, arts, or other classes, improving their own knowledge as well as that of their peers.

CHAPTER 5

TIMING

LAST PERIOD OF THE DAY, WHEN THEY'RE ANTSY. FIFTEEN MINUTES before lunch, when they're hungry. Fifteen minutes *after* lunch, when they're sleepy. I could go on—and so could you—listing cracks in the teaching day that need to be spackled. They aren't ideal moments to introduce a major concept, but you can't afford to waste a minute, not least because if you don't do something to engage students' attention when a crack opens, you'll lose them. And your mind.

Great-sentence study is the perfect activity for odd spaces in the school day. With the right sentence, you can pique students' curiosity and also achieve a pedagogical goal: honing a reading skill or demonstrating a technique students can employ in their own writing.

Further, sentence study easily stretches and contracts to fit the amount of time available. Spend five or ten minutes to convey one point, a full period to explain the intricacy of the author's syntax, or a week to explore varied sentence length. The subject matter can be one sentence or several. You can compare the effects of a single technique in the work of various authors or genres. Alternatively, you can show how several elements of writing (tone and point of view, for example) create synergy. Possibilities abound, and learning does, too.

In this section I suggest a few designs for short, medium, and long sentence-lessons. Take a cue from Goldilocks and look for the one that is "just right" for your needs. A word about time estimates: You know your class, and I don't. If you have a bunch of hand wavers eager to share their thoughts or, conversely, a shy group that must be coaxed into a discussion, add a few minutes to my time range.

THE MINI (5–10 MINUTES)

I often tuck mini-lessons into the "cracks" I mentioned at the beginning of this chapter, but my favorite ploy is to use them as settlers. Before each class I put a sentence on the board or screen. If I'm teaching virtually, I situate the sentence so that it's the first thing the students see when they log on. I pose one question about the sentence and, if necessary, I include a short note explaining the context. I may be specific ("Why *shattered* instead of *cracked*?") or general ("Write something about this sentence"). As students come to class, either in person or virtually, they jot down ideas.

It takes a few days to establish this "settling" pattern, but once they know what I expect, they're quietly working even before I formally begin the class, which is about a minute after the last student joins us. Two or three students read their responses; I emphasize one idea and then move on to the day's other work. If there's more to say or if I want them to apply a writing technique, I send them off with a homework question or I post the same sentence the following day, with a new prompt.

Regardless of whether it's a crack-filler or a settler, this pattern works for any mini-lesson:

- decoding: any unfamiliar words? Ask students to restate the sentence in their own words.
- grammar or style: make one point, guided by their observations or by your own goal.
- homework: modeling reinforces what they've learned in a mini-lesson.

Here's a sample mini-lesson based on a sentence from Frank Chin's short story "Railroad Standard Time":

> The music's run through Clorox and Simonized, beating so insistently right and regular that you feel to sing it will deodorize you, make you clean.

Class discussion centered on Chin's description of music. Most knew that *Clorox* is a brand of bleach and that to be *run through Clorox* is to be "whitened."

Only a few were familiar with *Simonized*, a word derived from the brand name of a cleaning-product company (Simoniz) that passed into the language as a verb meaning "polish with wax." Because this was a mini-lesson, I didn't explain that the protagonist of Chin's story struggles with his Chinese-American identity, a fact that gives *Clorox* an extra layer of meaning. That discussion is more suitable for a full-period lesson. Instead, I asked what sort of music these words bring to mind. How—or should—music *deodorize you* and *make you clean*? The homework assignment was to describe any sort of music and its effect, using Chin's sentence as a model for creative comparison. Typical student responses resemble these:

> **The music snarls like a Collie cooped up too long and then switches to a Doberman charging the fence.**

> **My cousin's singing makes mosquitos in my mind.**

> **The drum solo was like the whole world had one heart that was beating too fast.**

I didn't define *simile* or *metaphor*, but I could have done so during the initial discussion of Chin's sentence or the reading of student responses.

FULL PERIOD (45 MINUTES)

I rely on full-period sentence lessons when the class is between topics or books, a kind of educational palate cleanser. Because they're engaging stand-alones, sentence lessons also work well for the last day before vacation, when everyone's brains have already departed, or the first day back, when only some brain cells have returned.

An effective pattern for a full-period lesson:

- initial activity related to the element of style you're focusing on
- decoding of the sentence you want to present
- analysis of 3 or 4 elements of grammar or style in that sentence OR
- analysis of a single element of grammar or style in several different sentences
- short writing exercise, to be shared with the class

I find it helpful to think of a full-period sentence lesson as a set of modules, each containing an idea I want to emphasize or an exercise I want students to complete. I rank the modules, starting with the indispensable and ending with the disposable, which are the ones I don't mind leaving for another day or another sentence. Then I follow the students' comments, trusting them to lead me with their curiosity and insight. Before the class ends, though, I make sure we hit every item on my "must-do" list.

A full-period lesson permits group study, which logistically is not an option for mini-lessons. With a full period, you have time to divide the kids into compatible bunches and get them on task, which may be any of the following:

- Give every group the same sentence and the same question. This option maximizes the number of insights, because inevitably one group will catch something another has overlooked.
- Ask each group to answer a different question about the same sentence. One group dissects structure, another examines word choice, still another tackles sound, and so forth.
- Give a different sentence to each group. Every sentence is an exceptionally good example of the element of grammar or style you're focusing on. This approach lets them compare how different authors employ the same technique. Inevitably, they will like some sentences and dislike others, sparking an interesting discussion of tastes and standards.

NOTE: When groups share their results, I usually say something like "Did your group come up with something that no one else has mentioned?" By barring repeats, I save time and yawns while simultaneously requiring students to listen carefully to others' comments.

If time permits after the groups share their findings, I conclude with a writing exercise. Modeling, as described above, builds both writing and reading skills. Writing skills—well, that's obvious! But reading ability also improves when students write. They can more easily recognize the power of, say, parallel structure once they've slotted their own ideas into it.

Students can also use the assigned sentence as the starting point for an essay, a scene, or an extended description. This writing exercise also builds reading skills. Without context, students must extrapolate from what they've read, strengthening their inference skills as well as their imagination. Given Frank Chin's sentence, for example, they must determine the identity of *you* and decide whether the character wants to be *clean*. Also, exactly what *clean* means! There are no right or wrong answers to these questions, not even in Chin's story. He has his creation; the students have theirs.

Whether they've modeled one sentence or written a longer piece, I reserve a few minutes for sharing the results of their efforts—not just what they wrote but also why they decided to write it the way they did. I ask about ideas they considered and rejected. Doing so reinforces the idea of writing as a process, not a single leap from blank page to finished product.

THE MAXI

An extended unit of great-sentence study facilitates incremental growth; concentrated practice leads to mastery. That's the pedagogical rationale. There's also a practical reason for a great-sentence week or month. If you're slammed with grading or a time-consuming event saps your students' energy, great-sentence study alleviates some of the pressure. Consider the weeks when your students are taking high-stakes standardized tests or AP exams in other disciplines. They'll be out of class on the day of the exam and probably oblivious to everything but their AP prep for a week or so before. Writing, reading, and correcting sentences takes less time than tackling a full-length work. Plus, many schools now require students who are ill to self-quarantine. In these situations, students who miss class can easily join in the group lesson when they're ready. A win-win situation!

The design of a sentence-study unit (one or more weeks) depends on the goal. Here's a general pattern, minus timing estimates because this unit works best when you customize it to fit your class's needs:

- initial presentation (one activity)
- analysis of a single element of grammar or style in 5–10 sentences OR
- analysis of several elements of grammar or style in 4–5 sentences
- several short writing exercises or one longer exercise

- student presentations about the historical or literary context of the sentence
- student examples and analysis of the structure of a sentence they've found on the internet, in print, or in music, film, or television
- optional homework: read more, or all, of the work the sentence comes from

You can also create mini-courses with sentences on the same topic (presidential speeches, mystery stories, the environment, and so forth) or genre. In that last category, I like to select sentences from poems, and later have students hunt some down themselves. Readers sometimes forget that poetry has sentences in it, too, not just deep thoughts and emotive bursts! It's also fun to have them reread, with older eyes, sentences from works they loved as children. Dr. Seuss's playful language, the staid pronouncements of Paddington Bear, and the parallel structure of Ludwig Bemelmans's *Madeline* are good starting points. You can also ask them to bring in their favorite books and present a single sentence to their classmates.

PART II

SENTENCE ELEMENTS TO TEACH

CHAPTER 6
STRUCTURE

CROSSED SENTENCES

. . . .

What could be more human than an obsession with crossroads, which mattered as much to hunter-gatherers (Which way did the woolly mammoth go?) as it does to today's rush-hour commuter (Should I take a back road or hope the freeway clears up?). It's thus not surprising that many writers and speakers have employed crossed sentences, including Shakespeare, Lao Tsu, Mae West, Clare Booth Luce, John F. Kennedy, Cicero, Lin-Manuel Miranda, and a host of others.

A word about rhetoric: two terms may describe a crossed sentence, *chiasmus* (derived from the Greek letter *chi*, which resembles an X) and *antimetabole* (from the Greek words for "opposite direction" and "turning about"). The two overlap quite a bit, and they're often applied interchangeably. In general, both reverse ideas, antimetabole with the same words in each arm of the crossed structure and chiasmus with different words.

Regardless of what it's called, a crossed sentence excels at presenting two choices. A crossed sentence may also define via contrast or provoke delight through wordplay. I find that students grasp the structure of a crossed sentence immediately but appreciate its subtle, even subconscious, manipulation only with close examination—which is where we teachers come in.

TEACHING CROSSED SENTENCES: A GENERAL PLAN
Introduction (optional)
To introduce the power of a crossed sentence, try one of these exercises.

- Divide the class and distribute the first question to one half and the second question to the other:
  - Is it acceptable to pray while smoking?
  - Is it acceptable to smoke while praying?

Don't allow students to glimpse others' questions or to answer aloud. Count their written answers. Chances are most will answer yes to the first question and no to the second. Regardless of the outcome, discuss the significance of the change in word order. Segue from there into a discussion of crossed sentences.

- Ask for two opposite statements about one thing: an abstract quality, a group of people, or an endeavor. Challenge students to place both in one sentence. An example: "We create art, and then art creates us." Discuss the effect of crossing these ideas instead of stating them separately.

Decoding

- Have students identify the cross in the sentence and restate the meaning of each arm.
- Are the words the same in each arm? What's different? (the words or the order or both)

Analysis

- How do the "arms" relate to each other? (opposites, choices, definitions, and so forth)
- Is there wordplay? (puns, homonyms, double entendres, etc.)
- If the sentence were uncrossed and each idea presented separately, would the effect change? How? (varied answers)

TEACHING CROSSED SENTENCES: LESSON PLANS

> **William Shakespeare, *Macbeth* (Act 1, scene 1)**
>
> Fair is foul, and foul is fair:
> Hover through the fog and filthy air.

NOTE: The crossed elements are underlined.

Brief context: Three witches chant this sentence in the opening scene of the play.

Extended context: The witches plan to meet with the title character "when the hurly-burly's done." In the following scene, a bloody soldier describes Macbeth's heroism in defending King Duncan of Scotland in a battle ("the hurly-burly") against insurgents. In the next scene, Macbeth meets the three witches, who salute him with his current title (Thane of Glamis), the title of the rebel he defeated (Thane of Cawdor), and the ultimate honor (King). Macbeth is skeptical, but soon Duncan names him Thane of Cawdor, setting Macbeth on the path to the regicide and his own downfall.

Analysis

With brief context:

- What do you associate with *fair* and *foul*? (varied answers; elicit, if need be, sports and sensory definitions)
- What happens when *fair is foul*? (appearance/reality theme: what seems to be *fair* isn't; the rules have changed)
- What happens when *foul is fair*? (appearance and reality again: what looks bad isn't; standards break down; evil triumphs)
- Why say this twice, in a crossed structure? (reveals faulty perception and deceit; emphasizes unfairness and chaos; opens the door to two outcomes or opposing traits in one character)
- What does the end of the sentence, *hover through the fog and filthy air*, add to the sentence? (choices *hover*, awaiting decisions; the *fog* of confusion will descend; the kingdom will become *filthy* or tainted, as will Macbeth)

With extended context:

- Is Macbeth *fair* or *foul*? (*fair* because of his heroism but *foul* in his murder of the king)
- Are the witches *fair* or *foul*? (*foul* in that they've set out to subvert

Macbeth; *fair* in that they don't force him to commit a crime, just tempt him)

- How does the crossed structure relate to Macbeth's character? (faces a choice between good and evil; the king's murder turns a *fair* government to a *foul* one; Macbeth turns from *fair* to *foul* as he changes from hero to murderer)

SUPPLEMENTAL MATERIAL FOR *MACBETH*

Grammar

- Each arm of the crossed statement is an independent clause, joined by the conjunction *and.*
- A colon can introduce a list, but here it signals an explanation of what precedes the colon. The second line might be a command to the witches to wait (*hover*) in the miasma of evil that surrounds them (*fog and filthy air*) until Macbeth makes his choice.

Rhetoric

The *fair-foul* line is an example of *antimetabole.*

Additional Information and Activities

- If the class is reading or has read the play, it's easy to show how this crossed sentence applies to other events in *Macbeth.* Here are two: Lady Macbeth appears *fair* but is *foul*; Macbeth will *hover* between right and wrong until the witches' prophecy and Lady Macbeth's arguments tip him into *fog and filthy* action.
- Beliefs about witches in Shakespeare's time can be the basis for a history/language arts project.
- *Macbeth*, like all of Shakespeare's works, has been staged, filmed, cartooned, shortened, updated, and expressed in myriad forms and media. You might ask students to compare the witches' scene in two film versions (or in other media), concentrating on the presentation of the crossed line of dialogue.

Robert Graves, "Mammon"

If <u>there's no money in poetry</u>, <u>neither is there poetry in money</u>.

Brief context: This sentence comes from poet Robert Graves's 1963 speech to the London School of Economics.

Extended context: Graves's speech is a highly subjective, extended meditation on the role of money throughout history. The speech is entitled "Mammon," a term referring to great wealth or the desire for it. Also relevant: "Mammon" is often depicted as a false god. Graves begins his speech by explaining that the sentence about poetry and money was his retort to a business executive who urged Graves to "write a best-seller rather than poems which no ordinary mortal . . . could understand." Graves states firmly that "poets need never have empty purses." Just as military generals learn the logistics of warfare but nothing about "morale, weather, accident and miracle," economists should be reminded of "poetic and religious imponderables." Graves claims that finance "began as warm human love" and evolved into selfishness and a desire to dominate. He recounts a surprise gift of a hundred pounds that arrived when he was nearly penniless, sent from an acquaintance who wrote, "I like your poems, and I hear you are in difficulties." Graves always had enough money to live on but never enough to tempt him to stop working.

Analysis
With brief context:

• The words in this sentence are simple, but their connotations aren't. Ask students what they associate with *money* and *poetry*. How do those associations relate to the meaning of the sentence? (varied answers)
• What are some possible meanings of *there's no money in poetry*? (can't make a living as a poet; poets don't write about *money*; preoccupation with *money* precludes *poetry*)
• What are some possible meanings of *neither is there poetry in money*? (*money* pushes art aside; creativity has nothing to do with the pursuit of

money; deeper truths expressed in *poetry* don't come to light when the focus is on *money*)

• The sentence is framed as an implied *if/then* statement. Does Graves truly doubt that *there's no money in poetry*? (no clear answer, but the fact that Graves is speaking at the London School of Economics indicates high status and introduces the possibility that there *is money in poetry* for him)

• Graves's sentence implies an *if/then* situation, in which both or neither of the statements is true. What is the effect of this construction? (severs *money* from *poetry*; pits the financier against the artist; elevates the artist over the financier)

• In this crossed sentence, which path does Graves encourage? How do you know? (*poetry*, because he's a poet but also because *money* lacks *poetry*— artistry and creativity)

• Present Graves's statement with different words and no crossed structure: "Poets don't make money, and bankers seldom think about poetry." Does your reaction change? (uncrossed version is more neutral than Graves's sentence)

With extended context:

• Does knowing that Graves's statement rebutted a suggestion by a business executive affect your view of the sentence? (adds defensiveness)

• How does the title, "Mammon," influence your understanding of Graves's point of view? (allusion to the Bible—you can't worship both God and Mammon—you must choose)

• What's missing when *poetry* is absent, in Graves's view? (extrapolating from his comment on the military: emotion, serendipity, spirituality)

• Can you relate the crossed structure to other remarks by Graves in this speech? (unexpected gift arrives at a critical point—a crossroads; the poet chose his path and stayed on it—never stopped writing)

SUPPLEMENTAL MATERIAL FOR "MAMMON"

Grammar

- The first part of the cross is a dependent clause beginning with the conjunction *if.* The second part is an independent clause. This construction gives more importance to the lack of *poetry in money.*
- *Neither*, as a conjunction, generally pairs with *nor*, which is absent here. Instead, the first statement relies on *no money.* This break from a common pattern emphasizes the statement beginning with *neither.*
- *There's* (contraction of *there is*) in the first clause is paired with *is there* in the second. The reversal creates the cross.

Rhetoric

The statement is an example of *chiasmus.*

Additional Information and Activities

- Robert Graves's full lecture begins with the etymology of the word *money.* Consider having students research the etymology of any important word in the sentence or the lecture title, "Mammon."
- Is there any money in poetry? Calvin Trillin, known mainly for his prose work, once said that he was offered payment "in the high two figures" for a poem. Articles about poetry and money are fairly easy to find and may open a few students' eyes to the viability of this profession. Try not to discourage their literary aspirations, if you can. The world needs more poets, not fewer!

MORE CROSSES

Below are a few crossed sentences, with brief commentary, easily adaptable to the sort of lesson plan described above. The crossed elements are underlined.

> Nations don't distrust each other because they are armed; they are armed because they distrust each other.
>
> —Salvador de Madariaga, *Disarmament*

Salvador de Madariaga served as chief of the Disarmament Section of the League of Nations, the forerunner to the United Nations. He made this point about *distrust* in his book *Disarmament* and in a number of speeches; many other diplomats have made similar comments. Madariaga's crossed sentence places emotion (*distrust*) and danger (*armed*) in a shared reality but stresses that there are two opposite approaches to the problem. Madariaga's stance is that disarmament is impossible until the issue of *distrust* is resolved. A chilling note: *Disarmament* was published in 1929, only a decade before World War II broke out. The issue is no less pressing today.

> The value of marriage is <u>not that adults produce children</u>, but <u>that children produce adults</u>.   —Peter De Vries, *The Tunnel of Love*

In Peter De Vries's *The Tunnel of Love*, his 1954 novel set in suburbia, neighboring families (one with children, one hoping to adopt) cope with misunderstandings, career setbacks, and relationships. De Vries doesn't present a gauzy, aren't-they-adorable view of *children*: another sentence from the novel notes that parenthood often seems to be "nothing but feeding the mouth that bites you." In his crossed sentence, though, De Vries acknowledges the importance of the parent/child bond. Adults procreate (*produce children*), but their offspring bring them to maturity (*produce adults*). De Vries's novel was made into a film; the sentence might be the basis of a mixed-media study.

> I always say, <u>keep a diary</u> and someday <u>it'll keep you</u>.
>   —Mae West, *Every Day's a Holiday*

Mae West made a career playing bawdy women whose speech was rife with double entendres. In the 1937 film *Every Day's a Holiday*, which she wrote and acted in, she plays Peaches O'Day, who tangles with the law when she tries to sell the Brooklyn Bridge. Because the police captain gives her a break, she constructs an elaborate plot to help him win a mayoral election against an unscrupulous opponent. The implied meaning of West's crossed sentence is that the indiscretions recorded in a *diary* will *someday* yield sufficient blackmail payments to support the writer.

> **Better <u>to write for yourself and have no public</u>, than <u>to write for the public and have no self</u>.**   —Cyril Connolly, *New Statesman* article

The polar opposite of Mae West's comment about writing comes from literary critic Cyril Connolly, book reviewer for the *New Statesman* in the late 1920s and early 1930s. Connolly's principled stance, as expressed in this crossed sentence, depicts divergent paths: an *either/or* view that allows no subtlety. He never considers the possibility that what you *write for yourself* may attract a wide *public* audience. This sentence is a springboard to a discussion of writers' motivations.

> **No woman has ever <u>so comforted the distressed</u>—or <u>so distressed the comfortable</u>.**   —Clare Booth Luce (speaking of Eleanor Roosevelt)

Clare Booth Luce was an author and a diplomat; Eleanor Roosevelt was the First Lady during Franklin Roosevelt's administration and the first United States delegate to the United Nations General Assembly. In this crossed sentence, Luce acknowledges Roosevelt's strong commitment to human rights.

> **For one <u>gains by losing</u> and <u>loses by gaining</u>.**
>   —Lao Tsu, *Tao Te Ching*, translated by Gia-Fu Feng and Jane English

The *Tao Te Ching* is an ancient Chinese text attributed to Lao Tsu, a name that translates to "old master." The book lays down the basic tenets of Taoism, which advocates freedom from desire and a life in harmony with the natural order. Like many crosses in the *Tao Te Ching*, this sentence questions assumptions, specifically the nature of *losing* and *gaining*. *One*, an anonymous pronoun that stands in for a specific name, is an apt choice for this sentence. The self is lost, this crossed sentence states, but universality is gained. This sentence is a good starting point for an interdisciplinary project combining history, philosophy, and language arts.

> **<u>We didn't land on Plymouth Rock</u>; <u>the rock was landed on us</u>.**
>   —Malcolm X (1964 speech)

Activist Malcolm X used this line and variations of it several times to distinguish between descendants of the Pilgrims, who came to America voluntarily, and "people who formerly were African who were kidnapped and brought to America." Plymouth Rock, the landing site of the *Mayflower* voyagers and founders of Plymouth colony, is a symbol of power here. The crossed sentence stresses the power imbalance: in the first arm, the verb is active and negative (*didn't land*): *we* didn't wield power. The second arm also stresses the lack of power. The verb is passive: power was exercised *on us* (African Americans). This sentence structure reinforces Malcolm X's point: the history of African Americans differs from that of white Americans.

> I don't have <u>ugly ducklings turning into swans</u> in my stories; I have <u>ugly ducklings turning into confident ducks</u>.
>
> —Maeve Binchy (interview with *Current Biography*, 1995)

Many of Maeve Binchy's plots focus on family life and romantic entanglements (or disentanglements). Her crossed sentence here sums up her attitude toward her female protagonists. A Binchy heroine often starts out unsure and tries to change herself to attract love. That's the path expressed by the first arm of the sentence. At some point the character understands that nothing is better than accepting her true self. That is the second arm, Binchy's "moral of the story."

WRITING ASSIGNMENTS

Crossed sentences are like salt: a little goes a long way. You don't want your students to insert too many in their work, but in a well-chosen spot, a crossed sentence adds zip to speeches, essays, and stories. Have them practice with one or more of these exercises.

Unscrambling

Present all the words in a crossed sentence and ask students to put them in order, identifying the crossed element. Below are some suggestions, with solutions.

1. wherever whenever they they go go some others happiness cause
   ANSWER: Some cause happiness <u>wherever they go</u>; others <u>whenever they go</u>.   —Oscar Wilde
2. you you you remember remember forget forget want want to to what what and
   ANSWER: <u>You forget what you want to remember</u> and <u>you remember what you want to forget</u>.   —Cormac McCarthy, *The Road*
3. not but can can country country for for your your what what you you do do ask
   ANSWER: Ask not <u>what your country can do for you</u> but <u>what you can do for your country</u>.   —John F. Kennedy, inaugural address

Beyond the Dictionary

The dictionary definition decodes, but a true definition adds in the emotions and principles of the definer. Put students in that role by assigning an abstract concept (*justice, affection, friendship, success,* and so on). Ask them to state what it is and what it isn't, all in one crossed sentence. The pattern is as follows:

_____ is/does _____ not _____

Turning Point

Where did everything change, or when?

- Ask students to identify an important moment in their lives, perhaps a change or a choice.
- Have them jot down a few notes about what possibilities loomed or what choices were possible.
- Now ask them to fashion one statement about each of two possibilities or choices. Put them into a single sentence or, if need be, two sentences.
- Let them play with the wording until they have two "arms" of a crossed sentence.

Extra credit: Make the crossed sentence the basis for an essay or story about this important moment.

Act Now!

What matters to you? Ask your students that question and have them create a "call to action" in support of their cause or belief. The "call" should be a crossed sentence, showing the benefits of the students' position and the consequences of a different path. If you wish, extend the assignment by assigning research and further writing or mixed-media works in support of the actions the students advocate.

PARALLEL STRUCTURE

Your students can enjoy *texting and playing video games* but not *to write their English papers*—not in the same sentence, that is, unless they deviate from parallel structure. The principle of balance in a sentence, parallel structure is present when everything performing the same function in a sentence has the same grammatical identity. *Texting* and *playing video games* are parallel because they're both gerunds serving as direct objects. *To write their papers*, also a direct object, is an infinitive. Even if they're clueless about grammatical labels, students can hear the pattern break in *texting, playing video games*, and *to write their papers*.

Parallelism is a rule of formal English expression, and not a meaningless one: this structure unites and confers equal importance on the elements slotted into it. But the parallelism rule, like all rules, is often broken. That's fine when it's broken on purpose: to throw the reader off balance or to establish a hierarchy of importance. It's not so fine when nonparallel sentences are the result of sloppy writing. The goal is to show students how good writers conform with or break from parallel structure in order to align form and content.

TEACHING PARALLEL STRUCTURE: A GENERAL PLAN

Introduction (optional)

This activity introduces or reviews the concept of parallelism:

- For students unfamiliar with the concept, present a list of words or phrases that are generally parallel but break the pattern in one spot (*to jump, to shoot, to score, and winning the championship trophy*, for example).
- What pattern do they detect?
- Does anything break the pattern? What?
- Define the term *parallel* and have them correct the original list and perhaps generate some additional parallel lists.

Decoding

- After the usual decoding of unfamiliar words, ask students to isolate a list, if the sentence contains one.
- If no formal list appears, have students identify parts of the sentences that seem to belong together. Make a list of those items.
- Grammatical terminology isn't necessary, but if you prefer to use it, have students identify the parts of speech or functions of the items on the list.

Analysis

- Ask a student to read the list aloud. Can they hear a pattern? Does anything break the pattern?
- What do the items on the list or in the group have in common?
- If there's a break in the pattern, determine the reason. Why has the author separated that idea?

TEACHING PARALLEL SENTENCES: LESSON PLANS

After each sentence is a list of its parallel elements.

> ### "Unearth" by Alicia Elliott
>
> Even though she'd had her hair cut and her tongue tamed, even though she'd donned pantsuits and pearls and spoke English as well as either queen she was named for, even though she let people think she was Portuguese or Italian or Greek, even though she'd left the scarred memories of her childhood in a dark, unattended corner of her mind—her people still recognized her.

Parallels:

[had] *had her hair cut and her tongue tamed*
[had] *donned pantsuits and pearls*
spoke English as well as either queen she was named for
let people think she was Portuguese or Italian or Greek

> [had] *left the scarred memories of her childhood in a dark, unattended*
> *corner of her mind*

Brief context: The sentence represents the thoughts of a Canadian woman (*she*) when a stranger addresses her in Mohawk, the language *she* spoke as a child.

Extended context: Elizabeth (*she*) has received a call from a government official informing her that the bones of her brother Henry, who disappeared fifty-five years earlier at the age of five, have been unearthed at a construction site. Henry was taken to a boarding school along with other Mohawk children by Father Landry, a clergyman, to receive "a good education in the Lord." Henry doesn't return, and for several years neither does Father Landry. The mother's desperate inquiries to the church, the police, and other authorities yield no information. Elizabeth's mother deteriorates after Henry's disappearance. When Father Landry finally returns, the mother attacks him. She's incarcerated; he's held blameless.

Elizabeth has distanced herself from the events of her childhood and her Mohawk heritage. After her brother's remains are found, she returns to the reservation where she grew up. A young Mohawk woman addresses her as "Istha," or "auntie." When Elizabeth asks her how she knew, the woman replies, "You've got that tough Mohawk look to you." As the story ends, Elizabeth cooks Henry's favorite food, a traditional dish, and the reader is left with the sense that while she'll never regain what was taken from her, she may embrace what she herself jettisoned.

Analysis

With brief context:

- Which statements sound alike? (the four *even though* statements)
- What actions do these statements describe? (*cut, tamed, donned, spoke, let, left*)
- Which ones differ? (*cut, tamed*) How? (done to her, not by her)
- Evaluate the importance of each parallel element. Are they all on the same level? (Opinions will vary here: *tongue tamed* and *left . . . mind* may come up as more serious than the others)

- What common meaning do these statements have? (attempt to change appearance, personality, identity)
- Do any of the *even though* statements break the pattern? (*donned, spoke, let, left*—the verbs in the second, third, and fourth statements—are actions Elizabeth controls; in the first statement, *cut* and *tamed* are actions done to her)
- Examine the break in parallelism. Are *cut* and *tamed* of equal importance? (having one's hair *cut* is normal, having one's *tongue tamed* isn't)
- Why would someone have or need a *tongue tamed*? (fear of what will be said, enforcement of society's standards, emphasizing obedience and subjugation, assimilation)
- Think about the ending: *her people still recognized her.* What relationship may *her people* imply? (family, community, ethnicity, nationality, etc.)
- Does the sentence end on a positive note, or is recognition a negative event? (varied opinions)

With extended context, add these points to those above:

- How does the parallel list relate to Henry? (the actions in the *even though* statements may represent an attempt to avoid his fate by changing identity; harsh treatment broke not only bodies, such as Henry's, but also culture)
- Why try to pass for *Portuguese or Italian or Greek*? (perhaps perceived as less dangerous or more desirable than being *Mohawk*—by society and by Elizabeth herself)
- What is the significance of language? (*tongue tamed*—loss of native language, tamp down protest; also, speaking English *as well as either queen she was named for* represents complete assimilation)

SUPPLEMENTAL MATERIAL FOR "UNEARTH"

Grammar

- The *even though* statements are dependent clauses, subject-verb expressions that can't stand alone as complete thoughts.
- Dependent clauses reflect unequal power, as do the actions in the *even though* clauses. Mohawk communities had less power than the dominant, Euro-Canadian culture and government.

- The sentence gathers momentum with each clause, climaxing with the independent clause *her people still recognized her.* By placing *her people* in the independent clause, Elliott gives more importance to the group than to Elizabeth, the *she* of the dependent clauses. *She* may try to leave the group, but the group won't, and shouldn't, leave her.

Rhetoric

This sentence, with four consecutive *even though* statements, is an example of *anaphora*: the repetition of words or phrases at the beginning of sentences, phrases, or clauses.

Additional Information and Activities

- Elizabeth's story is fictional, but it's based on fact. From the late nineteenth through the late twentieth century, indigenous children were urged, even coerced, to attend residential schools throughout Canada. (Similar events also occurred in Native American communities.) In 2008, the Canadian government formally apologized for the disruption and harm these schools brought to indigenous communities. Have students consult the Truth and Reconciliation Commission of Canada to place Elizabeth's story in context.
- Children were forbidden to speak their native languages in residential schools. Discuss the role of language in unifying a community and transmitting its traditions. For a history/English research project, students can look into other banned languages: Basque, Catalan, and Galician in mid-twentieth-century Spain, for example, or Gaelic in Ireland and Scotland (beginning in the sixteenth and seventeenth centuries).

Michael Bond, *A Bear Called Paddington*

Without waiting for a reply, he caught hold of his wife's arm and pushed her through the crowd, around a cart laden with chocolate and cups of tea, past a bookstall, and through a gap in a pile of suitcases toward the Lost Property Office.

NOTE: The Paddington character has inspired films, cartoons, toys, and games. You may want to delay identification of the author and work until students have a chance to react to the sentence itself, without bringing other knowledge of Paddington into their analysis.

There are two sets of parallels in this sentence.
The first:

> *caught*
> *pushed*

The second:

> *through the crowd*
> *around a cart laden with chocolate and cups of tea*
> *past a bookstall*
> *through a gap in a pile of suitcases*
> *toward the Lost Property Office*

Brief context: The couple in this sentence are rushing through a train station to the *Lost Property Office* (Lost and Found).

Extended context: Mr. Brown has glimpsed a bear in a London railway station (Paddington, which becomes the bear's name). Mr. Brown is eager to show his wife the little fellow, who traveled as a stowaway from "darkest Peru" and wears a tag reading: "Please look after this bear." That's exactly what the Browns do. Like a young child, Paddington is well meaning, but he often doesn't understand where he is, what he's doing, and what the consequences of his actions will be. Adventures ensue, all with happy endings.

Michael Bond was inspired to write about Paddington when he saw children in Paddington Station during World War II. Some were displaced from other European countries; others were Londoners being evacuated to the countryside. The children wore identification tags similar to the one around Paddington's neck. It was the responsibility of British authorities to take care of these children, and they did, just as the Browns take care of the bear.

Analysis

With brief context:

• You may have to help non-British students decode *bookstall* (bookstore or kiosk) and *Lost Property Office* (Lost and Found).
• What actions did *he* do? (*caught* and *pushed*) Is *he* rude? Eager? Determined? (perhaps all three) Form a mental image of the movement described in the sentence. What do you associate with that image? (varied answers, many involving rushed movement along a crowded path)
• Suppose the sentence read: *caught hold of his wife's arm, pushing her.* Does the nonparallel version change your reaction? (varied answers)
• List the words marking the route *he* and *his wife* took. (answers above)
• Point out that they all begin with a directional word, or preposition (*through, around, past, through, toward*). Why? (delineates the couple's path)
• What is the effect of stringing together so many directions? (creates a sense of swift, heedless movement)
• Does any element of the phrase chain stand out? (*around . . . tea* is longer than the others) Why might the author distinguish this element from the others? (spotlights the refreshments)

With extended context:

• The parallel verbs describe the Browns' journey, but they also apply to the bear himself. Mr. Brown (*he*) *caught* and *pushed* his wife. (I should mention that Bond was trying to show eagerness, not dominance. Mrs. Brown makes most of the decisions in their household.) Paddington *caught* their hearts, because, well, who could resist him? He also *pushed* them—and himself—into entirely new experiences: "darkest Peru" and London are quite different, as is the Browns' family life after Paddington arrives.
• If students are familiar with the book, they can see that some parallel phrases also relate to Paddington:

> *through the crowd*: Paddington often attracts a *crowd*, such as when he wanders into a window display at a posh London store.

Around a cart laden with chocolate and cups of tea: Though marmalade is his favorite, Paddington loves all sorts of sweets.

Through a gap: If there's a way out of trouble—the tiniest *gap*—Paddington will find it. After a misunderstanding leads the bear to rub Mr. Brown's painting with turpentine, for instance, the altered picture wins an art contest.

In a pile of suitcases: Paddington starts off in London being treated like baggage.

Toward the Lost Property Office: He's not *property*, but Paddington is *lost* until he meets the Browns, and fairly frequently during his subsequent adventures.

• Even if students aren't familiar with the character, they can sense the comic-chase aspect of the sentence that resembles many scenes in children's books and films.

SUPPLEMENTAL MATERIAL FOR *A BEAR CALLED PADDINGTON*

Grammar

The sentence begins with two linked prepositional phrases (*Without waiting for a reply*) and ends with a chain of prepositional phrases (*through . . . Office*). The husband and wife are surrounded by these descriptions, just as they are surrounded by obstacles in their search for the bear.

Rhetoric

Bond has two sets of *parallels* here—one in the sentence and one implied by the setting, a railway station with parallel train tracks.

Additional Information and Activities

• The sentence can serve as the basis for media studies, with students comparing the book and one of the films or cartoons based on it.

- Paddington was inspired by the author's glimpse of displaced children. A history/English research project can explore this historical event. The website of Britain's Imperial War Museum is a good source.

> **Anthony Lane, review of *The Aeronauts***
>
> **The widow of another balloonist, she [Amelia Wren] knows (a) how to launch the lovely gas-filled globe and steer it toward the heavens, and (b) no fear.**

NOTE: I include this sentence, along with a brief analysis, as a counterpoint, because the sentence breaks parallel structure:

nonparallel items:

> *how to launch the lovely gas-filled globe and steer it toward the heavens*
> *no fear*

Anthony Lane's sentence comes from his review of *The Aeronauts*, a film about a mismatched pair of hot-air balloonists. Amelia Wren arrives at the launch riding atop the roof of her carriage; then she cartwheels around the balloon. Her partner is James Glaisher, a meteorologist who hopes to gather scientific data during the flight. Amelia's practical knowledge of ballooning, as well as her willingness to climb atop the balloon midflight to open a stuck valve, saves them both. Lane breaks parallelism with item (b), spotlighting Amelia Wren's daring. The parallel version would change *no fear* to something like *how to overcome fear and complete necessary tasks*. How stuffy! How un-Wren! Lane's *no fear* describes the character in a way that matches her personality.

MORE PARALLELS

The parallel elements are underlined, with some context following.

> With this faith we will be able <u>to work together</u>, <u>to pray together</u>, <u>to struggle together</u>, <u>to go to jail together</u>, <u>to stand up for freedom together</u>, knowing that we will be free one day.
>
> —Reverend Martin Luther King Jr., "I Have a Dream"

The Reverend Martin Luther King Jr. delivered this speech during the March on Washington in 1963, a massive, nonviolent protest against racial segregation and discrimination. King's speech is a call for justice for all Americans, a passionate plea that the nation live up to its ideals. The sentence is also a reassuring gesture of solidarity and comfort to civil rights activists who were risking their lives and freedom in nonviolent protests against unjust laws. King's speech had a wide audience, some of whom disagreed with his cause. The parallel infinitives of King's sentence juxtapose ordinary life activities (*work*, *pray*) and activism (*struggle, go to jail, stand up for freedom*). King links these two categories to stress that only protest against injustice will effect meaningful change and ensure that all Americans have an equal right to engage in everyday activities.

> I had to <u>go</u> out into the world and <u>see</u> it and <u>hear</u> it and <u>react</u> to it, before I knew at all <u>who I was</u>, <u>what I was</u>, <u>what I wanted to be</u>.
>
> —Mary Oliver, "Of Power and Time"

In this essay, Mary Oliver reflects on her evolution as a poet and as a person. The parallel infinitives (*go, see, hear, react*) are necessary tasks; the parallel noun clauses (*who I was, what I was, what I wanted to be*) chart her path to self-knowledge. Both lists are parallel, and therefore every item has equal importance. Oliver's strict adherence to this structure shows that she sees every stage of her journey, and every aspect of self-knowledge, as indispensable.

> We are <u>troubled</u> on every side, yet not <u>distressed</u>; we are <u>perplexed</u>, but not in despair;
> <u>Persecuted</u>, but not <u>forsaken</u>; cast down, but not <u>destroyed</u> . . .
>
> —Second Epistle to the Corinthians, King James Bible

This passage comes from the New Testament and is a letter (*epistle*) from Paul to the Christians of Corinth. Paul, a Christian, reflects on the suffering he and fellow believers undergo. Paul's letter acknowledges that he and his fellow Christians are fragile and can easily be harmed or killed. They find meaning in their faith and will not let persecution deflect them from their mission. Most of the verb forms in these lines are presented as parallel pairs of participles: *troubled, distressed; persecuted, forsaken; cast, destroyed*. Only in one spot does the pattern break: *perplexed* partners with a prepositional phrase, *in despair*. Why change the pattern with *despair*? Perhaps because *despair* is a dire state that merits special attention. To be *in despair* is to have no hope at all, worse than *destroyed* or *distressed*. It's important to note that all the pairs, strictly parallel or not, express optimism. The second element always includes *not*.

> **My heart's been borrowed and yours has been blue.**
>
> —Taylor Swift, "Lover"

Taylor Swift said she imagined a couple dancing at 3 a.m., too in love to stop, when she wrote this song. In an interview, she spoke about the fear and hope present in love, the "existential question" of committing to a shared life. In this line from the song, the conjunction *and* separates two parallel independent clauses, each describing the state of the lovers' hearts. Both have the same verb, *has been*. (The first *has* is part of the contraction *heart's*.) Swift's parallel structure places the lovers on equal footing. One lost a heart temporarily (*borrowed*), and the other was depressed (*blue*). *Has been* is in present-perfect tense, which connects the past and the present. The tense implies that the emotions expressed in each independent clause aren't completely absent. The singer is hoping their love will last but can't be certain that it will.

WRITING ASSIGNMENTS

Fill in the Blanks

Give students these general sentences and have them fill in the blanks with parallel elements:

My aunt _____ but _____.
What _____ and what _____ surprised everyone.
In the classroom where _____, where _____, and where
_____, the children were overjoyed.
Some _____, but others _____.

Second round: ask students to break the parallel pattern in order to emphasize a point.

Lists

Have students write a "to-do" list. They don't have to be truthful here. In fact, the more imaginative they are, the more fun they'll have and the stronger the lesson will be. Have them list parallel tasks of equal importance, as well as at least one nonparallel task that's more or less urgent than the others. Here's an example:

> **check smoke-detector battery**, because Esther is cooking tonight and her middle name may as well be "Burnadette"
> **make dinner reservation**, because I'll need real food after Esther's meal
> **antacid**, coupon?

As you see, the first two items are significant and parallel to each other. The last is less important (the list-writer can live without the medicine!) and breaks the parallel pattern.

Phone

This exercise is also more fun when it's completely fictional. Ask students to describe something on their phones. (Assure them that you won't check their devices.) Their descriptions should be parallel. An example:

> **My shortest playlist has songs guaranteed to annoy my father, who can't stand listening to anything but opera, and my longest has songs to entertain my friends, who love everything from hip-hop to rock to jazz.**

Song Hunting

For both rhythm and meaning, song lyrics are rife with parallels. Start students off listening to "They Can't Take That Away from Me" by George and Ira Gershwin (easily found on the internet). Then have them bring in examples of parallelism in their favorite songs.

POCKET STRUCTURE

"Pocket structure" is a term I coined to describe a sentence containing two expressions of the same idea, with information inserted between them. The "pocket" can be fashioned from a pair of words or from longer elements. Sometimes those words match, as they do in this sentence from Ralph Waldo Emerson's description of his aunt's approach to life:

<u>Do</u> what you are afraid to <u>do</u>.

In other sentences, such as this one from Richard Powers's novel *The Overstory*, closely related words form the pocket:

In summer, water rises through the xylem [of the tree] and <u>disperses</u> out of the million tiny mouths on the undersides of leaves, a hundred gallons a day <u>evaporating</u> from the tree's airy crown into the humid Iowa air.

The contents—everything between the words that form the pocket—are tucked away for a reason. Emerson envisions his aunt putting her fear where it can't interfere with her desire to *do* whatever challenges her. A pocket may also contain what can't be discarded: in Powers's sentence that's the awesome power of nature (*a hundred gallons a day*) and its fragility (*tiny mouths*).

Pockets, like most sentence structures, work on the unconscious level. Nevertheless, they have power—to reveal character, to highlight a theme, or to signal the presence of secrets.

TEACHING POCKET STRUCTURE: A GENERAL PLAN

Introduction (optional)

Before you turn to a specific sentence, you may want to take a moment to discuss the function of a pocket. Some possible questions:

- Apart from convenience, what are the advantages of a pocket?
- Have you ever carried anything you didn't need or didn't want to reveal? (I generally limit student responses to nods or a show of hands, to minimize giggles and to protect students' privacy.)
- What does the expression "full circle" mean? Discuss the effect of ending where you began and a common belief that "closure" is necessary, desirable, or possible.

Decoding

- Define unfamiliar words and ask for reactions and associations to key words.
- Direct their attention to ideas expressed twice, with the same or different words. Label that the pocket.
- Reread what lies between the pocket words. That's the contents.

Analysis

- Why would the contents be tucked away?
- Reword the sentence to eliminate the pocket. Does the reader reaction change? How?

TEACHING POCKET SENTENCES: LESSON PLANS

In each of these sentences, the pocket is underlined.

> ### John Boyne, *The Boy in the Striped Pajamas*
>
> "<u>What kind of job?</u>" asked Bruno, because if he was honest with himself—which he always tried to be—he wasn't entirely sure <u>what job Father did</u>.

The pocket contents give information about Bruno: *he was honest with himself, he always tried, he wasn't entirely sure.*

Alternate, nonpocket version:

> "What kind of job?" asked Bruno. He wasn't entirely sure what job Father did. Bruno admitted this because he always tried to be honest with himself.

NOTE: Students may have seen the film based on Boyne's novel. The film differs from the book significantly. For that reason, you may wish to withhold the title and author until students have analyzed the sentence.

Brief context: The sentence comes from a novel. The main character, Bruno, is a nine-year-old boy who has just discovered that his family must move because of his father's job.

Extended context: John Boyne's novel about the Holocaust, which he calls "a fable," is told from Bruno's point of view. Bruno is the son of a Nazi officer sent to run the concentration camp at Auschwitz because, his mother explains, "there's a very special job that needs doing there." Bruno dislikes his new home but is intrigued by a glimpse from his bedroom window of fenced-in people wearing "striped pajamas," inmates of the concentration camp. His father, who scares Bruno a bit, tells him that "they're not people at all . . . . not as we understand the term."

Bruno explores the area and meets an imprisoned boy, Shmuel. The children are separated by the fence but united by a common birthdate. They speak often. One day Shmuel appears in Bruno's kitchen, where he's been sent to work. Bruno offers the emaciated child some food and, when challenged by a Nazi officer, denies having done so, subjecting Shmuel to severe punishment for stealing. Later, at the fence, Bruno apologizes, and Shmuel eventually forgives him. When Shmuel's father disappears, Bruno promises to help Shmuel search for him. He squeezes under a gap in the fence, dons striped pajamas to avoid discovery by his father's soldiers and, during the search, is marched away with Shmuel and many others. The reader, but not the boys, knows that they're going to the gas chamber.

Analysis

With brief context:

- What word appears at both the beginning and the end of the sentence? (*job*)
- The pocket is a kind of boundary. How may a parent's job limit a child? (determines where the family lives, how much money the family has, how the family behaves)
- What's in the middle? (*honest with himself, tried to be, not entirely sure*)
- If that was all you knew, what would you think about the person these words describe? Would you want to be this person's friend? (varied answers)
- Why do you think the author "pocketed" this information? (personal qualities aren't always visible, but they're always present)
- What do the contents tell you about Bruno? (*honest with himself,* but the sentence says nothing about his honesty with others; *tried* implies some failure; *not entirely sure* suggests it may be easier to remain ignorant or that he's too intimidated to question the father, general atmosphere of secrecy)
- Is the effect of the "unpocketed" sentence different? If so, how and why? (*job* is more neutral, not presented as a boundary)

With extended context:

- Bruno betrayed Shmuel, denying that he gave food to his friend. Why? (knows he's not supposed to be friends with someone in "striped pajamas," afraid of father's reaction)
- Does being honest with himself matter if he lies to others? (varied opinions)
- Is the fact that Bruno always tried, but sometimes failed, a flaw or simply human nature? (varied opinions) Why might his attempts be pocketed? (failures trouble him, atmosphere of secrecy)
- Explore Bruno's ignorance with the class. (doesn't know anything about his father's job; isn't entirely sure what's happening—in the camp and the wider world; intuitively grasps the atmosphere of danger and the threat to Shmuel, but doesn't investigate) What obligation does Bruno have to ask more questions and inform himself? (varied opinions)

SUPPLEMENTAL MATERIAL FOR *THE BOY IN THE STRIPED PAJAMAS*

Grammar

- The sentence, as well as the pocket, begins with an independent clause: *"What kind of job?" asked Bruno.* Another independent clause ends the sentence and sews up the pocket: *he wasn't entirely sure what job Father did.* Independent clauses, which may stand alone as complete sentences, confer importance on the ideas they express.

- There are two dependent clauses (*because if he was honest with himself*, explaining why the question was *asked*, and *which he always tried to be*, explaining when Bruno *was honest with himself*). This type of clause subordinates the ideas it expresses, so why and when Bruno tries to be honest is less important than Father's *job*. This structure meshes well with the point Boyne is making, that the *job* has subverted integrity.

- The noun clause *what job Father did* can be viewed as the object of an implied preposition, *about.* Boyne also omits "he would admit that" as the lead-in to *he wasn't entirely sure what job Father did.* Boyne's elliptical approach in this sentence fits the way the author hints at events in the novel.

- A dash interrupts the flow and calls attention to the ideas it sets off. In this sentence, the interruption (*which he always tried to be*) emphasizes Bruno's effort. By saying *tried to be* instead of *was*, Boyne lets the reader know that Bruno is not a selfless, courageous hero. He's a flawed human being.

Rhetoric

The rhetorical term that best fits Boyne's pocket is *parembole*, defined as material related to the subject inserted into a single sentence, from the Greek words for "beside" and "throwing in."

Additional Information and Activities

- The pocket structure of John Boyne's sentence reflects the horrific reality of Nazi Germany. The father's *job*—the systematic extermination of Jews and others the Nazis deem "not people"—perverts everything society should treasure: family bonds, friendship, patriotism, and honor. Bruno's death is a consequence of his father's *job*, too, but the real tragedy is not one boy's fate but the entirety of the Holocaust. For guidance on discussing the Holocaust in an age-appropriate way, see the website of the United States Holocaust Museum or the teaching resources available at the Centre for Holocaust Education, a British group.

- The book and the film have been criticized for adopting Bruno's viewpoint and for the author's decision to give the character childlike ignorance. In class discussion, you can explore some of the objections critics raise and evaluate their validity.

Paul Laurence Dunbar, "Dreams"

What <u>dreams we have and how they fly</u>
Like rosy clouds across the sky;
Of wealth, of fame, of sure success,
Of love that comes to cheer and bless;
And how they wither, how they fade,
The waning wealth, the jilting jade—
The fame that for a moment gleams,
Then <u>flies forever,—dreams, ah</u>—<u>dreams</u>!

Brief context: This sentence is the first of a two-stanza poem published in 1903.

Extended context: Paul Laurence Dunbar was a poet, novelist, essayist, and playwright. While Dunbar was still in high school, his work was published in a local newspaper. After graduating, he applied for a number of jobs but was told that the positions were not open to African Americans. He eventually found work as an elevator operator, and he never stopped writing. His work gained recognition first in his home state of Ohio, then nationally and internationally.

Analysis

With brief context:

- Which words form the pocket? (the first and last line)
- Do the *dreams* differ in these lines? (first: more positive, related to future success; last: more negative as they're gone *forever*)
- What about *fly* and *flies*? Do they differ in meaning? (*fly* in the first line means "soar"; *flies* in the last line is closer to "flees" or "disappears")
- What about the contents of the pocket? What do they describe? (begin positively—*rosy clouds, wealth, fame, sure success, love, cheer, bless*—and then go negative—*wither, fade, waning, jilting jade, fame* that only *for a moment gleams*)
- How does the pocket structure relate to the meaning of the sentence? (hides hopeful *dreams*, perhaps to forestall embarrassment if the *dreams* don't come true; hides broken *dreams* out of shame)

With extended context:

- Poems aren't autobiographies, but some elements of Dunbar's life may have influenced this poem. Discuss this idea with the class. (began publishing while in high school—big *dreams*—but was rejected from jobs because of race)
- Did the poet achieve his *dreams*? (yes: fame and recognition for his writing)

SUPPLEMENTAL MATERIAL FOR "DREAMS"

Grammar

- This sentence contains several independent clauses: *What dreams we have, how they fly, how they wither, how they fade.* The order is reversed (object-subject-verb) because the sentence is exclamatory.
- Two adverbial phrases describe *fly*: *Like rosy clouds, across the sky*—unreachable locations in 1903.
- Four adjective phrases describe *dreams*: *Of wealth, of fame, of sure success,*

Of love. By attaching so many phrases to *dreams*, their importance is highlighted.

- The adjective clause *that for a moment gleams, Then flies forever* describes *fame.* A shorter adjective clause (*that comes to cheer and bless*) describes *love*, perhaps revealing that to the author, *love* is less important—or more easily defined—than *fame*.

- The first dash in the last line separates *dreams, ah—dreams* from the rest of the sentence. The poet is either addressing *dreams* or commenting on them. The second dash adds a moment of hesitation, perhaps a sigh.

Rhetoric

Like rosy clouds is a *simile*, and the address to *dreams* is an example of *apostrophe*.

Additional Information and Activities

- Paul Laurence Dunbar is perhaps most famous for his poem "Sympathy," one line of which is the title of the first volume of Maya Angelou's autobiography, *I Know Why the Caged Bird Sings*. Students might read that poem and compare it to "Dreams."

- Langston Hughes's poem "Harlem" discusses a "dream deferred." Students might compare Hughes's treatment of this subject with Dunbar's.

- "Dreams" lends itself to visual representation. For an arts/English project, have students illustrate the sentence.

MORE POCKETS

Pockets are versatile and, when you look for them, surprisingly common. Here are a few more examples, with pocket elements underlined and some context.

Getting Harold's engine running after so long took all of the <u>four hundred dollars</u> I'd saved over the course of my life—allowances, change ferreted away when Mom sent me down the street to buy something at the Circle K, summer work at Subway, Christmas

gifts from my grandparents—so, in a way, Harold was the culmination of my whole being, at least <u>financially speaking</u>.
—John Green, *Turtles All the Way Down*

The narrator, Aza, is still grieving the loss of her father and is battling obsessive-compulsive thoughts. Harold is the name she's given to her late father's car. Though not wealthy, Aza and her family have more money than Aza's friend Daisy, who has an after-school job she hates. Aza becomes involved with Davis Pickett, the son of a wealthy man who disappeared. Attitudes toward money and relationships with parents and others are major themes. As the story progresses, Aza must examine her priorities and relationships and come to terms with the ways in which her *whole being*, including her mental state, function in the world.

As she [Madame] <u>said</u> it, she knew that she knew of a better way; that there was something, altogether different, adult and inspired, that she could have said to Hilda to help her, and that one else but she, Madame, could say . . . because no one else has the knowledge, said Madame, but this second, willful, jealous, petty part in her would not let it be <u>said</u>.
—Rumer Godden, A Candle for St. Jude

Madame is the director of a ballet school. Hilda, a young and talented student, has choreographed a new ballet. The first part of the pocket refers to a rude dismissal of Hilda's ideas that Madame *said*. The second instance is her acknowledgment of guidance that she *would not let . . . be said*. The words are alike, as Madame and Hilda are (both talented and ambitious). Yet the context is different (Madame is at the end of her career and Hilda at the beginning). The contents show the struggle in Madame's mind to overcome her emotions and give Hilda appropriate guidance. The ellipses appear in the original and mirror the stops and starts of Madame's argument with herself.

So don't worry about it if you <u>write</u> out of sadness or hate or love—fear—or fascination, the most important thing, if you wish to do it, is to <u>write</u>.
—*The Selected Letters of Ralph Ellison*, edited by John F. Callahan and Marc C. Conner

In this sentence an established author, Ralph Ellison, offers advice to aspiring authors. His most famous work, *Invisible Man*, traces the evolution of the unnamed title character from an ambitious but naive African American youth through a stint with the American Communist Party to an underground bunker, where he lives surrounded by glowing lightbulbs, invisible to the society around him. Ellison taught at several universities and started a sequel to *Invisible Man*. When his manuscript burned in a fire, Ellison never returned to the project. How appropriate (and ironic) is this structure, then, given that Ellison's point is that the reasons to write are ultimately not *the most important thing*, which is simply *to write*.

> But his life was for other <u>things</u> now, he'd been desperately telling himself, beautiful and wondrous <u>things</u>.
>
> —Jamel Brinkley, "A Family"

The sentence represents the thoughts of the main character, Curtis, newly released from prison and struggling to establish a role for himself in the lives of two people affected by his crime: Lena, the lover of Curtis's dead friend, and her son. Curtis wants other *things*, namely to comfort Lena and help her son. He hides his feelings (*desperately telling himself*, not Lena or others). But the desperation is there, along with the need for *wondrous things* in the future Curtis imagines, strives for, and ultimately achieves: *a family*.

WRITING ASSIGNMENTS

Pocket Change

John Boyne's pocket sentence takes the reader into Bruno's mind and suits the character Boyne created. Give students a chance to change Bruno's character however they wish. They must start and end with Boyne's words:

> "What kind of job?" _____ job Father did.

Discuss how the contents they've created change the character. For example:

"What kind of job?" demanded Bruno, for he'd heard terrible reports of torture, forced labor, and murder, all part of the job Father did.

In this version, Bruno's not ignorant; he's defiant and horrified. His pocket doesn't conceal emotions or private thoughts. Instead, it keeps something important—his objections to Father's actions—close at hand.

NOTE: I've used *The Boy in the Striped Pajamas*, but you can assign any pocket sentence for this exercise.

Who's In the Pocket?

Give the students a pocket formed from two similar elements. Some possibilities:

Class ended _____ ended
The dog was barking _____ arf-arf
Alex smiled _____ grinned

Allow students to add or amend either part of the pocket, if they wish, as long as the two sides have matching ideas. Ask them to insert contents that reflect the character's thoughts and feelings. (You can try for theme, but that's harder to achieve in a single sentence.) Two examples:

Class ended, and Bill still didn't understand why anyone cared how much lemonade there was and why X somehow represented a beverage, but he did know that he was very glad indeed that class had ended.

Anna smiled as she took her seat in the theater—she told herself that if she could get through root canal she could survive anything—and told Max she was delighted to see his play, and grinned.

Discuss what the pocket contents reveal and why they might be tucked into a pocket. In the first example, Bill is sure about his emotions but unsure about math. He probably doesn't want to reveal his reaction to the teacher, so he pockets it. Anna, in the second example, is either protecting Max or hiding her opinion because she wants something from him.

Oh, What I Meant Was . . .

Some pockets contain corrections, like this one from Frederick Douglass's *My Life and Bondage*:

> I felt glad that they were released from prison, and from the dread prospect of a life (or death I should rather say) in the rice swamps.

Ask students to write a sentence with a pocket containing a correction. They can create their own sentences or work from these prompts:

> Luis took his vacation _____ two weeks off

> The babysitter cared for Robbie _____ the little boy

> Augusta wrote her essay _____ her essay

Sample answers:

> Luis took his vacation—well, if you consider taking business phone calls and answering 52 texts a day a vacation—but he did spend his two weeks off at a resort.

> The babysitter cared for Robbie—no, she loved the little boy.

> The first answer adds a touch of snark, the second an extra dose of affection.

Sewing

Distribute nonpocket sentences (from any source, on any subject) and ask students to turn them into pocket sentences. Have them read aloud the original and the pocketed versions and compare the effect on readers.

Un-Sewing

Ask students to "un-pocket" a pocket sentence. Follow the same pattern described above, distributing sentences from this chapter or other pocket sentences you've found.

PATTERN BREAKS

George Lucas knows what a credible alien life-form requires: an odd appearance and a strange way of speaking. Take Yoda, the diminutive Jedi master of the *Star Wars* films. Even without batwing ears, Yoda's sentence structure places the creature in "a galaxy far far away" because he reverses the common pattern of subject-verb-object/complement. In Yoda's speech, "You still have much to learn" becomes "Much to learn, you still have." But Yoda's syntax does more than situate him on another planet. It reinforces meaning: for a Jedi, the individual (*you*) doesn't take priority. Learning does—a goal we teachers share with Yoda.

Most sentence-pattern lessons rightly focus on variety, because changing things up attracts attention. But position in a sentence creates a hierarchy of importance. Bury an important idea in the middle of a string of modifiers and the reader walks away with a sense that something is overlooked or hidden. Place it first, and it captures attention. Move it to last, and you've got a punchline. Showing students how syntax aligns with meaning takes their writing and reading skills to the next level. A worthy goal, that is.

TEACHING PATTERN BREAKS: A GENERAL PLAN

Introduction (optional)

Select one of these activities to introduce pattern breaks:

- Show a video clip of Yoda. What do they detect in his speech? They'll mention the squeaky voice, of course, but many will go on to pattern, even if they can't label what they're hearing. Make a few points about syntax (with or without labels), as I did in the first paragraph of this section. Ask how deviations from the usual pattern affect their response. (I like to word the question this way: "This change affects you how?")
- In Lewis Carroll's *Alice's Adventures in Wonderland*, the March Hare tells the title character indignantly that "I see what I eat" is not the same as "I eat what I see." Is the March Hare correct? Discuss how word order affects perception and meaning.

Decoding

- After settling any vocabulary issues, have students restate the ideas in the sentence you've chosen.
- In a long or complicated sentence, ask students to identify "thought units"—the components of the sentence. For example, suppose they're working on Raymond Chandler's sentence: "Down these mean streets a man must go who is not himself mean, who is neither tarnished nor afraid." The sentence contains these components: (1) *Down these mean streets* (2) *a man must go* (3) *who is not himself mean* and (4) *who is neither tarnished nor afraid.*

NOTE: If students combine the last two, that's fine.

Analysis

- Which component is most important?
- Where is it in the sentence?
- Is that where you'd expect it to be? If so, why? If not, why not?
- How about the other components? Where are they located in relation to the most important idea? Is their location significant? In what way?
- Does the overall structure relate to the meaning of the sentence? How?

TEACHING PATTERN BREAKS: LESSON PLANS

> **J. R. R. Tolkien, *The Hobbit***
>
> **In a hole in the ground there lived a hobbit.**

Brief context: This is the opening sentence in a series about magical creatures.

Extended context: The hobbit of the sentence and title is Bilbo Baggins, and the hole is "not a nasty, dirty, wet hole" or a "dry, bare sandy" one but "a hobbit-hole, and that means comfort." Hobbits are about half the size of adult humans. Bilbo lives near the village of Hobbiton, but he generally prefers to stay in his cozy home, Bag End. When Bilbo is asked by a wizard,

Gandalf, to embark on a quest to rescue treasure stolen from a group of dwarves, he is at first reluctant. So are the dwarves, who doubt Bilbo's ability to help them. Gandalf insists that there is more to Bilbo than the dwarves can detect, in fact "a deal more than he has any idea of himself." Bilbo faces many perils during his journey to recover the dwarves' gold. He becomes stronger, craftier, and more heroic as the story unfolds, and he does indeed retrieve the treasure.

Analysis

With brief context:

- What's the effect of beginning the sentence with location? (emphasizes a different world, where readers don't know what to expect)
- What does *a hole in the ground* bring to mind? (small, makeshift, dirty, dark)
- In the natural world, what sorts of creatures live in *a hole in the ground*? (generally: small animals seeking shelter from predators or extreme weather; specifically: moles, chipmunks, most rabbit species, etc.)
- What's the effect of placing the creature at the end of the sentence, after the location of his home? (emphasizes location, puts distance between the creature and human life above ground, allows the reader to make assumptions about the creature's life and habitat)
- What does the reader expect *a hobbit* to be, given where the *hobbit* lives? (varied answers, some influenced by familiarity with the films—mention burrowing animals and magical beings)
- How would the effect of the sentence change if it read *A hobbit lived there in a hole in the ground*? (varied answers: focuses on the creature, location less important)
- Why include *there*? (extra emphasis on place)

With extended context:

- What's the significance of Bilbo's living *in a hole in the ground*? (he's protected there, must emerge to face danger and to grow)
- What's the effect of referring to *a hobbit*, not to "Bilbo"? (his identity is

unclear at first, relates to the wizard's assessment that there's more to him "than he has any idea of himself")

SUPPLEMENTAL MATERIAL FOR *THE HOBBIT*

Grammar

- The sentence is one independent clause, with the verb (*lived*) preceding the subject (*hobbit*). Inverting the normal order emphasizes that the reader has moved from normality to fantasy.
- Two prepositional phrases appear at the beginning of the sentence: *in a hole* and *in the ground*.

Rhetoric

The sentence is an example of *anastrophe*, a reversal of the usual word order, from the Greek for "turning about."

Additional Information and Activities

- Not of interest to students but definitely to their teachers: Tolkien said this sentence came to him as he was grading student papers. May the same inspiration strike all of us!
- Tolkien was a scholar and a linguist. *The Hobbit* and *The Lord of the Rings* draw from Norse mythology, *Beowulf*, and many traditions of the hero's journey. Consider assigning a research project on these sources.
- Because the films are so popular, students may enjoy comparing the opening sequence of one of the films to this sentence, the first in the book. How does the medium influence the message?
- Ask students to film this sentence. One of my students started with a wide, aboveground shot and narrowed slowly, burrowing underground until *a hobbit* appeared.

> ## Emily Dickinson, "Some Things That Fly There Be"
>
> Some things that fly there be,—
> Birds, hours, the bumble-bee:
> Of these no elegy.

Brief context: These three lines form the beginning of a short poem.

Extended context: This is the first of three stanzas in Emily Dickinson's poem. The second stanza discusses "things that stay" ("grief, hills, eternity") and the third refers to things that are "resting" and "rise" but remain a "riddle."

Analysis

With brief context:

- What are *Some things*? (*Birds, hours, the bumble-bee*)
- In the context of this sentence, what definitions apply to *fly*? (soar through the air, elapse, run away, disappear)
- What do these *things* have in common? (all parts of nature, all *fly*)
- In what way are they not alike? (*Birds* and *the bumble-bee* are animals that physically *fly*; *hours fly* figuratively—they pass quickly)
- The first line reverses the usual order, which would read "there be [are] some things that fly." How does the reversal change perception? (unusual order gives importance to *Some things*)
- What's the significance of starting with *Some things* and then naming them? (the whole is more important than the parts; individual identity is less important than the fact that they *fly* and are lost)
- Another reversal appears at the end of the sentence: *Of these no elegy.* What's the effect of this reversal? (maintains the rhyme, but also highlights *these*, again elevating the general over the specific)

With extended context:

- What do the "things that stay" have in common, according to the speaker? (permanence)
- How do they differ? (*Grief* and *eternity* are abstract, *hills* concrete; saying that *Grief* stays is a judgment, not a fact)
- What's the "riddle"? (why movement or change happens—"resting" and "rise")
- What's the significance of beginning the poem with *things that fly*? (most easily noticed, therefore most likely not given due respect)

SUPPLEMENTAL MATERIAL FOR "SOME THINGS THAT FLY THERE BE"

Grammar

- The comma and dash separate the subject *things* from its appositive (*Birds, hours, the bumble-bee*).
- The colon introduces an explanation of the first part of the sentence. There will be *no elegy* for *things that fly*.

Rhetoric

The sentence is an example of *anastrophe* (reversed order) or *hyperbaton*. These two are near-synonyms, but in hyperbaton the changed order creates a literary effect.

Additional Information and Activities

- Emily Dickinson's poem comprises only nine lines; consider showing students the entire work.
- Dickinson's punctuation is unusual, especially her use of dashes, which early editors of her work deleted or changed to commas. Although punctuation can be a dry subject, it can also be a fruitful area of research: who changed Dickinson's punctuation, when and why, and which version do students prefer?

> ## Barbara Kingsolver, "A Fist in the Eye of God"
>
> **When the lump had grown big enough—when some genetic trigger in her small brain said, "Now, that will do"—she stopped gathering and sat down on her little tuffet, waggling her wings and tiny rounded under-belly to shape the blob into a cup that would easily have fit inside my cupped hand.**

Brief context: The *she* in this sentence is a hummingbird, who built a nest in a tree as the author watched.

Extended context: In this essay Barbara Kingsolver explains why she fears genetically modified organisms (GMOs), primarily because they decrease the variety of genetic traits. In this sentence Kingsolver recounts watching a hummingbird painstakingly construct a nest from "wisps" of spiderweb silk that the bird "smoodged" onto a branch, making numerous trips until there was a "whitish lump" that the bird then shaped to fit her body. Following this sentence Kingsolver explains that the hummingbird added "fine filaments of shredded bark" and a "slap-dab or two of lichen." The last step: the bird licked the nest from the bottom to the top, then moved slightly and licked a new strip, over and over again until she cemented the entire nest. The hummingbird was now ready to lay her eggs.

Analysis

With brief context:

- Where is the bird, *she*, in the sentence? (in the middle)
- Which actions are explicitly paired with *she*? (*she stopped gathering and sat down on her little tuffet*)
- What comes before the *she* statement? (two long *when* statements)
- What comes after the *she* statement? (descriptive verb phrases: *waggling her wings and tiny rounded under-belly to shape the cup*)
- Where does a reference to the author appear in this sentence? (at the end: *my cupped hand*)

- How does the placement of *she* at the center of this sentence align with its meaning? (*she*, the bird, is at the center of the narrative; *she* is also at the center of the nest)
- Does the placement of the *when* statements reflect meaning? (the bird can't shape the central core until there's enough material; also, a nest is made only *when* the bird is ready for offspring)
- What's the significance of placing the human observer at the end of the sentence? (nature, in this instance, is more important than human beings)

With extended context:

- The bird builds the nest from delicate material, added bit by bit. How does the sentence reflect that process? (many phrases and clauses create the sentence)
- Why does the author mention that the cup could *easily have fit* in her *cupped hand*? (emphasize delicacy of the process and of the bird; implies the power of human beings to protect or destroy)
- How does the design of this sentence relate to the GMO issue? (the bird's *genetic trigger* appears early in the sentence and guides the bird's behavior; humans appear last in the sentence and have no role other than to observe the bird's nest-building technique)

SUPPLEMENTAL MATERIAL FOR "A FIST IN THE EYE OF GOD"

Grammar

- The syntax is complicated (as is the nest-building process!). First are two adverbial clauses, each beginning with *when*. Next is an independent clause, with *she* as the subject of *stopped* and *sat*. Then comes a participial phrase, *waggling . . . cup*. Last is an adjective clause, *that would easily . . . hand*, modifying *cup*.
- Dashes surround the second *when* statement, setting it apart from the rest of the sentence. This clause describes the *genetic trigger* and the bird's innate understanding of how big the *lump* must be. The essay addresses the issue of genetically modified organisms, so it's fitting that

the clause referring to *genetic trigger* gets special treatment. Also, GMOs are artificial, not a part of nature; the dashes set the clause apart from the rest of the sentence.

Rhetoric

The two *when* clauses are an example of *anaphora,* repetition of the same word or phrase at the beginning of two or more clauses.

Additional Information and Activities

- Barbara Kingsolver's essay constructs an intricate argument against GMOs. She calls biodiversity an "insurance policy" against mass extinction of food crops. The logical structure of the essay may serve as a model for other issue-oriented writing.
- Kingsolver's essay honors religious and ethical thinking as the proper motivators of scientific inquiry. A multidisciplinary project on science, morality, and language can easily arise from this sentence and essay.
- Have students compare Kingsolver's detailed description of the hummingbird's actions with photographic or video renditions of the nest-building process. How does the medium affect audience response?

MORE PATTERN BREAKS

Here are some sentences worth an in-depth, structural examination, along with brief commentary.

Asked to write about an icon in an essay collection of the same name, author Johanna Fateman wasn't sure whether to accept. She needed inspiration, which she described this way:

> **If it slams all the doors shut and chases you down a narrow corridor, if it rewrites your life in a matters of minutes, revealing everything that came before as an exercise to prepare you for its unique and superior challenges—well, then, that's the feeling I wanted.**

Ultimately Fateman chose feminist Andrea Dworkin as her topic. This sentence, with all those *if* clauses and qualifiers preceding their identification as *the feeling I wanted*, illustrates how difficult her decision was.

Poet John McCrae, an officer in World War I, was inspired to write "In Flanders Field" after a friend died. In the poem, the dead (*we*) speak:

> **Take up our quarrel with the foe:**
> **To you from failing hands we throw**
> **The torch; be yours to hold it high.**

The middle line places *To you from failing hands* before the subject-verb combination, *we throw*. *You* (the living) precede *we* (the dead), because *you* must now take up *the torch*, or cause.

The narrator of *Hotel du Lac*, a novel by Anita Brookner, has been involved in a scandal. To ride out the disgrace, she goes to a resort at her friend's insistence. The narrator writes:

> **A cold coming I had of it.**

She feels, she says, as if her disapproving friend was "escorting a prisoner from the dock to a maximum security wing." It's not surprising, therefore, that in Brookner's sentence a *cold coming* takes precedence over *I*.

As an English teacher, I'd like to think that writers concern themselves with only lofty ideas and impeccable syntax. As an author, I know that a long grocery list and a hamperful of dirty clothes take precedence—even for a writer as accomplished as Ralph Ellison. In a review of a collection of Ellison's letters, reviewer Kevin Young writes:

> **Shoes, a coat, old suits, his class ring: the requests to his mother**
> **and stepfather repeat like a scratched record that still itches.**

Young placed material goods first in this sentence, giving them the importance that Ellison himself gave them.

Rachel Carson, a founding figure of the environmental movement, wrote a pamphlet for the United States Bureau of Fisheries in 1935. That agency rejected her work because it was too lyrical for a government publication. Fortunately, *Atlantic* magazine published the piece, which contains this sentence:

Hard upon the retreating sea press invaders from the land.

The *invaders* in Carson's article are shore birds, crab, and other beach creatures. But her sentence underlines an essential theme of her essay: the *sea* is threatened or *press*[ed] by human *invaders from the land*, who are *hard upon the retreating sea*. In this context, *hard upon* means "soon," but the double meaning applies and justifies the prominent placement of the phrase.

One more, from Billie Eilish's song "I Love You":

Up all night on another red eye
I wish we never learned to fly.

A *red eye*, for readers fortunate enough not to have taken one, is an overnight flight. Eilish's enigmatic song concerns a couple reacting to the first declaration of love. Fear and vulnerability accompany that declaration, expressing a wish to return to an unforced and undefined state. Sleeplessness (*Up all night*) dominates the sentence and hints that worry and tears (*red eye*) will overshadow the relationship. Had they *never learned to fly* (declare love, or perhaps run away from love), everything would be easier.

WRITING ASSIGNMENTS

Fiddling with sentence patterns has its dangers: overuse of odd syntax makes that syntax normal—and, with the sole exception of Yoda, annoying. Nevertheless, practicing pattern breaks adds one more tool to your students' writing kits.

Back to Front

Ask students to select a sentence from their own, previously written work or from a textbook. Most likely they'll find that it follows the usual pattern: subject-verb-object or complement. (If you prefer not to use grammatical terms, identify the subject as the person or object being talked about, the verb as the action or state of being associated with the subject, and the object or complement as the natural completion of the idea begun by the subject and the verb. (For more on termless grammar, see Chapter 3.)

Once they've got a sentence, ask them to reword it so that the ideas are in a different order. They may have to adjust the wording a bit, but they should not stray too far from the original. An example:

> ORIGINAL: Despite the fact that the two species normally compete for space and food, a lioness adopted an orphaned baby leopard.
> REVISION: An orphaned baby leopard adopted by a lioness: not what you'd expect from two species that normally compete for space and food.

There's nothing wrong with the original, but the revision is more dramatic. Plus, starting with "an orphaned baby leopard" intensifies the "oh, how cute" response.

Centering

Ask students to think about someone who's at the center of a location or situation. Have them construct a sentence placing that person in a central position. Here's an example:

> **A juggler tossing multicolored bottles from hand to hand, the line of hungry patrons at the taco truck, and a toddler swinging from his big sister's arms whining for "one more, one more" surrounded Abdur, who thought how pleased the boss would be that one of his detectives had finally located the briefcase stolen from a high-security facility two days before.**

The detective is in the center of the sentence, the case, and the plaza. Content matches form!

U-TURNS

U-turns on the road are to be expected, but U-turns in sentences are generally a surprise. I coined this term, by the way, to label a sentence in which ideas flow in one direction and then suddenly reverse. Sometimes the U-turn subverts what precedes it, like a surprise attack or a punchline. Sometimes the turn is a foray into new territory. Why teach U-turns? Because they can reveal character, reinforce theme, or challenge assumptions. U-turns are also a staple of full-length works, and what students learn on the sentence level scales up easily.

TEACHING U-TURNS: A GENERAL PLAN

Introduction (optional)

Select one or more activities to introduce the "U-turn."

- Show the class only the first part of a U-turn sentence. What do they think comes next? Now reveal the second part. Are they surprised? Does the ending make sense?
- Discuss plot twists. Why are they so popular in stories? Introduce the idea that a single sentence may start off in one direction and veer into another.

Decoding

- Where does the sentence change direction?
- Restate the meaning of each part, before and after the change.

Analysis

- Define the direction that the first portion of the sentence seems to establish.
- Discuss how the second portion differs from the implied direction.
- What's the justification for a U-turn in the sentence? (varied answers: to begin where readers are comfortable before introducing new ideas, to undercut what's already been said, etc.)

- If the sentence were straightforward, expressing the idea without a U-turn, how would readers' reaction change?

TEACHING U-TURNS: LESSON PLANS

NOTE: A vertical line indicates where a new direction begins.

> ### Donna Leon, "Deformazione Professionale"
>
> **I have long been of the opinion that the only thing a person in the audience of an ongoing opera performance is allowed to say is, | "I'm having a heart attack."**

Brief context: This is a comment from an opera lover.

Extended context: The sentence is the first of the essay whose title translates to "Professional Deformation," with the last word being a synonym for "malformation" or "undesirable alteration." The second sentence of the essay is even more extreme than the first, stating that the "final two [words] will suffice" to avoid distracting the audience unnecessarily.

The essay is divided in two. The first part describes the author's indignation at the behavior of an older man in the audience who "was talking. And talking. And talking. And talking" to a silent companion during a performance that the author is also attending. At the conclusion of the performance the chatterbox seems to believe the applause is for his commentary, not for the singers. Later, Donna Leon discovers that the man was once the artistic director of the opera company. The second part of the essay recounts her own behavior at the post-opera party. A mystery novelist, Leon observes the guests. Is her host "strong enough to fight off two unarmed, though masked, robbers?" How would someone steal a handbag, and what would it contain? Or administer poison? The title of her essay implies that both she and the artistic director have been "deformed" by their careers, the talker conditioned to comment on the opera, the writer to observe and plot.

Analysis

With brief context:

• Focus on context. What sort of behavioral rules apply to an opera performance? (varied answers here, but in the interests of civility, please educate your students about courtesy in addition to writing style!)

• Where does the sentence divide? (at the quotation)

• What would you expect to follow the first portion of the sentence? (varied answers, perhaps "bravo" or similar praise)

• How does *I have long been of the opinion* contribute to readers' assumptions about content? (gives the impression that the opinion has been thoughtfully considered and that the sentence will offer a nuanced view)

• Why quote instead of paraphrase? (more dramatic)

• What is the tone? (comical, opinionated)

• Which words establish the tone? (the quotation is extreme, as are other words in the sentence: *long, only,* and *allowed*)

• How would the readers' reaction change if *is allowed to* were changed to *should*? (the original version commands, *should* makes a recommendation)

• Is the ending of the sentence intended to be read literally? (exaggerated)

• What does the ending reveal about the narrator? (loves opera, goes to extremes)

With extended context:

• Discuss the concept of *persona*, which the author of a first-person essay may adopt. How is creating a *persona* helpful to an author? (maintain privacy, free rein for creativity) Are there any disadvantages? (author may seem untrustworthy)

• How are the artistic director and the novelist "professionally deformed"? (job habits invade other areas of life, where they are inappropriate)

SUPPLEMENTAL MATERIAL FOR "DEFORMAZIONE PROFESSIONALE"

Grammar

- The adjective clause *that the only thing . . . heart attack* clarifies the meaning of *opinion*.
- Within that description, *I'm having a heart attack* is a subject complement, equivalent to *thing*. By leading with a general word (*thing*), Leon subtly encourages the reader to infer what the *thing* is. In this way, she sets up the U-turn before identifying the *thing* as *I am having a heart attack*.

Rhetoric

- *Hyperbole* is the use of exaggerated statements not intended to be taken literally. *I'm having a heart attack* is hyperbole (at least I hope it is!).
- *Persona* is the role an author or actor adopts and presents as the self. In Leon's sentence, it's likely she is less extreme than the *I* of her essay.

Additional Information and Activities

- Essays often begin with an account of a personal experience followed by an explanation of its significance. Leon's essay fits this pattern, opening with the opera and adding a second experience (the party) before interpreting the pair. Discuss the impact of self-revelation weighed against privacy concerns.
- For class discussion and/or an essay: Are the two examples of "deformation" (the artistic director, the mystery writer) really deformations? Alternate topic: Both examples are from creative activities. Are such careers more likely to "leak" into one's private life?

> **Justice Elena Kagan, Concurring Opinion in**
> *Florida v. Jardines*
>
> **Like the binoculars, a drug-detection dog is a specialized device for discovering objects not in plain view | (or plain smell).**

Brief context: This sentence comes from a Supreme Court opinion.

Extended context: The issue in the 2013 case of *Florida v. Jardines* was whether taking a drug-detection dog onto the porch of someone's house is subject to the Fourth Amendment's limits on searches. The Supreme Court ruled that the officer and the dog were indeed conducting a search and therefore the Fourth Amendment's requirements apply.

Justice Elena Kagan sided with the majority but expanded on her reasoning in a concurring opinion. She equates the search in this case to a stranger's stepping onto a homeowner's porch "carrying super-high-powered binoculars." Without knocking or greeting the resident, Kagan continues, the stranger peers through the windows and sees intimate details of someone's life. The use of binoculars goes against the homeowner's "reasonable expectation of privacy." So does the use of a trained, drug-detection dog.

Kagan plays with an often-used term, *plain view*, by adding *plain smell*. (Legally, something *in plain view* may provide grounds for a warrantless search. In the Jardines case, the drugs were not *in plain view*.) Kagan dismisses one opposing argument, that dogs are common in American households and therefore the drug-sniffing dog's presence is not unusual. She writes that the officer's dog in the Jardines case was "not your neighbor's pet, come to your porch on a leisurely stroll." She notes that likening a drug-detection dog to "the poodle down the street" is equating "high-powered binoculars" to "a piece of plain glass."

Analysis

With brief context:

- Students may need help decoding the "title" of the piece. Criminal charges are brought by the government, in this case the state of *Florida*. *Jardines* is the defendant in the case. You may also have to explain, or have them research, the abbreviation *v.* (for "versus") and this specific usage of *plain* ("open, unhidden").
- What is the purpose of *binoculars*? (to sharpen sight, increase visibility) What about a *drug-detection dog*? (to find drugs)
- What is the purpose of beginning with *Like the binoculars*? (sets up a comparison)
- Have you heard the expression *in plain view* or its variation *in plain*

sight? What do they mean? (visible without a search) How about *plain smell*? (unusual, most likely never heard it) Why pair the common with the uncommon? (extends established ideas)

- How is *plain sight* similar to *plain smell*? (no special effort required)
- What does the phrase *specialized device* mean in this context? (the drug-detection dog is trained to signal the presence of drugs)
- What's the likely meaning of *objects* in the context of this sentence? (evidence of a crime, specifically drugs or drug-related paraphernalia)
- If the sentence ended with *objects*, would your reaction to it change? (varied answers)

With extended context:

- What is the legal significance of *not in plain view*? (probable cause and warrant needed)
- How does Kagan's sentence relate *plain smell* to the law? (equates *not in plain view* to human eyes with [*not in*] *plain smell* to an untrained, normal nose)
- How does Kagan's sentence reflect the role of the Supreme Court? (hard one! My answer: the Court applies the principles laid down in the Constitution, as well as legal precedents, to their cases. The Founders could not have imagined all aspects of modern life, so the Court must look for equivalents, such as *plain sight* and *plain smell*.)

SUPPLEMENTAL MATERIAL FOR CONCURRING OPINION

Grammar

- Prepositional phrases express relationships. *Like the binoculars* relates the optical instrument to the drug-detection dog. (Elsewhere in her opinion Kagan reiterates the link, writing that "the equipment they [the police] used was animal, not mineral.")
- The sentence has a linking verb, *is*, which connects the subject (*dog*) to the subject complement (*device*). This underscores Kagan's point: the dog isn't a pet but a *device* to detect drugs.

Rhetoric

Kagan's sentence creates an *analogy*, or comparison, between the *drug-detection dog* and the *binoculars*.

Additional Information and Activities

- Several other Supreme Court cases have addressed the use of drug-detection dogs: *United States v. Place* (1983), *City of Indianapolis v. Edmond* (2000), *Illinois v. Caballes* (2005), and *Florida v. Harris* (2013). A history/English project might inquire into the legal principles governing what these animals are permitted to do.
- Kagan's opinion is a fairly easy read, even for nonlawyers. The entire case—a summary, the majority opinion, Justice Kagan's concurring opinion, and the dissent—can be accessed at https://supreme.justia.com/cases/federal/us/569/1/.

Siegfried Sassoon, "Glory of Women"

You love us when we're heroes, home on leave,
Or wounded in a | mentionable place.

Brief context: This poem was written by a war veteran.

Extended context: Siegfried Sassoon is one of the preeminent poets of World War I, a decorated soldier so disillusioned by the horrors he witnessed in battle that he wrote a letter to his commanding officer entitled "Finished with the War: A Soldier's Declaration." He could have been imprisoned for treason for writing it but instead was sent to a psychiatric hospital and eventually returned to duty. Sassoon was critical of the oblivious or even callous reactions of civilians on the home front. One example: British veterans' hospitals of the era often grouped patients with disfiguring injuries in a separate wing, hiding the patients from the general public.

Analysis

With brief context:

- Where is the U-turn? (just before *mentionable*)
- What impression do the words before the U-turn give? (idealized image: brave warriors returning from the front, welcomed by patriotic women who *love* them, *love* the *wounded*)
- What function does *when* have in this sentence? (limits the time period or conditions under which *you love us*)
- The word *unmentionable* is an old-fashioned euphemism for underwear and the parts of the body that underwear covers. Explore the meaning of *mentionable.* (not in common use, means "able to be talked about")
- Why are some things not talked about? (what you don't want to know or can't bear to think about)
- What's the tone? (cynical, bitter)
- What's the effect of the U-turn? (subverts the implied patriotism of the first part of the sentence)
- How does the sentence reflect the soldiers' reality? (nonsoldiers seldom understand what soldiers face)

With extended context:

- How might the pronoun *us* relate to the author's message? (a veteran, Sassoon is included in *us*, speaks with authority)
- What's *mentionable* and *unmentionable* about war? (varied answers: the wounded soldiers, censored criticism of war, treason charge and psychiatric treatment)

SUPPLEMENTAL MATERIAL FOR "GLORY OF WOMEN"

Grammar

The verb in the independent clause (*love*) is modified by *when . . . place.* This structure emphasizes that the women's *love* is not unconditional.

Additional Information and Activities

- World War I brought forth an outpouring of poetry. Consider assigning poems from Sassoon, Wilfred Owen, Rupert Brooks, and others. Reading in chronological order, students may note how many poets started out writing patriotic poems and then made a U-turn into cynicism.
- For an arts/English project, have students watch a scene from a film set during World War I or look at some photographs. They can compare the effect of Sassoon's poem to the visual presentation in those media.

EXPECT THE UNEXPECTED: MORE U-TURNS

In these U-turn sentences, I've added a bit of context where needed. The U-turn is marked with a vertical line.

That mood remained on them for three miles during which they made reasonably good progress, | being forced to make for shore—before they sank—only four times.
> —Farley Mowat, *The Dog Who Wouldn't Be* (description of the maiden—and only—voyage of the boat his neighbor built)

Every morning, he would tear out a page from his English dictionary, memorize it, and | eat it.
> —Yoon Choi, "The Art of Losing" (about an immigrant who must improve his English skills in order to continue his career as a college professor)

Today Greenland has 56,000 residents, 12,000 Internet connections, 50 farms, and, by American standards, | no trees.
> —Elizabeth Kolbert, "A Song of Ice"

The total freedom of writers in this country can be | distressing.
> —Walker Percy, "Why I Live Where I Live"

Jim Kay's favorite part of drawing is | right before
he makes a mark.
                    —Alexandra Alter, "Illustrating Magic and Harry Potter"

Nancy Drew, the girl detective who could pick a lock, play the
bagpipes, tap Morse Code in high heels and drive her blue roadster
like a Daytona champ, | turns 90 next year.
                    —Alexis Soloski, "The Case of Enduring Popularity"

Players across the majors have reported to spring training this year
with gloves, bats, and | barbs.
                    —Tyler Kepner, "Astros Scandal Linger. That's the Real Shame"

[Christian] Menn was a professor of structural engineering
at the Swiss Federal Institute of Technology in Zurich, where
Albert Einstein got his diploma in math and natural sciences,
where the mathematician John von Neumann got his in chemical
engineering, and where the Chinese-born paleoclimatologist Ken
Hsü got his | umlaut.   —John McPhee, "Tabula Rasa"

The earth is running out of | places to go.
                    —Stanley Reed, "Saudi Arabia Wants Your Next Vacation"

Blackstone declined to turn Sarah into an elephant—either he
couldn't or he wouldn't, I've always said in my carefully balanced
account of the incident—but he declined with great aplomb,
pointing out to me that an elephant is one of the few beasts that
require more upkeep than | a teenager.
                    —Calvin Trillin, "A Couple of Eccentric Guys"

WRITING ASSIGNMENTS

Modeling U-turns is surprisingly easy. To that basic assignment, add some of
these, all of which take a little more time.

Definitions Redefined

Choose a random word, or ask students to select one. Have them find a dictionary definition and restate it in their own words and then state it once more so that it matches their idea of the word. This is a playful assignment, so give them free rein. Two sample answers:

> Maturity is "the fullness of growth or development," or, what parents seldom recognize in their offspring.

> Insurance is a "plan for compensation in case of loss," like taking ten sharpened #2 pencils to a standardized test.

Some suggestions: *convenience, flirting, poetry, hipster, delicious,* and *news.*

Surprise, With or Without Delight

Ask students to think of a situation that turned out differently from what they expected, delighting or disappointing them. Have them write a sentence with the unexpected element at the end. For example:

> Joe valued honesty above all else, and his campaign slogan—"I'll achieve modest results!"—proved true on election day.

Skewers

Some authors sound polite just before they tear their characters apart. Have students write sentences that begin positively and then take a nose-dive. An example:

> Bob spoke to Amy at length about his strong support for feminism and then left the woman he'd repeatedly interrupted in order to give a lecture entitled "Female Voices Matter."

Stats

As Elizabeth Kolbert does in her sentence about Greenland, ask students to incorporate statistics in a sentence on any topic they choose, moving from the expected to the unexpected. They may need research time for this assignment. Here's an example:

> One factor determining the creature with the best sense of smell is the number of olfactory receptor genes, of which humans have 396, dogs 811, cows 1186, African elephants 1948, and sperm whales 0.

Got you with that last one, right? The statistical progression moves upward, until it crashes with a U-turn.

VISUAL PRESENTATION

This section requires a warning label: once you set students to work on the visual presentation of a sentence, you'll have to pry them away from the topic with a crowbar. That's how appealing the link between image and text is.

Not that the topic is a new one, as the proliferation of memes on social media sites shows. Beyond memes, though, much remains to be seen: the artwork of Jenny Holzer, Tauba Auerbach, René Magritte, and Roy Lichtenstein, just to name a few who incorporate sentences into their visual creations. Sentences with playful fonts, all caps, and offbeat layouts make it onto library shelves, too, especially in children's or young adult books such as Jeff Kinney's *The Diary of a Wimpy Kid* and *P.S. Longer Letter Later* by Paula Danziger and Ann M. Martin. Graphic novels make good use of image and text (take a look at *Persepolis* and *Maus*, if you haven't already), and poets have long experimented with, well, everything to do with words, including the physical image their sentences create.

In short: no one can dismiss the visual presentation of sentences as gimmicky, though in all fairness, I must admit that sometimes it can be. But in the hands of masterful writers, visual presentation weds art to meaning, intensifying the power of a sentence in a unique way. I don't need an emoji to explain that students live in a sea of images. We all know that, just as we know that our job is to teach them to swim.

TEACHING VISUAL PRESENTATION: A GENERAL PLAN

Introduction (optional)

Select an image/text. First, show students only the text. Gather reactions. Next, read it aloud, if possible. (Some visually presented sentences don't easily fit the spoken-word format. One I discuss later in this chapter—E. E. Cummings's "1(a"—falls into this category.) Gather reactions to the oral presentation. Finally, present the image and text together, as the creator of the sentence intended. What's lost or gained with each format?

Decoding

- This task may be especially challenging, depending on how the words appear. Some image/text sentences have no punctuation, with only capital or lowercase letters, and many ignore the usual horizontal, left-to-right, reading pattern. It may be impossible to determine where an unconventional sentence begins and ends. As the students decode, discuss all reasonable interpretations with the class.
- Decoding this sort of sentence involves addressing the image as well as the words. What impressions does the image convey?

Analysis

- It's likely that the artist/author made a number of choices: font, size, placement, margins, color, image type and size, and so forth. Identify and discuss every element that appears.
- How does the visual presentation as a whole reflect, subvert, or otherwise interact with the text's meaning?

TEACHING VISUAL PRESENTATION: LESSON PLANS

> ### William Goldman, *The Princess Bride*
>
> But—
> —in the farthest corner of the Great Square—
> —in the highest building in the land—
> —deep in the deepest shadow—
> —the man in black stood waiting.

Brief context: This sentence appears in a scene in which a prince announces his engagement and his fiancée walks across the Great Square, where his subjects greet her joyfully.

Extended context: The fiancée, Buttercup, has agreed to marry Prince Humperdinck only because she believes the man she loves, Westley, is dead. Westley worked for Buttercup's family for many years. Buttercup treated him disdain-fully until, one day, she realized that she loved him. Westley went off to make his fortune in preparation for marrying Buttercup, but his ship sank. This sentence follows a description of the prince's engagement announcement and Buttercup's walk through the Great Square. Buttercup has many adventures, some dangerous, before she discovers the identity of *the man in black*.

Analysis

With brief context:

- What's the effect of placing *But*— at the beginning of the sentence, alone on a line? (a teaser, a warning, suspense, loneliness)
- The next four lines are indented. How does that design affect the reader? (leaning forward, more suspense)
- Dashes abound in this sentence. What do they add, visually? (resemble daggers or spears or cuts)
- The sentence is presented on five lines, though it is part of a novel, not a poem. How does that arrangement affect the reader? (teases the reader, dripping out information bit by bit, as the plot does)
- The last line expresses a complete thought and could stand alone as a sentence. How does that placement, in relation to the four lines preceding it, affect readers' perception? (delayed independence, sense that the line is important for as-yet-unknown reasons)

With extended context:

- The sentence builds up to *the man in black* but doesn't identify him. Why? (adds to the mystery, readers want to know who he is)
- The words in this sentence are extreme (*farthest, Great, highest, deepest*). How do those word choices affect readers' assumptions about *the man in black*? (he's extreme in personality or has had extreme experiences)
- How might Buttercup's adventures relate to the extreme language of the sentence? (some are "dangerous" or extreme, like the language)

- How does the visual image of the sentence relate to events in the story? (Buttercup will have a series of adventures—layout of the lines suggests a series)

SUPPLEMENTAL MATERIAL FOR *THE PRINCESS BRIDE*

Grammar

- The sentence begins with a conjunction: *But.* Many writers begin sentences this way, but the strictest grammarians maintain that this usage is incorrect.
- With the above exception noted, the sentence is a single independent clause.
- Five prepositional phrases, all giving location, precede the clause *the man in black stood waiting.* Prepositional phrases are arguably less important than clauses, so this structure implies that the man's location is less important than the fact that he's there and *waiting*.

Rhetoric

There are no conjunctions between phrases, so the term *asyndeton* applies to this sentence.

Additional Information and Activities

- Spoiler alert: *the man in black* is Westley, who did not die when his ship sank and instead earned his fortune as the "Dread Pirate Roberts." He is waiting to see whether Buttercup still loves him. She does, and they share the adventures referred to in the "extended context" section. (I'm giving you this information in case you wish to correct student speculation about the identity of *the man in black*.)
- The novel was made into a film, making this sentence a fine basis for a visual arts/English discussion. How is *the man in black* shown in the film? Which is more dramatic, the sentence or the film? Why?
- Goldman is the author of the novel but also a character in it, making the book a good focus for a study of *metafiction*, in which the author refers to the piece of writing, or the process of writing, within the work.

Marjane Satrapi, *Persepolis 2*

THE HARDER I TRIED TO ASSIMILATE, THE MORE I HAD THE FEELING THAT I WAS DISTANCING MYSELF FROM MY CULTURE, BETRAYING MY PARENTS AND MY ORIGINS, THAT I WAS PLAYING A GAME BY SOMEBODY ELSE'S RULES.

Brief context: A young Iranian woman living in Austria explains how she feels in this graphic autobiography.

Extended context: Marjane Satrapi's graphic autobiographies, *Persepolis* and its sequel, *Persepolis 2*, recount her childhood in Iran and, later, in exile. Her family opposed the harsh rule of the Shah and the equally harsh rule of the Islamic fundamentalists who toppled him and established a theocracy. To save Satrapi from the dangers of the Iran–Iraq war and the limitations on women of Iranian society, her parents sent her to live with a friend in Austria. She changes schools and living arrangements several times, always the outsider. For a while she tries to fit in, but as her sentence and accompanying drawing show, this is not the path for her.

Analysis

With brief context:

- What do you see in the drawing? (large figure taking a giant step away from two people represented by faceless, dark shapes)
- Who's who? (large figure—narrator; dark shapes—parents)
- How do the legs appear? (extended beyond what's natural or possible in real life; the front leg at the limit of the panel)

- How does the presentation of the legs reflect the narrator's emotions? (stretching for a new identity contorts her, takes her away from her parents)
- What about her feet? How do they relate to her situation? (front foot stretches outward and away from her parents, back foot drifts above the ground—she's isn't with them, and she's drifting)
- Look at her arms. Do they relate to her sentence? (curved downward, fingers splayed as if searching for a handrail and stability: *playing a game by somebody else's rules*).
- What does the drawing add to the sentence? (image makes the author's emotional life visible and intensely personal)

With extended context:

- How does the figure in the foreground relate to the author's life? (wearing pants, hair uncovered and very short: distanced from the strict traditions for women in Iran, more Westernized)
- How about the figures in the background? How do they relate to the author's life? (united, mother wearing a short skirt—not conforming to Iran's strict dress code for women; a solid shape that the girl can't see—her sense of alienation)

SUPPLEMENTAL MATERIAL FOR *PERSEPOLIS 2*

Grammar

- The sentence begins with a parallel comparison: *The harder I . . . the more I.*
- *Feeling* is modified by two clauses beginning with *that*. Devoting so much space to these modifiers conveys an urgent need to explain the emotion.
- Another modifier, *betraying . . . origins* is a participial phrase that further explains *feeling*. It breaks the parallel pattern of modifiers, perhaps because it is the most extreme of the three explanations of how she feels.

Rhetoric

The statement about *playing a game* is a *metaphor*. As noted above, there are two *parallel* modifiers and one that breaks the pattern.

Additional Information and Activities

- It's easy to comprehend, intellectually, that assimilation comes with loss. You might ask students to imagine another illustration depicting something else the author has had to leave behind: a tradition, a favorite location or event, and so on. They can describe the loss with one sentence and illustrate it. (Stick figures are fine, or descriptions of what they would draw if they had the ability.)
- For a history/English research project, students can look into Iranian history: the fall of the Shah, the installation of a theocracy, relations with other countries, and so forth.

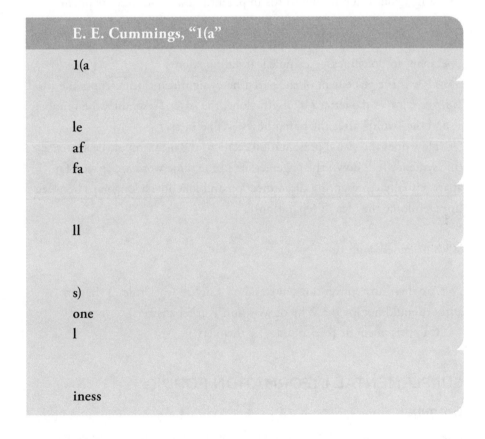

E. E. Cummings, "l(a"

l(a

le
af
fa

ll

s)
one
l

iness

Brief context: E. E. Cummings's poem, arranged horizontally, is "l(a leaf falls)oneliness."

Extended context: E. E. Cummings dispensed with the usual rules of punctuation, spelling, and grammar for artistic effect. This poem has no title and is known by its first line. Presented as a visual image, the poem makes a strong statement. Read aloud—no easy task!—the poem changes.

Analysis

With brief context:

- When you omit the words in parentheses, what does the poem express? (*loneliness*)
- When you read only the words in parentheses, what does the poem express? (*a leaf falls*)
- How is the parenthetical expression related to the rest of the sentence? (metaphor for loneliness—a single leaf, falling alone)
- How is the placement of the parentheses significant? (interrupts the word *loneliness*, leaves the letter *l* by itself, alone; the letter *l* resembles the number 1, and the "word" after the parentheses is "oneliness")
- How does the visual presentation relate to the meaning of the sentence? (the sentence falls down the page; letters in the same word are spaced far apart, visually representing disconnection and loneliness; long gaps between lines reinforce the idea of separation)

With extended context:

- Are there any conventions of standard English (the "rules") that an author should not break? Why or why not? (varied answers)
- Can this poem be read aloud? (let them try!)

SUPPLEMENTAL INFORMATION FOR "l(a"

Grammar

Students sometimes ask me whether the poem "l(a" is really a sentence. The *Oxford English Dictionary* defines a sentence as "a series of words in connected speech or writing, forming the grammatically complete expression of a single thought." A secondary definition specifies that a sentence has a subject and a predicate. The words in parentheses satisfy the requirements of both defini-tions. True, *a leaf falls* is embedded within the word *loneliness*. But that arrangement only strengthens the case for "1(a" as a sentence fitting the crite-ria in the primary definition. The grammatical disconnection of *loneliness* from *a leaf falls* strongly connects the word to the "expression of a single thought" about the nature of *loneliness*.

Rhetoric

The words in parentheses, *a leaf falls*, are a *metaphor* for loneliness.

Additional Information and Activities

- E. E. Cummings was an innovative poet, one of the most popular of the twentieth century. More of his work is available on the Poetry Foundation website.
- Cummings was part of a larger artistic movement, modernism. For an interdisciplinary research project on modernism, have students compare Cummings's work with that of modernist painters such as Pablo Picasso, Henri Matisse, or Georgia O'Keeffe.

MORE VISUAL PRESENTATIONS

Whether on a page or a screen—or billboards or clothing or anywhere else—visual presentations of sentences are easy to find. Here are a few more, with some questions and comments.

> **A. A. Milne, "The Christening"**
>
> I sometimes call him Terrible John,
> 'Cos his tail goes on—
> And on—
> And on.

This sentence comes from a poetry collection entitled *When We Were Very Young* by Alan Alexander Milne. The preface to the book asks readers to imagine that the speaker is Christopher Robin, a character in the author's Winnie the Pooh stories and, not coincidentally, the name of the author's young son. The speaker ponders the names he applies to his "dear little dormouse" (*him*) whose tail is "e-nor-mouse." (You may need to explain that a *dormouse* is quite different from the sort of mouse often kept as a pet.) In other parts of the poem, the speaker calls the pet "Terrible Jack" and "Terrible James" because "he likes me calling him names." At the end, though, the speaker says he will call the dormouse "Jim" because he is "so fond of him."

Analysis

- How does the appearance of this sentence relate to its meaning? (each line is shorter than the one preceding it, resembling a tapering tail)
- What is the function of *Terrible John* in this sentence? (sets up the rhyme for *on / and on*)
- Why *Terrible*? (no evidence that the pet is badly behaved, but the speaker says that the dormouse "likes me calling him names")
- Does this sentence have the same effect if it's read aloud, but not seen? (aloud, the rhyme dominates; seeing it adds the impression of a *tail*)

> ### Thomas Hardy, "The Convergence of the Twain"
>
> **And as the smart ship grew**
> **In stature, grace, and hue,**
> **In shadowy silent distance grew the Iceberg too.**

Thomas Hardy wrote "The Convergence of the Twain" shortly after the *Titanic* sank in April 1912. *Twain*, or "two," refers to the ship and the iceberg. Every stanza in the poem is one sentence, arranged on the page like this one. The poem begins with images of the sunken ship, contrasting the pride and luxury that were part of the creation of the vessel with the decay of the wreck. The poet sees their meeting, or *convergence*, as destined by "the Immanent Will," not necessarily God but a powerful, determining force.

Analysis

- How does the visual presentation of this sentence relate to its subject? (resembles a ship; the longest line is the last, and most of an iceberg's mass is below water)
- Read the sentence aloud. What do you hear? How does the sound relate to meaning? (end rhymes unite the lines; lines refer to the *ship* and to the *Iceberg*, thus they're also united—the *convergence* of the title)
- The sentence begins with *And*. What do you imagine comes before this sentence? (information about the ship and the iceberg precedes this sentence)
- Which is more important—to hear or to see this sentence? (to see, because you can't hear the image; with the image, the ship is more dominant than the iceberg—ironic, as the iceberg sinks the ship)

WRITING ASSIGNMENTS

Modeling assignments for visual presentation will stretch students'—and your—definition of "sentence." My approach is to declare a cease-fire in my war for correct grammar and permit whatever they like, so long as it's neither hurtful (always banned) nor incomprehensible. In reviewing the responses, I recommend asking students to explain the rationale for every sentence after their peers have had a chance to weigh in on meaning. Read on, for a few more prompts.

Atmosphere

Taking a cue from William Goldman, whose sentence about *the man in black* is suspenseful and mysterious, ask for a sentence that creates an atmosphere. Goldman employs horizontal lines, but your class doesn't have to do the same. A sentence about a love triangle might actually be a triangle, with sharp words and sharp punctuation (dashes or exclamation points) emphasizing rivalry. A joyful sentence might feature an increasingly large font for each word, perhaps moving from light italics to deep bold. Here's one about a job interview:

I won't get it; **I have a good resume,** but I still don't think I'll get it.

Anxiety, determination, self-help mantra . . . all come through via font.

Definition

With a nod to E. E. Cummings, ask students to write a sentence defining the word it is embedded in. Matching the visual aspect of the sentence with the words should be their focus. Here's a definition of "crowding":

CR|can'tmove|OW|toomanypeoplesteppingonmytoes|DING

What I like about this response is the way "crowding" is divided. *CR* sounds like the beginning of a comment that hits a barrier. Next up is what's happening to provoke the comment: "can'tmove" presented without a space. Now another bit of "crowding" (*OW*) sounding like a yelp of pain. Why? Keep reading: "toomanypeoplesteppingonmytoes" which is, of course, squeezed together. The line ends, like a boxing round, with the "ding" of a bell.

Paths

Where does language go if it doesn't follow the usual rules? To confusion, maybe, but also perhaps to possibility. Ask students to select three words, or give them three with no punctuation and with every letter capitalized. Have them arrange the words so that more than one path opens up. For example: start with JACK LOVES JILL. If these words are arranged in a circle or placed on the sides of a triangle, several interpretations are possible:

Jill loves Jack.
Jack loves Jill?
Jill loves, Jack!
Loves: Jack, Jill

CHAPTER 7
DICTION

VALUABLE VERBS

. . . .

One of my favorite lessons, which I unleash about a month into my writing class, involves asking a student—one who trusts me enough to challenge me—to *walk* to the door. When the student is halfway there, I say, "No, you're not doing what I asked. Please *walk* back to your seat." With a slight adjustment—faster, slower, jauntier, more determined, whatever—the student completes the journey. I reject that effort, too, and repeat the request: *walk* to the door, seat, and door again. At some point the student will round on me with a what-are-you-crazy? look and blurt, "You just said *walk*! That could be anything!" Ah. Now I solicit better verbs from the class. My chosen helper has to *stomp*, *plod*, *strut*, *saunter*, *stroll* . . . you get the point. And so does the class.

That's a basic lesson in verb selection: specific is better. More lessons follow: how a verb can illustrate character and mood, echo a theme, convey an attitude. These roles are generally easy to see in a single sentence.

Before I continue, I should address terminology: I'm calling an action word that powers a sentence a *verb*, well aware that some English teachers prefer *simple predicate*. That's fine. Substitute the term you normally use when you teach the potential of *verbs* (or *predicates*). As students examine sentences someone else has written and write their own, the goal is the same: to grasp how an apt choice adds value and how a poor selection mars the reading experience.

TEACHING VALUABLE VERBS: A GENERAL PLAN

Introduction (optional)

Use the activity described above to introduce the concept of a valuable verb, or select one of these:

- A less physical variation of the *walk* exercise (well suited to online learning) involves *say*, with the command being "say your name." Continue telling the students they're wrong until they snap. Then have them *murmur, whisper, shout, declare, offer*, and so forth.
- Ask students to write a sentence about one thing they did recently. Comb through the answers and select one that might benefit from a more interesting verb. Read the sentence aloud and ask the writer a question about the event. Then challenge the class to substitute a better verb that incorporates the new information. Here's an example, with the verbs underlined:

SENTENCE: I watched a *Star Wars* marathon on Saturday.
QUESTION: Do you like those films?
ANSWER: Absolutely! I love them! I sat in front of the TV all day.
REVISED SENTENCE: I devoured the *Star Wars* marathon on Saturday.
ALTERNATE: I glued myself to the *Star Wars* marathon on Saturday.

Decoding

- Before they can analyze the verb, they have to find it. The usual question— what's the action in the sentence?—is a good starting point.
- Unless you want to incorporate a grammar lesson on complete sentences, don't stress out about differentiating between the simple predicate (the main verb in the sentence) and participles functioning as modifiers. Also, it doesn't matter if they fail to identify the entire verb phrase, overlooking *do, has, must, can*, and the *like*. Keep their attention on the words expressing action.
- Linking verbs may be present in the sentence. In general, they're not as fruitful an area of study as action verbs. True, *seems* and *is* convey

different degrees of certainty. In my experience, students come to see this
on their own and select the verb that best suits what they're trying to say.

- Once they've identified the verbs, check that they understand the entire
sentence.

Analysis

- Discuss connotation, if appropriate.
- Is the verb in active voice (*threw*) or passive (*was thrown*)? How does
voice affect the sentence?
- Identify the tense. How does it reflect the meaning of the sentence?
- If more than one verb is present, do you see a shift? If so, why has the
author changed from active to passive, from present to past, and so forth?

TEACHING VALUABLE VERBS: LESSON PLANS

I've selected these sentences because the verbs highlight character, theme, and
action in precise and forceful ways. The verbs I discuss are underlined.

> ### Brook Larmer, "Li Na: China's Tennis Rebel"
>
> **Now Li, the former French Open champion and sixth-ranked
> player in the world, <u>teetered</u> one game away from a third-round
> loss to the Czech veteran Klara Zakopalova.**

Brief context: This sentence describes a tennis match between two professional
tennis players.

Extended context: Li Na was enrolled in China's state-controlled sports program when she was only five. Throughout her childhood she endured a gru-
eling training regimen with little personal freedom. She achieved great
international success, winning two important championships. As the article's
title implies, Li Na often rebelled against her role as sports star and national
icon. She pointedly noted in an interview that "nobody bothered to ask"

whether she wanted to play tennis. Her career had ups and downs, matching her relationship with the Chinese media, who alternately praised and criticized her. She eventually attained a degree of independence, paying her own expenses in return for the right to choose her coach, take more control of her personal life, and keep a percentage of her winnings. She dropped out of tennis once, returned to the game, threatened to drop out again, and finally retired in 2014. In 2019 she became the first player born in Asia to enter the International Tennis Hall of Fame.

Analysis

With brief context:

- What image does the verb *teetered* call to mind? (children's playground equipment—a teeter-totter or seesaw)
- How does *teetered* fit Li Na's potential defeat? (the game could go either way, her rank up or down; also, figuratively she's on the edge of a cliff, ripe for falling out of the tournament, alluding to the common expression *teetering on the brink*)
- Substitute *was* for *teetered*. How does the sentence change? (*was* is more neutral; *teetered* implies unsteadiness, more predictive of a fall)
- The sentence begins with *Now*, but the verb is in past tense. How do these two time markers go together? (creates a "you are there" approach, directs readers' attention to a fixed a moment in the past)

With extended context:

- How does *teetered* apply to Li Na's career? (her career has had highs and lows, like the motion of a seesaw; she's been in and out of the sport, implying a wavering desire to play)
- How does *teetered* apply to Li Na's relationship with the media? (media wavers between praise and criticism)

SUPPLEMENTAL MATERIAL FOR "LI NA: CHINA'S TENNIS REBEL"

Grammar

- The subject of the sentence is *Li Na*. Her name is followed by a lengthy appositive (*the former French . . . world*) that tells the reader who she is.
- The second player, *Klara Zakopalova*, is identified only as a *Czech veteran*. The disparity in length fittingly gives the subject of the article, *Li Na*, more importance.

Additional Information and Activities

- This sentence comes from an article on tennis. What about other sports? Ask students to list verbs that may usefully describe soccer, basketball, and any other sport. Additional challenge: find verbs that apply to the athlete's career, not just to the action described.
- This article is a good fit for an interdisciplinary research project combining psychology and English. Many studies have been done on the relationship between stress, mindset, and performance. Alternatively, students can look specifically at children's responses to training regimens.
- Li Na was part of a national, government-sponsored program. For a social studies/English research project, students can examine the benefit or harm that has come from this institution in China and in other countries with similar programs.

Adele, "Million Years Ago"

To <u>earn</u> my stripes I'd have to <u>pay</u> / And <u>bear</u> my soul.

Brief context: Adele sings this song, which she and Gregory Kurstin cowrote. The singer (*I*) looks at her childhood, the time before she was famous, with longing and regret.

Extended context: The narrator longs for what she's lost from her childhood. Her friends, as well as strangers, react to her differently now that she's a celebrity. She sees her youth as a time when everything seemed to be possible, a nonstop party. She knows that she's made mistakes and that being an adult requires coming to terms with them and expressing regret. This song represents a way to do so.

Analysis

With brief context:

- What does *earn my stripes* mean? (reach a higher level, a reference to military uniforms where *stripes* indicate rank)
- What must the singer *pay* to *earn* [her] *stripes*? (not money, but painful feelings and difficult experiences)
- The official lyrics include *bear*, a homonym for *bare*, the spelling that appears in some printed versions of the song. Listeners, of course, can't tell whether the line reads *bear* or *bare*. How does the meaning change with each word? (*bear my soul*—accept the burden on my spirit; *bare my soul*—reveal my inner self)
- Which word fits the theme of regret? (both, but in different ways: *bear* shows the burden of regret, *bare* a way to accept responsibility and to heal)
- The main verb of the sentence isn't the interesting one (*would have*, with *would* folded into the contraction *I'd*). What's the effect of shifting the focus to the infinitives *pay* and *bear*? (fame is an illusion, catching all the attention and obscuring what really matters—in this case, *pay* and *bear*)

With extended context:

- How does *earn my stripes* relate to the singer's expression of regret? (to *earn* a higher level of maturity she has to deal with the past)
- What has she had to *pay*? (loss of old relationships, changes in current relationships, reality instead of dreams)
- How does the singer's view of life change? (not a party but something to be treasured, things will inevitably be lost and should be appreciated while they exist)
- How does the title relate to the sentence? (shows the gap between childhood and adulthood)

SUPPLEMENTAL MATERIAL FOR "MILLION YEARS AGO"

Grammar

- The core independent clause is *I* [would] *have to pay / and bear my soul.*
- *To earn my stripes* is an infinitive phrase describing the verb *would have*, answering the question *why*.
- The sentence has three infinitives, *to earn, to pay, bear*. The last is, fittingly, *bare* because the *to* is implied.

Rhetoric

The title, which appears often in the song, is an example of *hyperbole*, or exaggeration.

Additional Information and Activities

- Have students listen to the song before they see the sentence. Did they assume the word was "bear" or "bare"? Why?
- If students read the sentence before hearing the song, what do they imagine it will sound like? What tempo, volume, and instruments do they expect? Why?

> **Ransom Riggs, *Miss Peregrine's Home for Peculiar Children***
>
> Fireplaces were <u>throttled</u> with vines that had <u>descended</u> from the roof and begun to <u>spread</u> across the floors like alien tentacles.

Brief context: A young boy explores the ruins of a house his late grandfather often described to him.

Extended context: Unknowingly, the boy is exploring a portal to the past, a good match for his name, Jacob *Port*man. The "peculiar children" of the title live in the house on a single day in 1940, in a time loop that the title character magically resets just before a German bomb destroys the house. Jacob's trip there was suggested by his psychiatrist, who has told him that seeing the place his grandfather spoke about will help Jacob recover from grief. The grandfather, who was murdered by tentacled monsters, often told Jacob stories of children with special powers. Jacob didn't believe him, but the stories were true. The novel is illustrated by photos that supposedly represent the children his grandfather knew. (The author collects old photos, some of which inspired this story and appear in the book.) The plot centers on the conflict between the peculiar children and the monsters, who seek to kill and eat them in order to acquire human physical traits.

Analysis

With brief context:

• Identify the verbs. If you heard these three words, what sort of story would you imagine? (*throttled*—crime, thriller; *descended*—mystery, tale of evil; *spread*—natural disaster or plague)
• The first verb, *were throttled*, is in passive voice. What effect does that have on the reader? (hides the guilty one: the sentence says that the *fireplaces were throttled with vines*, not *by vines* and certainly not *vines throttled the fireplaces*).
• What can you tell about the *vines* from the information in this sentence? (sound menacing because of the three verbs; the *vines* are a growing menace; *vines* are compared to *alien tentacles*)
• Why are *fireplaces* a symbolic target? (hearth, traditional symbol of home)

With extended context, add these points:

• How does the verb *throttle* relate to the monsters who killed Jacob's grandfather? (someone is *throttled* with a long, thin implement; the grandfather was murdered by tentacled monsters; *vines* and *tentacles* are long and thin)
• How does *descended* add to the effect of the sentence? (moving down from the roof changes perspective, and Jacob's belief in his grandfather's

story changes his perspective; *descended*—downward motion often associated with evil)

- How about *spread*? (unless stopped, the monsters' evil will *spread*)

SUPPLEMENTAL MATERIAL FOR *MISS PEREGRINE'S HOME FOR PECULIAR CHILDREN*

Grammar

The first verb (*throttled*) is in the past tense. The next two (*had descended*, [had] *begun*) are in past-perfect tense, which places them further in the past. These tenses relate to the sequence of events in the plot. The bomb *had descended* and the destruction from the monsters *had begun to spread* before the house was ruined and the vines grew.

Rhetoric

The direct comparison, *like alien monsters*, is a *simile*.

Additional Information and Activities

- Because the book was inspired by, and includes, old photographs, this sentence could be part of an interdisciplinary language arts/photography project.
- The book, the first in a trilogy, was made into a film and a graphic novel. The sentence can be the starting point for an art/language arts unit.

MORE VERBS WITH VALUE

Here I've provided no lesson plans, but enough context for the underlined verbs to allow you to create your own.

> And then the thing beneath the hood, whatever it was, <u>drew</u> a long, slow, <u>rattling</u> breath, as though it were <u>trying to suck</u> something more than air from its surroundings.
>
> — J. K. Rowling, *Harry Potter and the Prisoner of Azkaban*

The *thing* in J. K. Rowling's sentence is a dementor, a magical creature that physically represents the feelings of depression. The dementors have been assigned to protect Hogwarts, the wizarding academy, from the supposed threat of an escaped prisoner. The simple definition of *drew* in this context is "to pull in air," but the word carries the connotation of force. A secondary meaning of the verb is "to distort." The dementors indeed distort reality. When they approach, their victims feel intense hopelessness, as if, in one character's words, they'd "never be cheerful again." The verb form *rattling* (a participle) literally represents a noise, but it also implies how shaken the victim feels. The last verb shows the dementors' true intent: to *suck* life and hope away. Fortunately for Harry Potter, they are *trying*, but they fail.

> That time of year thou <u>mayst</u> in me <u>behold</u>
> When yellow leaves, or none, or few, <u>do hang</u>
> Upon those boughs which <u>shake</u> against the cold,
> Bare ruin'd choirs, where late the sweet birds <u>sang</u>.
>
> —William Shakespeare, Sonnet 73

These lines, the first quatrain, come from a speaker who thinks himself old, perhaps near death. Comparing himself to late autumn, he employs three present-tense verbs: *behold, hang,* and *shake.* The speaker's lover *mayst behold* the damage time has inflicted. Not many leaves still *hang,* just as not many opportunities for growth or survival remain for the speaker. There's some fear, too (*shake*). The single past-tense verb, *sang,* reflects the speaker's youthful joy—and perhaps the words he shaped into beautiful poetry at an earlier age. *The sweet birds sang,* but their *choirs* are now *bare* and *ruin'd.* The verbs fit both the *time of year* and the ending stage of life.

> Her imagination is impeccable the way it <u>cuts</u> and <u>scrapes</u> the bone
> never <u>touching</u> the marrow where that dirty feeling <u>is thrumming</u>
> like a fiddle for fear its strings will <u>break</u> and <u>screech</u> the loss of its
> tune since for her permanent ignorance is so much better than the
> quick of life.   —Toni Morrison, *God Help the Child*

The pronoun *her* in this sentence refers to Bride. Raised by a disdainful and cold mother, Bride has secrets that cause a rupture between her and Booker, whose journal contains this sentence. Booker thinks he knows the source of Bride's pain—racism and the self-hate it has caused—but he's wrong. He's right, however, that Bride has long been in *fear* of expressing the truth about events of her childhood, which will indeed *break* and *screech*. The *cuts* and *scrapes* and *touching* echo events she's participated in (spoiler alert): Bride was so desperate for a gesture of affection from her mother that she lied about a teacher she said was *touching* her inappropriately. Years later, when the woman is released from prison, Bride brings her gifts. The enraged woman *cuts* and *scrapes* Bride. Bride's *dirty feeling is thrumming* because of the lie she told, and when she finally confesses to Booker (*break* and *screech* apply to that scene), he at first rejects but eventually accepts her.

> As I **balloon** with disbelief that I created this, that everyone is seeing my true world, I can see from where I'm sitting that Ryan **crumples.**   —Leah Henderson, "Warning: Color May Fade"

The speaker is a shy art student; Ryan is another student who claimed credit for the speaker's work. Angry at herself for not speaking up, the speaker creates a collage of her private drawings that awes the audience. The speaker's self-esteem grows (*balloon*) and Ryan, who thought she'd win the art competition, *crumples.*

> An ambassador is an honest man sent to **lie** abroad for the good of his country.   —Sir Henry Wotton, note

Henry Wotton (1568–1639) was an English author and diplomat. All you need to know about this sentence from a note Wotton wrote to a friend is that the verb *lie* once meant "to reside in a foreign country." It also meant what it means now: "to say something that is not true." Wotton undoubtedly appreciated both meanings and expected his reader to do so also. His comment caused some displeasure to a fellow diplomat, who wrote an entire book denouncing it.

WRITING ASSIGNMENTS

The easiest and shortest path to more valuable verbs is to have students swap out some tired specimens from sentences that could use a little extra zip. There is, sadly, way too much material for them to work on: a glance at the internet or one of their textbooks will surely provide a sentence or two that they can revise. Here are a few other possible assignments.

Mental Narration

I myself engage in this exercise at faculty meetings, but you can ask students to work on it in the cafeteria or during their free time. They should look and listen carefully to people around them and mentally apply great verbs. Some examples: that fellow in the corner is *spouting* opinions to his companion, whose eyes are *darting* around in search of an escape route. The teacher on duty in the lunchroom *trudges* from table to table, *tamping* and *clamping* down on restless eaters.

Furniture

Pick something in the room and ask students to write a sentence describing it. I like to place a chair atop my desk (drama queen here). As they read the sentences aloud, I tally the verbs; forms of *be* and *have* predominate: The chair <u>has</u> dull brown color varnish on it, it <u>has</u> ink stains on the arms, the back <u>is</u> slightly curved, and so forth. Next I challenge them to rewrite their sentences without any form of *be* or *have*. Sample results: Dull brown varnish <u>colors</u> the chair, ink <u>splotches</u> or <u>stains</u> the arms, the back <u>curves</u> slightly.

Sports, Arts, Science

All fields are fertile when it comes to writing great sentences, but somehow these three seem particularly helpful when it comes to inspiring students to opt for expressive verbs. Show them a clip of a game, a performance, or a scientific achievement. Tell them to describe the action they're watching, paying special attention to the verbs. Examples, based on typical student responses:

Brian tapped the basketball with his fingertips and flicked it sideways before Geno could pierce the air with his usual devastating jump shot.

Mom swooped across the room and bent over the recliner where Henry had entombed himself.

The purple grains we dribbled into the solution gasped out so much acrid smoke that we stampeded out of the chem lab.

DESCRIPTIVE DETAILS

• •

The common expression "the devil is in the details" doesn't apply to writing. In fact, the opposite is true. Carefully chosen details are angels that add grace to a sentence; they make a topic come alive, deliver an understandable message, and, in the hands of the best authors, create an indelible impression. Pushing students first to notice and then to incorporate well-crafted, detailed descriptions is a worthy goal. Sentences are an ideal medium for reaching it.

TEACHING DESCRIPTIVE DETAILS: A GENERAL PLAN

Introduction (optional)

Descriptions are everywhere, and some of them are undeniably bad. Take advantage of that fact:

- Ask your students to write a "bad" description—one that's poorly expressed.
- Select a response that's vague, such as "Maggie is nice."
- Have everyone in the class write a sentence supporting the idea that Maggie is nice. (Note: Maggie is fictional, so they're making up answers.)
- Read a couple of responses, which will vary. One may say that Maggie "always helps her friends" and another that "she never steals or lies."
- Pick a response ("Maggie always helps her friends") and have everyone in the class express the same idea with specific (and fictional) details. These responses will vary: "she makes her friends personal playlists for their birthdays," "Maggie helps me with my physics homework," and so forth.
- Discuss what each answer reveals about Maggie. Which sentence would you include in a paragraph about this character? Why?

Decoding

In addition to the usual decoding, ask students to identify descriptions. Direct them to think about content, not part of speech, so they'll move beyond simple adjectives and adverbs.

Analysis

- What's being described?
- What information does each description give you?
- What type of description is it? (visual, behavioral, evaluative, emotional, etc.)
- Is the author conveying exactly what's there or adding a dose of imagination?
- How does the description affect the reader's impression of what's being described?
- Can the description be interpreted in more than one way? If yes, is that a problem? Why or why not?

TEACHING DESCRIPTIVE DETAILS: LESSON PLANS

Carl Hiaasen, *Hoot*

His mother caught him climbing out the window with his snowboard and a plastic tackle box in which he had packed underwear, socks, a fleece ski jacket, and a $100 savings bond his grandfather had given him as a birthday present.

Brief context: Told that the family must move from Montana to Florida because of his father's promotion, twelve-year-old Roy Eberhardt decides to run away.

Extended context: Roy loved Montana's "snaggled-peaked mountains" and "braided green rivers." He's not interested in going to the mall or to an amusement park; mostly he's trying to manage middle-school social life and survive the school bully's attacks. During one bus ride to school, Roy glimpses a running boy wearing a "faded Miami Heat basketball jersey and dirty khaki shorts" but no shoes. Intrigued, Roy vows to find him. Roy meets the boy's sister and later the boy himself and eventually participates in the running boy's mission: to stop a new branch of a pancake franchise from being constructed atop the habitat of an endangered species.

Analysis

With brief context:

- What is Roy taking with him when he tries to run away from home? (*snowboard, tackle box, underwear, socks, ski jacket, savings bond*)
- What does this collection tell you about Roy? (impractical, isn't prepared to live on his own)
  - Which items are expected? (*underwear, socks, jacket*)
  - Which item is least useful? (*savings bond*—can't be spent like cash)
- What else do you learn about Roy from this sentence? (disobedient—climbs out a window to run away; innocent—no idea what to take; ingenious—uses a tackle box for a suitcase)

With extended context:

- How does Roy's attempt to run away relate to the rest of the story? (independent-minded and adventurous—tries to run away, finds the barefoot boy, joins the environmental protest)
- How is the *savings bond* connected to the rest of the story? (the *savings bond* is an investment for the future—Roy's protest is meant to protect the future of an endangered species)
- How does the collection as a whole relate to Roy's experience in Florida? (*snowboard, ski jacket*—represent loss of things he loved in Montana; *underwear, socks*—has to deal with reality)
- How does the author's use of detail in this sentence relate to the style of other quoted material? (mix of general and specific—*mountains, rivers, Miami Heat jersey, khaki shorts*)

SUPPLEMENTAL MATERIAL FOR *HOOT*

Grammar

- The basic independent clause, *His mother caught him*, has a chain of descriptions attached to it. Roy's attempt to run away, had it been successful, would have set a chain of events in motion, which the family's move to Florida does.

- The *mother* is dominant, as the subject of the independent clause. Roy's actions are described in a dependent element, a participial phrase. This structure echoes Roy's dependence on his parents' decisions.
- The *savings bond* is from the past (*his grandfather had given* [it to] *him as a birthday present*). Roy's family ties are, in a sense, a part of his past. He thinks more about his friends, as most people his age do.

Additional Information and Activities

- Carl Hiaasen's books feature a variety of eccentric characters, some pretentious and others well-meaning but clueless. *Hoot* is no exception. The running boy, for example, is called "Mullet Fingers" because he can catch fish with his bare hands. Students may want to read the entire book to see how Hiaasen employs details to set a scene and establish character.
- As in many books intended for young adults, the authority figures (parents, school officials, police) are largely absent or ineffective. For a psychology/English project, have students research this stage of the maturation process to see how the dynamic plays out in real life.
- The school bully looms large in the story. For a psychology/English project, students might research why some people become bullies and what actions are most effective in response to them.
- *Hoot* deals with environmental issues and activism: a good basis for a science/English project.

Charles Dickens, *David Copperfield*

I recollect Peggotty and I peeping out at them from my little window; I recollect how closely they seemed to be examining the sweetbriar between them, as they strolled along; and how, from being in a perfectly angelic temper, Peggotty turned cross in a moment, and brushed my hair the wrong way, excessively hard.

Brief context: The narrator is a small boy, the son of a widow. Peggotty is an employee watching *them*—the mother and a man who will soon propose marriage to her.

Extended context: The narrator is the title character, called "Davy" by his mother, and Peggotty, the housekeeper. His father died shortly before Davy was born. When the narrator is seven, Mr. Murdstone begins to court the mother and eventually marries her, despite Peggotty's warnings to Davy's mother. Mr. Murdstone, and later Miss Murdstone, his sister, treat Davy and his mother harshly.

Analysis

With brief context:

• Which words tell you about Peggotty? (*peeping, angelic temper, turned cross in a moment, brushed my hair the wrong way, excessively hard*)
• What do you learn about Peggotty from these descriptions? (*peeping*—can't act openly; *angelic temper*—good mood; *turned cross in a moment*—saw something upsetting; *brushed my hair . . . excessively hard*—expresses her anxiety and anger through action, not words)
• What can you infer about Peggotty's opinion of the mother and her soon-to-be fiancé? (doesn't like him: her mood changes when she sees that the two were *closely . . . examining the sweetbriar*, and that they *strolled* together)
• What's the significance of *brushed my hair the wrong way*? (literal: Peggotty is upset; figurative: the fiancé irritates her; the relationship is going the *wrong way*)
• What do you learn about the child from this sentence? (innocent, ignorant; he observes but can't interpret)

With extended context:

• What's the significance of *peeping*? (Davy and Peggotty have little power; they're on the edge, *peeping*, not included in the decision that will affect their lives)
• How does this sentence foreshadow the plot? (*angelic* caretaker is lost to Davy when the Murdstones take over; their lives will be *turned cross*; the Murdstones will irritate, or *brush the wrong way*; the Murdstones will be *excessively hard* on Davy)

SUPPLEMENTAL MATERIAL
FOR *DAVID COPPERFIELD*

Grammar

- Two independent clauses appear in the sentence, both beginning with *I recollect*. This structure emphasizes timing and stage of life: a mature, independent adult *recollect*[s] his childhood.
- Two dependent clauses beginning with *how* describe what happens to the little boy, who, as a child, is dependent.

Additional Information and Activities

- *David Copperfield* is not an autobiographical novel, but elements of Charles Dickens's experiences appear. The class might discuss whether it's helpful to know about the author. If so, in what way?
- Dickens incorporates realistic elements of Victorian society in his novels. A history/English project might arise from this fact, especially if students read the entire book. Even if they do not, consider a research project on Victorian views of childhood.

> ### Mary Taylor Simeti, *On Persephone's Island*
>
> Strong and harsh and ever so slightly bitter, but with all the flavor and the color of the olive intact, Sicilian olive oil is a far cry from the pale insipid stuff that is exported to the States, and a slice of freshly baked Sicilian bread, sprinkled with oil and salt and preferably still hot from an oven that has been fired with almond shells, would beat ambrosia any day.

Brief context: The sentence comes from a book about Sicily in southern Italy.

Extended context: The author was born in the United States but has lived in Sicily her entire adult life. *On Persephone's Island* weaves autobiographical detail with descriptions of place, food, and culture, as well as Greek and

Roman mythology. The sentence comes from a chapter about the olive harvest and traditional methods of processing the crop into oil. The author also describes recipes and other ways in which olive oil is used. After the sentence above, the author adds that eating Sicilian bread "with the first oil of the new crop assumes the solemnity of a ritual."

Analysis

With brief context:

• What do you learn about Sicilian olive oil from this sentence? (*strong and harsh* as compared to oil exported to *the States*; delicious eaten with *freshly baked Sicilian bread*, with *oil and salt*)
• What do you learn about the bread? (author prefers it *still hot from an oven that has been fired with almond shells*)
• What's the author's opinion of the bread, oil, and salt eaten together? (better than *ambrosia*, the food of the gods)
• Which detail stands out? Why? (varied answers; for me, it's the *almond shells*, which are an unusual fuel)
• What do you learn from that detail? (varied answers; for me, that nothing is wasted and that traditional methods endure)

With extended context:

• What is the significance of *ambrosia*? (food of the gods, shows the author's knowledge of mythology as well as her appreciation of this food)
• What does this sentence tell you about the author? (implies appreciation for extremes—*strong and harsh . . . bitter*, shows that she understands the process as well as the product—*oven . . . fired with almond shells*; elevates simple things in life—"solemnity of a ritual")

SUPPLEMENTAL MATERIAL
FOR *ON PERSEPHONE'S ISLAND*

Grammar

- The core of the first independent clause (*Sicilian olive oil is a far cry*) is surrounded by descriptions. The subject is *olive oil*, the verb *is*, the complement *far cry*.
- The description attached to the first independent clause precedes it. It's long, conferring importance on the details within. That suits the content, which prioritizes the qualities of the oil. More description follows the core (*from the pale . . . States*). That structure also matches meaning, as the oil *exported to the States*, in the author's opinion, ranks below the oil eaten in Sicily.
- The second independent clause in the sentence begins with *a slice*. Here, too, content and structure align. The core of the clause is *bread* (subject) *would beat* (verb) *ambrosia* (object). Woven into that core are descriptive details: *freshly baked, sprinkled with oil and salt, fired with almond shells*, etc. The experience of eating the bread, oil, and salt cannot be broken apart or, the author claims, exported.

Rhetoric

The author makes an allusion to Greek mythology with *ambrosia*.

Additional Information and Activities

- Greek mythology appears in this sentence as well as in the title of the book. Have students research *Persephone* and *ambrosia*.
- Writing about food is an art, practiced by many writers throughout the centuries. Have students look into cookbooks or online recipe sites. How is the food described? Ask them to compare their findings.
- Sicily, *Persephone's Island*, is the author's real subject. For a social studies/ English research project, have students find out more about this island.

MORE DESCRIPTIVE DETAILS

Here are a few more sentences with great details. I've underlined my favorite spots, but feel free to focus on other words.

> Liza was in a bad temper, for she was mixing the Christmas puddings in the kitchen, and had been drawn from them, <u>with a raisin still on her cheek</u>, by Nana's absurd suspicions.
>
> —J. M. Barrie, *Peter Pan* (Nana, the nursemaid-dog, calls the cook because Peter Pan is in the children's room)

> The grizzled vendor saw where my wandering eyes had settled, peeled a pink plastic bag emblazoned with "Thank you for your patronage—Have a nice day" from the thick stack hanging from a meathook overhead and, with <u>a practiced snap of the wrist</u>, ballooned the sack with air.
>
> —Leslie Li, "Empty Bamboo" (narrator buying fruit)

> The sole decorations other than a thirsty-looking potted plant were two black-and-white photos depicting the Yosemite Valley, of the sort you might find hanging above the Keurig machine at a business hotel, and a red neon sign spelling out "10,000 Hours"— the pop-science creative-labor catchphrase made famous by Malcolm Gladwell—that <u>would fit in nicely above the kombucha tap at a co-working space</u>.
>
> —Jonah Weiner, "How Billie Eilish Rode Teenage Weirdness to Stardom" (description of the home of Billie Eilish's brother, who works with her on her music)

> Once she returned from a walk with a dead painted turtle she'd found on the side of the road, placed it on our backyard picnic table, pulled out a makeshift assortment of surgical tools—a

screwdriver, dinner forks, a butcher knife—and announced we
were having science class.

>—Meghan O'Gieblyn, "Homeschool" (dissection lesson from
>the author's mother, who homeschooled her children)

She nodded, and he ran forward again, almost stumbling, an
unlaced shoe coming off, to seize his son, and hold him, while
he shouted wildly, incoherently, for the village and the world
to hear his joy.

>—Alexander McCall Smith, *The No. 1 Ladies' Detective
>Agency* (a kidnap victim is returned to his
>father [*he*] by the detective [*she*])

WRITING ASSIGNMENTS

Fifty percent of skillful use of detail is *noticing*. Once students open their
senses—all of them!—they take in an enormous amount of information. The
other fifty percent is *selecting*. Rather than reporting everything, they must
winnow the pile until only revealing information remains. Try these exercises.

Daily Life

Ask students to watch a scene from a film or TV show or to sit in a public
place for a few minutes. Have them list everything they see, hear, smell, experience tactilely (temperature, texture, etc.), and, if relevant, taste. Which
details best capture the action or setting? Have them work those details into a
sentence. Here's a composite of student responses to a library visit:

ton of kids, tan shelves, a curved check-out desk with 6 books
on top and 9 magazines, one petite librarian wearing high heels
and a clerk with a blue shirt. "Shshshsh! Be quiet!" Giggles
from two middle-schoolers with backpacks as big as their backs.
Brrrriiiinnnggg. "Turn your phone off!" The smell of pizza and
doughnuts from a fundraising booth outside the door. Chilly, too
much air conditioning. "This is a week overdue." "Dude, that's my
calculator, not yours."

Here are the underlined details, inserted into a sentence:

> **The librarian stood tall on her four-inch heels and scolded the giggling middle-schoolers stooping under backpacks as big as their backs: "Turn your phones off!"**

Action!

The smallest detail sometimes reveals the strongest emotions. In Tim O'Brien's *The Things They Carried*, for example, a soldier reads and rereads a letter from home, holding it "with the tips of his fingers." Homesickness and vulnerability have seldom been portrayed more accurately. Ask students to write sentences, and then perhaps a scene, in which an emotion comes across through a physical action or reaction, such as the following:

> **When the fire alarm went off, I jumped out of my seat and grabbed my phone, forgetting that it was plugged in.**

Fact Meets Art

History, science, math, cooking—anything in which facts are conveyed—can benefit from a dash of art in the form of a well-chosen detail. Ask students to write a sentence giving information from one of those areas, employing specific and vivid detail.

TONE

● ●

Long before infants learn language, they distinguish between a soothing murmur and an irritated growl. The words "there there" and "don't you ever sleep?"
may be meaningless to a baby, but the tone is not. Yet somehow it's hard for
students to identify tone in a written work, even when they reach the don't-
take-that-tone-with-me stage, also known as adolescence. Perhaps tone is complex because it springs from myriad decisions the author makes about diction,
syntax, punctuation, and content. When I teach tone, I address these factors,
but I also acknowledge that tone comprises less tangible qualities and that reasonable people can interpret a sentence in more than one way. This is not necessarily a disadvantage, in my view. It's an opening for discussion.

TEACHING TONE: A GENERAL PLAN

Introduction (optional)

I like to begin the study of tone with this exercise:

- Select three words, such as *George, home,* and *go,* and tell the class they
  must incorporate the ideas they represent (though not necessarily the
  exact words) in a sentence.
- Randomly assign tones, one per student: regretful, elated, condescending,
  aggressive, sympathetic, and so forth. Do so quietly, so no one but the
  writer knows which tone has been assigned.
- Have students write their sentences on index cards or submit them
  online. Collect and redistribute the sentences. Ask them to identify the
  tone of the sentence they received.
- Reveal the result to the writer. Discuss how accurate each answer is.
- As writers, let them explain why they chose the words they did. As
  readers, have them explain the impressions they gathered from the
  sentence.

Decoding

- Connotation is paramount in a tone lesson, so allot a little more time than usual for this step.
- Point of view is also key. If the sentence is in first person or quotes someone, who's speaking or narrating? If it's in second person, identify *you*. Who's speaking or writing to *you*? If the author has chosen third-person limited, in which only one character's thoughts and feelings are presented, identify the character. If it's third-person omniscient, which gives the reader access to the inner lives of all the characters, simply point out that fact and move on.

Analysis

- Word choice: have students consider the connotations of significant words in the sentence. Any common threads? Perhaps several words have positive connotations, creating a laudatory or inspirational tone. Are there "fighting" words? Then the tone may be aggressive or belligerent.
- Syntax: Is the order of words unusual in any way? If so, what is the effect on the sentence? For example: "Why did George go home?" is neutral compared to "George went home why?"
- Clauses: If the sentence has more than one subject-verb unit, which is independent and which dependent? How does that structure highlight or downplay the importance of the information?
- Punctuation and capitalization: Anything unusual? If so, what's the effect on tone?
- Content: Do you see a cause-effect relationship? Spatial or chronological order? Comparison or contrast? An assertion that's affirmed or denied?
- Imagine that you're hearing the sentence. What tone do you hear? How did you make that decision?

TEACHING TONE: LESSON PLANS

Ring Lardner, "Why Ring Stopped Covering Baseball"

A couple yrs. ago a ball player named Baby Ruth that was a pitcher by birth was made into an outfielder on acct. of how he could bust them and he begin breaking records for long distants hits and etc. and he become a big drawing card and the master minds that controls baseball says to themselfs that if it is home runs that the public wants to see, why leave us give them home runs so they fixed up a ball that if you don't miss it entirely it will clear the fence and the result is that ball players which use to specialize in hump back liners to the pitcher is now amongst our leading sluggers when by rights they couldn't take a ball in their hands and throw it past the base umpire.

Brief context: A sportswriter, perfectly grammatical when he wants to be, writes about his belief that the composition of a baseball was altered to produce more home runs.

Extended context: *Baby Ruth* is Babe Ruth, a legendary baseball player who began his career as a pitcher. The crowds went wild whenever he hit a home run, which was often. An inferior player might hit a ball that rises slightly and then drops, an easy out. With the altered ball, such a player might become a slugger, hitting home runs. In Ring Lardner's sports journalism he himself is a character, a stand-in for sports fans.

Analysis

With brief context:

• Do you notice any unusual words or words used in an unusual way? Why might the author have chosen them? (*yrs., acct., bust, become, distants, and etc., themselfs, leave, use, hump back liners*—varied reasons: to sound

uneducated, to surprise, to create an eccentric character, to show a change
from the norm—as the baseball has also been changed, in the author's view)

- Why use abbreviations? (out of breath, in a hurry, doesn't care about
the niceties of language, something's missing from the word—something's
missing from the game)

- Consider the way the sentence is organized. Again, look for anything
unusual. What's the purpose? (very long—creates momentum, as if the writer
won't let the reader go until the point is made; cause and effect—moves
from the home runs hit by *Baby Ruth* to *big drawing card* to *leading sluggers*;
sentence breaks grammar rules, just as changing the baseball breaks the
game's rules)

- Anything unusual about the punctuation? What's the effect of the
author's choices here? (many commas omitted, several sentences run
together—momentum, also unstoppable, and the sentence is about a baseball
that travels too fast and too far)

- Consider the overall content. How does it relate to the title?
(sportswriter's fed up with the changes that serve financial interests, not the
game)

- How would you characterize the tone of this sentence? (tongue-in-cheek,
ironic, mocking, cynical)

With extended context:

- Why refer to *Baby Ruth*? (play on words for Babe Ruth, famous homerun
hitter)

- How does a *hump back liner* fit the tone? (visual image, more interesting
than "line drive," fits the eccentric persona; comic effect because no one
wants to *specialize* in easy outs)

- What persona has the author created? (disenchanted journalist, frustrated
fan, cynical observer)

- Why create a persona? (more interesting, perhaps to reach a wider
audience, lets readers in on the joke)

- How does the persona affect the tone? (intensifies the tone by assuming
that readers, like the writer, are cynical; also, comic tone highlighted)

SUPPLEMENTAL MATERIAL FOR "WHY RING STOPPED COVERING BASEBALL"

Grammar

Lots of broken rules here, to create the persona of an uneducated writer:

- inappropriate abbreviation (*yrs., acct., and etc.*)
- wrong word (*Baby, that, bust, distants, master minds, themselfs, leave*)
- incorrect verb form (*begin, become, controls, says, use, is*)
- run-on sentence
- odd expressions (*a pitcher by birth, a ball that if,* etc.)

Rhetoric

Hump back liners is a metaphor.

Additional Information and Activities

- Rewrite time: have students correct the grammar and spelling. How does the tone change? Which do they like better?
- Baseball and other sports often deal with "juiced-ball" controversies. A research project on the altered-ball theory of the early 1920s (when this article appeared) and the late 2010s might interest sports fans. A research project on the business of sports is another possibility.
- Ring Lardner's writing on sports, theater, politics, and other topics is worth exploring further. The pieces tend to be short and are fun to read. His short stories are also worth a look.

Margery Williams, *The Velveteen Rabbit*

"When a child loves you for a long, long time, not just to play with, but REALLY loves you, then you become Real."

Brief context: The Velveteen Rabbit, a stuffed toy, asks a leather rocking horse what "real" is. This sentence is the horse's answer.

Extended context: The Rabbit was the best Christmas present to "the Boy" for "at least two hours." Then the Boy was distracted, and the Rabbit was left alone, snubbed by most of the other toys. He befriends the "Skin Horse" (a leather rocking horse), who explains that real "isn't how you are made" but what "happens to you" over a long time, and not often to those who "break easily" or "have to be carefully kept." One day Nana gives the Boy the Rabbit at bedtime. The Boy and the Rabbit become inseparable until the Boy becomes ill. After his recovery, the doctor decrees that all bedding, including stuffed toys, be burned to prevent further infection. In the rubbish heap, the Rabbit cries as he remembers his time with the Boy, "the flower-bed, the quiet evenings in the wood when he lay in the bracken and the little ants ran over his paws; the wonderful day when he first knew that he was Real." From his tear sprouts a flower, which opens to disclose a fairy, who turns the Velveteen Rabbit into a real animal. A year passes and the Boy, playing in the yard, sees a rabbit that reminds him of his beloved toy—but he never learns that "it really was his own Bunny, come back to look at the child who had first helped him to be Real."

Analysis

With brief context:

- What do you notice about the words in this sentence? (simple, some repeated, some capitalized where you would expect lower case)
- What's the effect of repeating *long*? (sounds childlike, shows an extended amount of time)
- Do the two instances of *love* have the same definition? (first *love* is general, akin to "like a lot"; the second is unconditional)
- Why are *REALLY* and *Real* capitalized? (the first: emphasis, the second: special status or achievement)
- What does *not just to play with* add to the sentence? (a condition, imposes a stringent requirement for becoming *Real*)
- What is the definition of *Real*? (connected to another by true love)
- Why *become* and not *are*? (indicates a process)
- "Listen" to this sentence. What tone do you hear? (varied answers: wise elder gently instructing the young; factual, direct, simple)

With extended context:

• Do the featured sentence and the other quotations from the story have the same tone? If not, how do they differ? (the quotation from the Skin Horse has the same tone, but the others don't)

   • What's the tone of the quotation about liking the present for "about two hours"? How do you know? (gently mocking, sounds like a parent speaking affectionately about a child's short attention span)

   • What's the tone of the other quotations? How do you know? (nostalgic and sad, reflective—remembers shared experiences, crying)

SUPPLEMENTAL MATERIAL FOR
THE VELVETEEN RABBIT

Grammar

The independent clause (*then you become Real*) appears last. This structure suits the meaning, because certain conditions must be met before achieving that state. Those conditions appear in the dependent clause at the beginning of the sentence: *When . . . you.*

Rhetoric

Two iterations of *loves you* is an example of *diacope*, repetition of a word or phrase separated by other words. *REALLY* and *Real* are an example of *antanaclasis*, repetition of similar words but with different meanings.

Additional Information and Activities

• *The Velveteen Rabbit* is a children's book, but the author doesn't condescend to her audience. The horse imparts wise counsel: what you're made of (mechanical parts or expensive fabric, for example) doesn't mean anything. You become Real through unconditional love (the Boy's love for the Rabbit) and vulnerability (the Rabbit's tears). Life brings change; parts wear out and materials fade. Illness threatens. But those changes don't change real love. A philosophy/English discussion may center on this sentence (What's real? How do you know?)

- A psychology/English project on fantasy and its role in the human psyche can begin with this sentence.
- Life-threatening situations appear often in children's stories, especially older ones. Consider assigning a compare/contrast essay based on *The Velveteen Rabbit* and a modern fantasy work, such as *Toy Story* or *Finding Nemo*. Students can discuss where danger lies, how characters escape (or not), and what adversity teaches.

A TONAL ASSORTMENT

With little or no context, students can experience an array of tones by examining these sentences.

Disdainful, critical

In spite of your wide and generous disregard of my communications on the subject of the script of *Strangers on a Train* and your failure to make any comment on it, and in spite of not having heard a word from you since I began the writing of the actual screenplay—for all of which I might say I bear no malice, since this sort of procedure seems to be part of the standard Hollywood depravity—in spite of this extremely cumbersome sentence, I feel that I should, just for the record, pass you a few comments on what is termed the final script.

> —Raymond Chandler, screenwriter (letter to Alfred Hitchcock, director, about the film *Strangers on a Train*)

Mournful

Every day I open the door, it takes just a minute 'fore I remember I won't hear Mama getting supper started, or hear her humming— His eye is on the sparrow, and I know He watches me—and just a little bit longer to remember I won't see Mama ever again.

> —Lesa Cline-Ransome, *Finding Langston* (a novel about a bereaved father and his young child, who narrates)

Self-mocking

Frankly, I didn't want to pay for anything I wouldn't need at the exact moment in time I was at the store buying it.

—Miranda Berman and Gaby Moskowitz, *Hot Mess Kitchen* (about buying pots and pans in a cookbook for people who need a chapter entitled "Welcome to Your Kitchen! It's Okay If You've Never Been In Here Before")

Encouraging, playful

Be butterfly stroke in a pool of freestylers.

—Renée Watson and Ellen Hagan, *Watch Us Rise* (a high school girl's reminder to herself that it's okay to challenge others' expectations)

Determined, passionate

To be free—to walk the good American earth as equal citizens, to live without fear, to enjoy the fruits of our toil, to give our children every opportunity in life—that dream which we have held so long in our hearts is today the destiny that we hold in our hands.

—Paul Robeson, *Here I Stand* (the civil rights activist, in his autobiography)

Reflective, pensive

Much later, when I looked back on the flight, it seemed to me that we had been two lost souls in an immense netherworld, traveling toward an arbitrary goal, wondering which of us was more forsaken: the navigator who didn't care where we were going, or the pilot who didn't care if we ever got there.

—Jane Mendelsohn, *I Was Amelia Earhart* (a novel about the aviator, the narrator)

Ironic, humorous

Every time the waiter would offer you something, you'd give it right back to him, because you said that he was your long-lost

brother, changed in the cradle by a gypsy band, and that anything
you had was his.

—Dorothy Parker, "You Were Perfectly Fine" (a short story about a hungover
young man hearing about his actions the night before, which he
doesn't remember, from a young woman who assures him that
he was "perfectly fine")

Indignant

You then proceeded to crouch down to the floor and dump
everything out of your bag, and I mean . . . *everything!* . . . leaking
packets of sequins and gummed stars, sea shells, odd pieces of
fur, crochet hooks, a monarch butterfly embedded in plastic,
dental floss, antique glass buttons, small jingling bells, lace . . . I
thought I'd die!

—Tina Howe, *Painting Churches* (a line from a character berating her
mother for the mother's behavior at the daughter's gallery opening)

Argumentative

It's not that rats have become parasitic to human cities; it's more
correct to say they have become parasitic to the disturbance, waste,
construction, and destruction that we humans have long produced.

—Becca Cudmore, "The Case for Leaving City Rats Alone" (an article
explaining unintended consequences of pest control measures)

Wry, humorous

Our good ship appears to be drifting somewhere, but we are not
looking at the same maps, cannot agree on the direction of the
prevailing winds, and several of us claim to have scurvy while
others dispute the existence of scurvy and believe it is a hoax
invented by the Chinese.

—*The Best American Non-Required Reading 2017*, edited by Sarah Vowell
(from the introduction commenting on polarized viewpoints)

WRITING ASSIGNMENTS

I like to assign two writing exercises, one focused on the author's tone and one on an individual's tone (a character in a work of fiction or someone quoted in nonfiction). The assignments below can, with a few tweaks, serve either purpose.

Arguments

Ask students to select a sentence from an essay that they or someone else has written. You can also use internet posts or comments (teacher-screened, to weed out objectionable material). Have students identify the overall tone and select a sentence that exemplifies it. Now tell them to switch tones. The first example tinkers with the author's tone, the second a quoted expert (fictional):

> ORIGINAL: Travelers don't understand that they're ruining the planet every time they get on a plane. (condescending)
> REVISION: Air travel accounts for 2.5% of the world's carbon dioxide emissions, enough to have a negative impact on the environment. (informative)

> ORIGINAL: "Although planes are more fuel efficient than ever, only decreasing the number of flights will sufficiently lower the carbon footprint," explained Joseph Sloan, an environmental activist. (authoritative, assertive)
> REVISION: "You fly, the planet dies," declared Joseph Sloan, an environmental activist (passionate)

NOTE: Students don't have to agree with the statements, original or revised.

Reports

Ask students to select a daily activity (texting a friend, eating lunch, and so on). Assign two or more tones and have them fashion sentences reporting the activity using those tones. A possible response:

> ACTIVITY: uploading homework to the class website
> TONES: relieved, annoyed

George pressed the "submit" button and sighed as he turned, at long last, to the cat who'd been demanding attention for the last hour.

"Take that, Dr. Finlay!" snapped George as he pressed the "submit" button and simultaneously dumped the cat yet again from his lap.

Extra credit: Allow students to place the incident in context by writing a story.

Shifts

How are you feeling? If you're human, the answer to that question (and the tone in which the answer is given) changes rapidly. Start the day with a growl or a smile and chances are something will happen to flip one to the other. Reflect this reality through a change in tone, in one or more sentences. A few possible shifts:

skeptical → convinced
detached → sympathetic
patronizing → humble

WORD SHIFTS

• •

Here's my favorite teaching fantasy:

Setting: my classroom. Student with vocabulary book, me with a coffee cup. Student: "Who decides what a word means?" I begin to formulate an age-appropriate explanation of linguistics. Fortunately, I'm too slow. She goes on. "I mean, some of the words on this list mean more than one thing." I'm still putting together a response—I haven't had the coffee yet!—when she adds, "The same word could mean a bunch of things. Like *light*. It's that kind of *light*." She points at the fluorescent bulbs above. "And this kind of *light*." She picks up a sheet of paper as if weighing it. "Then there's the other *light*, like *light of my life*." I take a sip of coffee. I consider jumping in with a figurative-language comment, but she's on a roll, and I'd like to see how far she can get. "It's like Othello. He hits the switch and puts out the *light* and then he kills his wife, the *light* in his life goes out. I like that they go together and make you think."

I round off the dream by replacing the coffee in my cup with champagne, as I mentally toast this *light* of my class. Anachronism aside (how would a student know when light switches were invented?), she's figured out why word shifts work—because they "go together and make you think." So does a shift in a part of speech, as when the same root shows up in more than one form (*force* and *forceful*, for example). The similarity puts the words into the same realm; the shift makes each more vivid. I don't have to teach students the value of word shifts, because Shakespeare does it for me. In this chapter are sentences from other writers who can also teach this concept to your students.

TEACHING WORD SHIFTS: A GENERAL PLAN

Introduction (optional)

Try this activity to introduce students to word shifts:

Present a word that has more than one meaning. Challenge students to come up with a sentence using the same word in two different ways. An example:

"Don't <u>play</u> with the <u>play</u>!" shouted the director as the actors began to ad-lib.

"Every word in the <u>play</u> is exactly <u>right</u>," added the <u>playwright</u>.

Discuss the wordplay. Do they like it? Why or why not? Answers will vary. Students often mention the fun factor, but a few may grasp that a shift both unites and separates—the literary version of having your cake and eating it, too.

Decoding

- After checking that students understand what the sentence means, focus on the repeated or similar words. List possible definitions of the word(s).
- Which definitions are relevant in the context of the sentence?
- Optional: Does the part of speech change?

Analysis

- What ideas does the sentence express? (generally two or more)
- Underline and label the words that express each idea (the "thought units" created by clauses or phrases).
- Where are the repeated or similar words? (usually one in each "thought unit")
- Does the meaning of the repeated word or word part shift? How?
- How does the shift of meaning affect the sentence?
- Optional: If the part of speech has changed, which word is more important? (nouns and verbs tend to be more important than adjectives and adverbs, which modify other words)
- Does their position in the sentence relate to the importance of the ideas expressed? How?

TEACHING WORD SHIFTS: LESSON PLANS

In each sentence the words that shift are underlined.

> **Potter Stewart, Dissenting Opinion in *Henderson v. Bannan***
>
> <u>Swift</u> <u>justice</u> demands more than <u>just</u> <u>swiftness</u>.

Brief context: Potter Stewart, appointed to the Supreme Court in 1958, was an appeals court judge when he wrote this sentence about a man who was arrested, tried, and sentenced to life in prison within an eight-hour period.

Extended context: Potter Stewart wrote this dissenting opinion in the case of James Henderson. Stewart begins with the facts of the case. Late one afternoon, Henderson testified, he heard that the police were looking for him. Henderson went to the station, was taken into custody, and was sent to jail around 8:30 p.m. Stewart continues, "two and a half hours later he had been sentenced to prison for the rest of his life." Stewart notes that the defendant was "friendless and alone" and was never "advised by the judge or by anyone else" that he had a right to an attorney or that he might receive a life sentence.

The justice system sets limits on the amount of time for various steps to take place, based on the principle that "justice delayed is justice denied." Stewart's sentence sums up his belief that the rushed court proceedings in Henderson's case were grounds to overturn his conviction. The other two judges on the panel disagreed, and Henderson remained in prison.

Decoding

- The title may be obscure to some students: an *opinion* presents the reasoning and precedents that led to the court's decision. A judge who does not agree with the majority decision may write a *dissenting opinion*.
- The abbreviation *v.* stands for *versus*, which separates the opposing sides of the case.
- The names in the title are those of the opposing sides: James *Henderson*,

the man in prison, and William H. *Bannan*, the warden and representative of the state.

Analysis

With brief context:

- Which words repeat and shift in this sentence? (*swift, swiftness* and *justice, just*)
  - What two ideas does the sentence express? (*swift justice* and *just swiftness*)
  - What does *just* mean? ("fair" and "only")
  - On the literal level, which definition applies to this sentence? ("only")
  - How does the other definition of *just* apply to the sentence? (echoes *justice*, the principle of fairness)
  - What about *swift* and *swiftness*? Why use both? (to connect both halves of the sentence, to evaluate speed as a factor in the judicial process)

With extended context:

- What is the meaning of the legal principle that "justice delayed is justice denied"? (waiting too long for a decision is unfair)
  - Does Stewart agree with that principle? (not completely—other factors matter also)
  - How do you know? (*justice* requires *more than just swiftness*)

SUPPLEMENTAL MATERIAL FOR DISSENTING OPINION

Grammar

- The sentence is a single independent clause that adheres to the most common pattern: subject-verb-object. The subject is *justice*, the verb *demands*, and the object *swiftness*. The basic syntax matches the fact that Stewart is discussing a basic principle of *justice*.
- The subject, *justice*, is also the subject (topic) of the court proceedings.
- Parts of speech shift in this sentence: *swift* (adjective) → *swiftness* (noun), *justice* (noun) → *just* (adjective). The last pair is significant: *justice* is

the goal, and a noun can stand by itself, independently. An adjective, though, modifies another word—in this sentence, *swiftness.* The shift in part of speech implies that *swiftness* has overpowered *justice* in Henderson's case.

Rhetoric

The shifts in this sentence are an example of *polyptoton,* using different forms of the same root word.

Additional Information and Activities

- The court's decision, including Potter Stewart's dissenting opinion, can be found at https://www.courtlistener.com/opinion/245396/james -henderson-v-william-h-bannan-warden/. It's not an easy read, but the portions dealing with the facts of the case are relatively clear.
- James Henderson was arrested in 1942. The appeals court decided his case in 1958. These two facts can be the basis for a discussion of the meaning of *swift justice.*

Kelly Barnhill, *The Witch's Boy*

It's a terrible thing when a <u>fool</u> with <u>power</u> <u>fools</u> with <u>power</u>.

Brief context: Someone who has made a bad choice reflects on the action and its consequences.

Extended context: Kelly Barnhill's novel has a magical setting: there's a witch, the witch's son, and a small clay pot of magic. Also a bandit's daughter, a wolf that saves the boy, who in turn unites with the girl to rescue two kingdoms from an immature king, an evil royal advisor, and various other threats. Along the way, the boy and the girl help their parents, too. The sentence comes from a stone creature, one of several who were once alive in a different form until they attempted to achieve immortality. That ill-advised action turned them to stone, motionless but capable of thought.

Analysis

With brief context:

- What two ideas appear in the sentence? (*fool with power* and *fools with power*)
- What are the characteristics of a *fool*? (varied answers: funny, thoughtless, unwise, gullible, silly)
- Which definitions of the noun *fool* apply to this sentence? (*fool*: someone who is unwise or thoughtless)
- What does the verb *fool* mean? (to trick, to play around with, to amuse, to use unwisely)
- Which definitions of the verb *fool* apply to this sentence? (to play around with, to use unwisely)
- Does *power* change in meaning? (no)

With extended context:

- Given the context, what sort of *power* would you expect this sentence to refer to? (political—the king and advisor; magical—the clay pot and stone beings; and emotional—parent/child bonds)
- How would a *fool* misuse, or *fool with*, power? (without precautions, without thinking of the consequences to self and others)
- What might be the *terrible thing*? (turning to stone)
- Overall, what does the sentence say about *power*? (must be used wisely)

SUPPLEMENTAL MATERIAL FOR *THE WITCH'S BOY*

Grammar

- The sentence contains two clauses: *it's a terrible thing* is independent, and *when a fool with power fools with power* is dependent. This structure stresses *terrible* and creates some suspense. What's *terrible*?
- The subject-verb pair of the independent clause is *it is* (contracted to *it's*). The linking verb *is* connects *it* to *terrible thing*. Both are equivalent to *when a fool with power fools with power*.
- Beginning with a vague pronoun (*it*, folded into *it's*) and then supplying

the meaning echoes the message of the sentence: think about the consequences (*terrible*) before acting (*fool with power*).

Rhetoric

The shift from the noun *fool* to the verb *fools* is an example of *polyptoton*, which repeats and therefore emphasizes the root word.

Additional Information and Activities

- Kelly Barnhill's young adult novel considers *power* in general but also the power of words in particular. The witch's boy, Ned, has trouble speaking because his grieving mother stitched his dying brother's soul to him when both were in danger of death. Not until the brother's spirit has been released is Ned able to speak. Ned's father can't speak of his love for Ned until he, too, is released—in his case from guilt over his other son's death and fear of losing his remaining son. One character says that "a word, after all, is a kind of magic." Discuss the power and vulnerability of verbal expression.
- Fantasy books are wildly popular, especially with young adults. A psychology/English project might explore why.
- Many fantasy books (though not *The Witch's Boy*) have been made into films. Students might compare two versions of the same scene (from the *Harry Potter* series or *The Lord of the Rings* series, for example) for a visual arts/English project.

Chris Colin, "This Sand Is Your Sand"

> I thought that if we could just keep talking, we'd find some <u>common</u> <u>ground</u>, even if we never agreed that his <u>ground</u> was <u>common</u>.

Brief context: The narrator is on public land talking with the owner of a home nearby, who believes the land is part of his private property.

Extended context: In this nonfiction article, the author travels the length of the Russian River in California. According to law, all land a certain distance from the low-water line of the river belongs to the public. Many homeowners don't know the law (which is rather complicated and vague) and feel strongly that they own the riverfront land that abuts their property. During his journey, Chris Colin anchors his boat and sits on one stretch of public shore after another, often tangling with residents who think he's trespassing. He politely explains the law, with varied results. One hits golf balls at him! Others are genuinely surprised to find out that what they thought was their private property wasn't private at all.

Analysis

With brief context:

- Identify two ideas in the sentence. (keep talking to find agreement, agree to disagree about who owns the land)
- What does *common* mean? ("shared," "ordinary," "occurring frequently")
- Which definition of *common* applies in this sentence? ("shared")
- Define *ground*. ("earth or land," "lowest level," "fundamental principle or idea")
- Does the meaning of *common* shift? (no)
- How about *ground*? (yes, the first *ground* is a "fundamental principle or idea," the second is "earth or land")
- How does the repetition of words affect the reader? (unites the two—they're both in the discussion)
- What idea does the shift reinforce? (Colin and the homeowner have different opinions)

With extended context:

- What does the expression *common ground* mean? (shared ideas, open to the public)
- Which meanings apply to the discussion on the banks of the Russian River? (both: the first *common ground* is the agreement the narrator seeks, the second is a legal principle governing land near the river)

SUPPLEMENTAL MATERIAL FOR "THIS SAND IS YOUR SAND"

Grammar

- The sentence begins with an independent clause, *I thought . . . ground.*
- Within that clause is a dependent clause, *that . . . we'd find some common ground*, which functions as the object of the verb *thought.*
- A dependent clause, *if we could just keep talking*, describes the verb *would find.* (The *would* is tucked into the contraction, *we'd.*) Another dependent clause, *even if . . . common*, also describes *would find.* Both explain the conditions under which *we'd find.*
- The tangle of clauses here resembles the tangle of interests: the public's right to the river area, the homeowner's expectation of privacy, and vague laws.

Rhetoric

The shifting definition of *ground* is an example of *antanaclasis.*

Additional Information and Activities

- The title of the article alludes to Woody Guthrie's song "This Land Is Your Land." This sentence might be the basis of an arts/English project, as the song asserts the public's right to the land and, by extension, to the nation.
- The sentence, as well as the article it comes from, could spark research into easement, the legal term for public/private property rights.

MORE SHIFTS

Here are a few other sentences illustrating word shifts, which are underlined.

> We're not primarily put on this earth to <u>see through one another</u>, but to <u>see one another through</u>.
>
> —Peter De Vries, *Let Me Count the Ways*

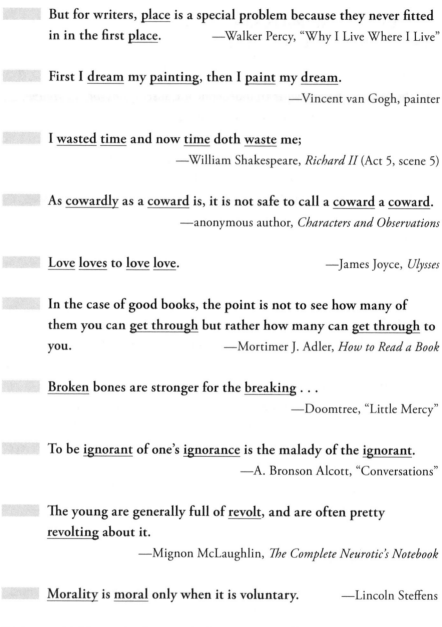

But for writers, <u>place</u> is a special problem because they never fitted in in the first <u>place</u>.   —Walker Percy, "Why I Live Where I Live"

First I <u>dream</u> my <u>painting</u>, then I <u>paint</u> my <u>dream</u>.
                                                                        —Vincent van Gogh, painter

I <u>wasted</u> <u>time</u> and now <u>time</u> doth <u>waste</u> me;
                                              —William Shakespeare, *Richard II* (Act 5, scene 5)

As <u>cowardly</u> as a <u>coward</u> is, it is not safe to call a <u>coward</u> a <u>coward</u>.
                                         —anonymous author, *Characters and Observations*

<u>Love</u> <u>loves</u> to <u>love</u> <u>love</u>.   —James Joyce, *Ulysses*

In the case of good books, the point is not to see how many of them you can <u>get through</u> but rather how many can <u>get through</u> to you.   —Mortimer J. Adler, *How to Read a Book*

<u>Broken</u> bones are stronger for the <u>breaking</u> . . .
                                                                        —Doomtree, "Little Mercy"

To be <u>ignorant</u> of one's <u>ignorance</u> is the malady of the <u>ignorant</u>.
                                                              —A. Bronson Alcott, "Conversations"

The young are generally full of <u>revolt</u>, and are often pretty <u>revolting</u> about it.
                                         —Mignon McLaughlin, *The Complete Neurotic's Notebook*

<u>Morality</u> is <u>moral</u> only when it is voluntary.   —Lincoln Steffens

Had enough? If not, check your playlist. Music is rife with word shifts: Stevie Wonder's "Love's in Need of Love Today" and the Beatles's "Please Please Me" are on mine. Your students will likely suggest more.

WRITING ASSIGNMENTS

You and your class can have some fun with these word-shift exercises.

Math

Ask students to look through their math textbooks for terms that are also common English words with different definitions. Fashion sentences that combine both. An example:

> After rating their comments on social media, I found that the
> <u>mean</u> was very <u>mean</u>.

Although I made this up, I find that the average internet comment is far too cruel, unfortunately.

Family Ties

Give the class a word and ask them to brainstorm all the members of its family, including common expressions. Start with *large*, for example, and add *largely, by and large, in large part, at large,* and *largesse.* How many forms can they insert in one sentence? A sample answer:

> By and large, I prefer not to accept a large gift from a robber
> still at large.

I Believe

You probably noticed that many word shifts appear in statements of principle. I sometimes think this happens because shifting words tend to create memorable sentences, and nothing is more important to remember than core values. Ask students to write a sentence that expresses what they believe. (Potter Stewart's sentence is a good model here.) One possible response:

> If we <u>trust</u> people to be <u>trustworthy</u>, they will be.

This assignment can stop at the sentence level, but it may also serve as the foundation for an essay.

Marketing

The best ads catch your attention and hold it. Word shifts also catch attention. Pretty good match, don't you think? Send students to a market, a store, or a shopping site on the internet. Have them look for a brand name that they can shift into a word, which in turn can become a sentence for an advertisement or a commercial. An example:

SETTING: Soccer game

SCENE 1 ACTION: Player runs across a muddy field and slips.

SCENE 2 ACTION: Player stuffs the dirty uniform into a washing machine and adds detergent, All.

DIALOGUE: <u>All</u> is <u>all</u> I need to clean my clothes!

COINAGE

From *analogy* to *zygote*, we teachers take pride in expanding our students' vocabulary. We nudge our classes to dictionaries and glossaries, and most of us don't care whether they opt for paper or plastic (keyboards) or the nearest human who knows the definition. We want to steep our students in the rich tradition of the English language.

But what about words that don't appear in a dictionary—the ones that authors (and everyone else!) create to fill a need, to give life to an imaginary world, or to provoke delight and other emotions? We seldom teach them, and even less often do we give our students license to coin. Yet every word in the dictionary was once new, perhaps scorned as incorrect or unnecessary until it became not only proper but indispensable. Moreover, the definitions of many words have evolved over time. Just ask the folks who labor over new editions of *Webster's Online Dictionary*, among others.

I vote to celebrate and cultivate linguistic invention: I am in favor of showing students sentences in which a new word appears or an old one is repurposed. Kids love thinking up new terms, and they also enjoy seeing many authors do the same.

TEACHING COINAGE: A GENERAL PLAN

Introduction (optional)

One or more of these activities introduce the concept of coinage.

- Where do new words come from? Who defines them? How do they change?
- If any students have read Andrew Clements's novel *Frindle*, ask them to speak about the book, which recounts how a fifth grader persuades first his class, then his town, and then many others to call a *pen* a *frindle*. Place a copy in your classroom library if you teach middle-schoolers or adults with a good sense of humor.
- Read a few lines from Lewis Carroll's "Jabberwocky." What do they think "brillig" means? What sort of animals are "slithy toves"? What

clues led to their answers? (Answers will vary, but when you respond, make the connection between sentence structure and part of speech. The position of "slithy," for example, implies a description of "toves," suggesting an adjective-noun sequence.)

Decoding

- Distribute words from the sentence, one per student. Some will immediately find an answer, but the one who receives the coined word will probably be stuck. Ask for a guess.
- What clues led to the guess? Is there a consensus? Now's the time for you to weigh in with some context, if you know the work or the author's intention.

Analysis

- Is the coined word completely original, or is it a new usage of an established word?
- Is there a standard word or expression to replace the coined term?
- Why coin, if a standard word can say the same thing? (builds an alternate universe, establishes the world of the characters, reinforces a theme)
- What are the advantages of a coined word in this sentence? (varied answers)

TEACHING COINAGE: LESSON PLANS

Underlining indicates coined word(s).

> **Lois Lowry, *The Giver***
>
> **Yet he felt it: felt that <u>Elsewhere</u> was not far away.**

Brief context: The sentence describes the feelings of a young boy, *he*, who has run away from home.

Extended context: The *he* in the sentence is Jonas, the protagonist of Lois Lowry's novel depicting a regimented society where, at age twelve, children are removed from the families that raised them and placed in professional groups to train for whatever profession the Elders of the community choose. Generations ago, the Elders somehow contrived to remove emotions from daily life, along with memories of the experiences that gave rise to intense feelings. Joyful sled rides are gone, as are the horrors of war. Only one person in the community knows the past and retains the emotional range everyone else has been denied. He's the title character, who's tasked with passing on his knowledge to Jonas. One day Jonas learns that a baby, Gabriel, is set to be "released" because he has failed to conform to the developmental norms for his age. When Jonas realizes that those who are "released" are sent Elsewhere—killed or exiled—he grabs Gabriel and runs away. The sentence occurs at a moment in the journey when Jonas is hungry and tired, but hopeful. As the book ends, Jonas does indeed glimpse *Elsewhere*.

Analysis

With brief context:

- What does the word *elsewhere* mean? ("in some other place")
- How is the word *elsewhere* normally used in a sentence? (elicit some examples, pointing out that the word generally describes a location but does not name a place)
- Is Lowry's use of *Elsewhere* unusual? In what way? (capitalized, the name of a place)
- If a more conventional term were in this sentence—the name of a town or a country, perhaps—would the effect be the same? Why? (Lowry's usage divides the world into two categories: Jonas's birth community and the rest of the world, or *Elsewhere*)

With extended context:

- What's the effect of *Yet* at the beginning of the sentence? (implies pressure to think otherwise, emphasizes Jonas's rebellious escape)
- Lowry uses the negative form, *not far away*, instead of the positive, *near*.

What does this add to the sentence? (almost an internal argument—"you won't make it," "yes I will, it's *not far away*")

- What's the effect of this unusual presentation of the word *elsewhere*? (gains importance and mystery)

- *Elsewhere* is normally an adverb, a description. How does changing it to a proper noun affect readers' reactions? (*Elsewhere* becomes a specific place, emphasizes that it's outside the regimented society)

SUPPLEMENTAL MATERIAL FOR *THE GIVER*

Grammar

- The pronoun *it* is general. The reader waits in suspense for the meaning: *that Elsewhere was not far away.* Jonas, too, is in suspense. He doesn't know what awaits him *Elsewhere*.

- Jonas *felt*, or believed, that he and Gabriel were almost at their destination. Because there are no feelings in the community they've left, this verb choice is significant. Jonas can feel; members of his former community cannot.

Rhetoric

Anthimeria is the rhetorical term for shifting the part of speech, in this case from adverb to noun.

Additional Information and Activities

- *The Giver* is part of the utopian/dystopian tradition. The Elders set up their community to free residents from suffering (utopian) but erased the emotional highs along with the lows. The quest for "Sameness"—a society in which everyone has a defined role to fill and conflict doesn't arise—erases identity and creates dystopia. Discuss the students' visions of utopia and dystopia.

- The novel was published in 1993, two years after the collapse of the Soviet Union. Parallels can be drawn between any totalitarian society and Jonas's community, a good basis for a history/English research project.

> ## William Shakespeare, *King Lear* (Act 4, scene 3)
>
> A sovereign shame so <u>elbows</u> him.

Brief context: The pronoun *him* refers to King Lear, who is ashamed of the way he treated one of his daughters.

Extended context: As the play begins, Lear announces his intention to cede power to his daughters, first asking them to declare their devotion to him. Two offer effusive praise; in an aside, the youngest, Cordelia, says she must "Love, and be silent" because she doesn't express herself easily. Enraged because Cordelia will not praise him, Lear splits the kingdom between his other daughters and disowns Cordelia, who soon marries the King of France. The older daughters treat their father cruelly, and he descends into madness. They treat their subjects unjustly also, and the country suffers. The Duke of Kent, loyal to Lear, says this line after Cordelia and her French troops have returned to England to rescue her father. Kent believes that Lear "by no means / Will yield to see his daughter" because Lear is ashamed of the way he treated Cordelia.

Analysis

With brief context:

- Ask for definitions of *elbow* (arm joint, to poke with that joint)
- Discuss the evolution of *elbow*. According to the *Oxford English Dictionary*, *elbow* has been used as the name of a body part (a noun) for more than a thousand years. Shakespeare was the first to employ *elbow* as an action (a verb).
- What happens when you *elbow* someone? (don't demonstrate on a real person: mime the action and prepare for giggles)
- How is *elbow* different from "punch" or "hit"? (less aggressive, intended to push someone aside, shows a power imbalance—you don't generally *elbow* a superior)

• What happens if *shame*, not a person, *elbows* Lear? (emotional reference, he's pushed aside by his own feelings)

With extended context, add these points:

• Would the sentence change if *sovereign* were replaced by "overpowering" or "great"? (*sovereign* emphasizes Lear's former status as king; Lear's shame is not only that he mistreated his daughter but also that he failed to live up to his responsibilities as *sovereign* of his people)
• Why *elbows* and not "inhibits"? (the *elbow* is a junction, a point of movement in several directions; Lear understands how his actions hurt Cordelia—a turning point for him; several actions are possible, but his *shame* pushes him away from the best course—to meet with her and reconcile)

SUPPLEMENTAL MATERIAL FOR *KING LEAR*

Grammar

The sentence is a sole independent clause. This form suits Lear: disowning his faithful daughter and being scorned by her sisters leaves him alone. The shame that keeps him away from Cordelia ensures that he remains alone.

Rhetoric

Shame is *personified* in this sentence, because Shakespeare has given human attributes (*elbows*) to an emotion. Changing *elbow* from noun to verb is an example of *anthimeria*.

Additional Information and Activities

• Cordelia finds it hard to express her emotions. Do any students feel the same? What are the consequences and advantages of silence or minimal expression?
• A history/English research project could shed light on the role of the sovereign and the politics of Shakespeare's time.

> ## Nick Wolven, "Caspar D. Luckinbill, What Are You Going to Do?"
>
> **You've got to be ubi, <u>omni</u>, <u>toto</u>, round-the-clock.**

Brief context: Comment from an executive about marketing.

Extended context: Nick Wolven's science-fiction story takes aspects of modern life (marketing, social media, the internet of things, loss of privacy, and terrorism) and stretches them to absurdity. The title character works for "the contractor for the external relations department of the financial branch of a marketing subsidiary of a worldwide conglomerate that makes NVC-recognition software"—NVC being "nonverbal communication," the step beyond facial recognition. Caspar's personality is as obscure as his job description until he becomes a victim of "mediaterrorism"; every screen he nears (and screens are everywhere) broadcasts scenes of violence and death, blaming him and asking what he's going to do about the carnage he's supposedly caused. Caspar hasn't done anything, but his efforts to end the mediaterrorism campaign and establish his innocence are futile. He loses his job (coworkers complain about the images they see and the screams they hear when he's around), his friends (same reason), and his wife (also the same, but with a dose of blame: Why doesn't he do something? Doesn't he care?). Caspar does care, but nothing changes until he makes a documentary about being a victim of mediaterrorism, which turns him into a viral phenomenon. The sentence comes from Caspar's mind as he thinks about his media campaign to be the signature mediaterrorism victim.

Analysis

With brief context:

- Have students guess what *ubi*, *omni*, and *toto* mean. (The first is an actual word, though rare: *ubi* means "permanent or present location." *Omni* is normally a prefix, meaning "in all ways or places." *In toto* is a common expression meaning "in all," but *toto* by itself is a coinage.
- Do these coined words sound like any words you know? ("ubiquitous"—

found everywhere, "omnibus"—public conveyance or a collection of things, "toto"—total or, as mentioned above, "in toto")

- How do they relate to *round-the-clock*? (all have elements of everywhere, including everything, all the time)
- What sort of marketing campaign do these words suggest? (24/7 coverage, saturating every market)
- Who could *you* represent? (marketing executive speaking to employees, self, or client)

With extended context:

- How do these coined words apply to today's media? Future media? (ever more pervasive)
- How would the readers' reactions differ if the sentence had substituted "everywhere, all the time" for the descriptions of what *you* must be? (varied answers)
- Suppose the writer had coined "unstop" and inserted it in place of *round-the-clock*? Which do you like better? (varied opinions; "unstop" is a word meaning "uncap or uncork"; using it instead of *round-the-clock* would connote exertion or release from confinement)
- How do coined words fit the science-fiction genre of this story? (imagined worlds, imagined words)

SUPPLEMENTAL MATERIAL FOR "CASPAR D. LUCKINBILL, WHAT ARE YOU GOING TO DO?"

Grammar

Ubi, *omni*, *toto*, and *round-the-clock* are adjectives, completing the infinitive phrase *to be*.

Rhetoric

Anthimeria is the rhetorical term for changing the part of speech of a word.

Additional Information and Activities

- A project on the techniques and effects of marketing is a good follow-up to an analysis of this sentence and/or the story it comes from.

- Science fiction, set in another reality, nevertheless comments on the reality we live in. Discuss what Wolven's sentence says about social media: its pitfalls and positive contributions.

MORE COINAGE

Apply the general design of the lesson plans above to these sentences with coined words, which are underlined. The words are either entirely new or shifted from their usual definition or part of speech.

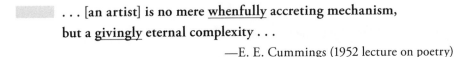 . . . [an artist] is no mere <u>whenfully</u> accreting mechanism, but a <u>givingly</u> eternal complexity . . .

—E. E. Cummings (1952 lecture on poetry)

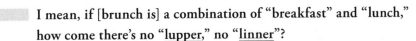 I mean, if [brunch is] a combination of "breakfast" and "lunch," how come there's no "<u>lupper</u>," no "<u>linner</u>"?

—*Seinfeld*, television comedy

The arts <u>babblative</u> and <u>scribblative</u>.

—Robert Southey, *Colloquies on the Progress and Prospects of Society*

The minister's wife leaned toward me, her long yellow face full of <u>sorry</u>.   —Maya Angelou, *I Know Why the Caged Bird Sings*

<u>Jaw-jaw</u> is better than <u>war-war</u>.

—Harold Macmillan (British prime minister, 1957–63)

Even if I thought it would be fun to <u>Kerouac</u> about in America for a while, I had no particular desire to leave Sarajevo.

—Aleksander Hemon, *The Book of My Lives* (allusion to Jack Kerouac, the Beat author of *On the Road*)

      Your _only_ ended there.
        —Jacqueline Woodson, "The Distance" (coach rejecting a player's excuse
          that, as an only child, he has trouble coordinating a relay
            race with teammates; italics in the original)

      **I hesitated before long, gooey strings of bacteria dangling from the
ceiling—affectionately known as "<u>snotsicles</u>"—but the sewer was
less repellent than I'd expected.**
        —Will Hunt, _Underground_ (nonfiction account of
          exploring under the surface of the earth)

Other good sources of coined words:

- News reports of scandals (anything ending with _-gate_) and disasters (words ending with _-geddon_ or _-ado_)
- Stories about celebrity couples (look for combined names of couples— _Brangelina, Javanka_—or names attached to current events—_Brexit, Megxit_)
- Children's songs and books
- Science fiction, fantasy, and utopian/dystopian films
- Poetry

WRITING ASSIGNMENTS

A few long and short exercises to strengthen the coinage muscles.

Alterations

The _Washington Post_ sponsors many wordplay contests. One asks entrants to select an existing word and change its meaning. Here are some entries I never got around to submitting:

    locomotor—erratic, self-driving car
    sausage—wise carpenter

Ask students to browse through a dictionary or thesaurus and redefine some words. Or, have them create a new word by swapping one or more letters from an existing word. Some examples, from a different *Washington Post* contest:

> *locabore*—person who insists on telling you where every food item is from (play on *locavore*, "someone who eats locally produced food")
>
> *sarchasm*—the gulf between a sarcastic wit and the listener who doesn't get the joke

Word Creator

Have you ever tied yourself up in sentences trying to describe something that has no name? Ask students to create a word for the currently nameless. Begin with school items. What are these?

> a twenty-pound textbook the teacher makes you bring to class but never use
>
> the loose, pointy tip of the spiral from an old spiral-bound notebook

Move on to extracurriculars. Have them find a word for each of these:

> a soccer player's hands
>
> the club member who attends only when yearbook photos are taken

Now get personal:

> a playlist your grandmother swears you'll love
>
> seat selection for a holiday dinner with a boring relative

Kidnapping

"Kidnap" a character from a novel, play, film, or television show. In one column, name the character and add a description. In the other column, turn the name or description into an action. Or, in the first column write an occupation, and then follow the same steps. For example, while *Harry potters* around

Hogwarts, a *lyrical* songwriter *lyrics* a love song. Extra credit: write a scene in which the character displays the qualities you've assigned, employing the word you coined.

Current Eventing

What's happening? Have students watch the news or check the internet and then write a news story, or just a headline, with a coinage that reflects one event. A balanced budget, for example, might be reported this way: "The town council incomed the outflow." The report of an awards ceremony (particularly one in show business) might list the "saltshakers," or weeping winners.

CHAPTER 8
SOUND

ONOMATOPOEIA

. . . .

If I'm the judge, *onomatopoeia* wins the award for "Most Fun Rhetorical Device." The term refers to words that mimic the sound of their meaning: *swoosh* for a mop's slide across the floor, *beep* for an auto horn, and *moo* for a cow's comment. These are all standard words, by the way, but onomatopoeia is closely related to coinage, which I discuss in Chapter 7. Both practices probably date from the "where can I find a cave?" era, and, as a glance at the internet reveals, both continue today.

Why teach *onomatopoeia*, apart from its entertainment value? (And it *is* entertaining. You may have to wrench the class away from *oinks* and *clatters*.) A few reasons: to show how writers work with sound, to demonstrate that words act on the ear as well as on the eye (even if read silently), and to reach beneath conscious thought. That last one needs a bit of explanation. It's likely that we hear before we see, perhaps even before birth: some studies show that a baby's cries follow the intonations of the mother's language. Clearly, sounds tap into a deep well of associations. One last reason: onomatopoeia, taught in the context of a sentence, forces students to consider rhythm. By examining where the word appears in the sentence and what precedes or follows it, students grasp the synergy between sound and content in a great sentence.

TEACHING ONOMATOPOEIA: A GENERAL PLAN

Introduction (optional)

To begin a study of onomatopoeia, ask students for some words that sound like what they mean. I like to start with animal noises or machines, but other prompts work well, too. I pair their onomatopoetic words with something general: for *clicks* and *whirrs* I offer *engine noises*, for example. Which do they prefer? Why? Is the answer dependent on context, audience, or purpose?

Decoding

Check whether students understand the overall meaning of the sentence. Then ask them to find an example of onomatopoeia. Is it an established word or the author's coinage?

Analysis

- Reword the sentence, subtracting the onomatopoeia and, if need be, inserting a substitute. How does the sentence change? (more formal, less childlike, less vivid)
- Read the sentence aloud. Do you hear a rhythmic pattern in the sentence? How does the onomatopoeia fit or break that pattern?
- Place the sentence in context, identifying, if possible, audience and purpose. Does the onomatopoeia relate to the context? How?

TEACHING ONOMATOPOEIA: LESSON PLANS

In these sentences, examples of onomatopoeia are underlined.

> ### George Plimpton, *Shadow Box*
>
> One heard the sound before one's eyes acclimatized: the <u>slap-slap</u> of the ropes being <u>skipped</u>, the <u>thud</u> of leather into the big heavy bags that <u>squeaked</u> from their chains as they swung, the <u>rattle</u> of the speed bags, the <u>muffled</u> sounds of gym shoes on the canvas of the rings (there were two rings), the <u>snuffles</u> of the fighters

> **breathing out through their noses, and every three minutes, the sharp <u>clang</u> of the ring bell.**

Brief context: The author visits a boxing gym.

Extended context: George Plimpton specialized in participatory journalism. On assignment to write about boxing, he hired a trainer, frequented gyms where boxers sparred and exercised, and eventually went three rounds with Archie Moore, a champion fighter.

Analysis

With brief context:

- The italics appear in the original. Of all the examples of onomatopoeia in this sentence, why do you think the author selected italics for this word? (coinage)
- Have one student read the sentence aloud, or read it aloud yourself. Students may easily identify *slap-slap* but perhaps not some of the other words I underlined above. Press them until all the words have emerged. Ask them why they'd originally skipped *skipped*. (common word, not noticeable)
- Why did the author insert so many onomatopoetic words into one sentence? (creates a "soundscape," adds to the perception of the boxers' world)
- Had the author described the scene visually, without onomatopoeia, would you perceive it the same way? (varied answers)
- There's no dialogue here, just sounds of movement and breath. Do you imagine that no one in the room is talking? Why highlight nonverbal sounds? (boxing becomes more about the body, less about the mind)

With extended context:

- Could Plimpton have written this sentence from secondhand observation—perhaps a recording? (varied answers)
- Does knowing that Plimpton participated as an amateur in the sports he wrote about change your view of this sentence? (varied answers)

SUPPLEMENTAL MATERIAL FOR *SHADOW BOX*

Grammar

- The subject is *one*, a substitute for *I* that's often associated with the upper classes, especially in British English. (George Plimpton was born into a wealthy American family.) *One* is also employed to express a universal experience. In this sentence both meanings apply to *one* and the possessive, *one's*.
- The words in parentheses are an independent clause, as are all the words *not* in parentheses. This structure extracts the visual observation (*there were two rings*) from the auditory.
- The colon begins a list, each item serving to expand on *sound*. The entire list is an appositive of *sound*, moving from that general category to specifics.

Rhetoric

The dominant rhetorical device is *onomatopoeia*, but Plimpton also uses *ring* as both a noun and an adjective, an example of *antanaclasis* (repetition of a word with a shift in meaning). *Rings* are the square structures where boxers fight; *ring*, as used in this sentence, describes *bell*, as in the bell located in the boxing *ring*. Plimpton is playful here, citing *ring bell* as an object that *rings*.

Additional Information and Activities

- How do other sports sound? Have students look for onomatopoeia in sports pages or websites.
- Play a clip from a boxing film (*Rocky, Million Dollar Baby, Fight Club*, etc.) Have students listen, eyes closed. Compare their reactions to Plimpton's descriptions.
- George Plimpton's forays into professional sports may be the basis of an interdisciplinary study. Among his books are *Out of My League* (baseball), *Paper Lion* (football), *The Bogey Man* (golf), and *Open Net* (ice hockey).

> ### E. B. White, *Stuart Little*
>
> So every morning, after climbing to the basin, he would seize his hammer and pound the faucet, and the other members of the household, dozing in their beds, would hear the bright sharp *plink plink plink* of Stuart's hammer, like a faraway blacksmith, telling them that day had come and that Stuart was trying to brush his teeth.

Brief context: The title character, *he* in this sentence, is a mouse born into a human family. His paws are too small to turn the faucet on, so he uses a hammer.

Extended context: A beloved character (and protagonist of a film series), Stuart is so small that he "could have been sent by first class mail for three cents." The book describing his life, *Stuart Little*, requires the suspension of disbelief common to children's literature. Mrs. Little is surprised when she gives birth to a mouse, but she copes. So does Stuart, who gamely figures out how to navigate life as a very little creature in a very large world. The book details his adventures, including some not-too-scary encounters with a cat. No matter what happens, Stuart always perseveres and emerges safe and sound.

Analysis

With brief context:

- Why has the author written *plink plink plink* instead of "hammering"? (varied answers)
- Hammering can be represented by other onomatopoetic words. Ask for some substitutes and discuss why E. B. White might have chosen *plink plink plink* instead. How does White's choice fit the meaning? (sounds less forceful than *thunk* or *thud*, and Stuart has little strength)
- How do the sounds of *bright* and *sharp* add to the hammer effect? (single syllables, each ending with an abrupt sound, like a hammer blow)
- How does the fact that the sentence is long relate to its content? (an ordinary activity, like tooth brushing, is a long process for Stuart)

With extended context:

- How does the sentence as a whole add to the reader's understanding of Stuart's character? (doesn't give up on tooth brushing, persistent)
- How does *plink plink plink* affect the reader's impression of Stuart? (sound emphasized Stuart's efforts)

SUPPLEMENTAL MATERIAL FOR *STUART LITTLE*

Grammar

- The subject of the first independent clause in the sentence is *he*, paired with the verb *would seize*. It's fitting that *he* (Stuart) is in an independent clause, as his efforts to brush his teeth by himself are a sign of his determination to be independent.
- *He* appears after two time descriptions, *every morning* (adverbial noun *morning* modified by another adverb, *every*) and *after climbing to the basin* (two prepositional phrases, the first with a gerund, *climbing*, as the object of *after* and the second, *to the basin*, modifying the gerund). By beginning with these time expressions, the author emphasizes the amount of time Stuart must spend on this task.
- The subject of the next independent clause is *the other members of the household*, the simple subject being *members*. They, too, have a life independent of Stuart. They're *dozing in their beds* while he's going about his morning routine.
- The verbs *would seize* and *would hear* (the verbs paired with *he* and *members*) emphasize a habitual action. Both Stuart and his family have a routine that works, albeit an odd one.
- A participial phrase, *telling them . . . teeth*, modifies *plink plink plink*. Stuart is small (the tiny sounds of his hammer) but he matters: they hear him.
- Two noun clauses act as direct objects of the *telling*: *that day had come* and *that Stuart was trying to brush his teeth*. The mouse's significance comes through here, also. His *telling them that day had come* is grammatically equal to his hygiene. Both are part of the family's daily life.

Rhetoric

Apart from onomatopoeia, *like a faraway blacksmith* is an example of a *simile*, a direct comparison. *Bright sharp plink plink plink* is an example of *synesthesia*, sensory crossover.

Additional Information and Activities

- White's book has been adapted for film. Comparing the two sheds light on the advantages and disadvantages of each medium.
- *Stuart Little* calls for a suspension of disbelief: a mouse born to a human mother and father. Discuss why children's books so often turn to fantasy. Consider assigning a psychology/English research project on the topic.

Ronald Harwood, *The Dresser*

**To carry on Cordelia, dead, to cry like the wind,
<u>howl, howl, howl</u>.**

Brief context: An actor playing King Lear talks about what he must do when the character he's playing, King Lear, carries the body of Cordelia, the king's daughter, onto the stage.

Extended context: Ronald Harwood's play takes the backstage view, as Norman, an assistant and the dresser of the title, talks with the star, an aging actor known only as "Sir." Sir is gradually deteriorating. The world around them is doing the same thing; the bombs of the Blitz (aerial bombardment by German planes) can be heard inside the theater, but Sir maintains that the show must go on. The play is a meditation on old age, perspective (the actor's and the assistant's), and the meaning of a life's work.

Analysis

With brief context:

- Where do you hear onomatopoeia? (*howl, howl, howl*)
- What do those words mean in this sentence? (the actor's tone of voice;

note that students might be confused here, as *King Lear* has a famous storm scene, but Sir is talking about what he has to do on stage, and that's *howl*)

- What's the effect of saying *like the wind*? (clarifies that it's not the storm but the actor who must *howl*)
- Look at the beginning of the sentence. Does *to carry on* contribute to the significance of the onomatopoeia? (*To carry on*—double meaning: "to rant" and "to physically lift and move"; the second definition is what Sir refers to, but the first is what he's actually doing in this speech)
- Look closely at *Cordelia, dead.* Is that the usual word order? How does that order affect the impact of the sentence? (single-word descriptions more commonly precede what they describe; unusual order emphasizes unpredictability—Lear didn't expect his daughter to be *dead*)
- What about *to cry*? How does that add to the meaning? (here Sir means *cry* as loud, piercing speech, but the phrase also alludes to tears)
- Why three *howls*? (extremes of emotion, fits Sir's personality)

With extended context, add these points:

- To the question about *Cordelia, dead* above, prompt them to think about the bombs falling. (unpredictable, many are dead because of the bombing, Sir is old and whether he can survive and continue to act is also unpredictable)
- To the question about *cry*, prompt them to expand their answers to take into account the people suffering losses from the Blitz.
- How does the phrase *To carry on* relate to what is going on in the war? (British people must *carry on*—continue, despite danger from the Blitz; famous slogan "Keep calm and carry on")

SUPPLEMENTAL MATERIAL FOR *THE DRESSER*

Grammar
- The "sentence," according to traditional grammarians, isn't actually a sentence but rather a fragment: two infinitive phrases.
- *Howl, howl, howl* might be an infinitive phrase with an implied *to*. Or, the expression is the object of the infinitive *to cry*.

Rhetoric

Like the wind is a simile; the three *howl*s are examples of onomatopoeia.

Additional Information and Activities

- To place the setting of the play in its historical context, have students research the Blitz, perhaps on the websites of the Imperial War Museum or the British Broadcasting Corporation.
- Theater tradition is "the show must go on," a maxim applied in other situations as well. Class discussion: Is this a good rule? What conditions call for the show *not* to go on, either literally or figuratively?

MORE ONOMATOPOEIA

I've underlined examples of onomatopoeia in the sentences below and provided just enough context so you can design a lesson modeled on those above.

Among the Hemons, the intensity of the <u>slurping</u> is proportional to the enjoyment of food, and the borscht that day yielded a symphony.   —Aleksandar Hemon, *The Book of My Lives*

I am Sir Brian! (<u>sper-lash</u>)
I am Sir Brian! (<u>sper-losh</u>)   —A. A. Milne, *When We Were Very Young*

It did not build as in a Berlioz cantata or culminate from a collection of small, meaningless gestures—a <u>whistle</u>, a <u>hiss</u>, a persistent <u>rattle</u>—in a cacophony of tearing metal, <u>snapping</u> cables, and <u>shattering</u> glass.
                    —Bernadette Esposito, "A-LOC" (a plane's engine explodes)

Ducks say "<u>quack</u>"
And fish go "<u>blub</u>"   —Ylvis, "The Fox"

Then I put two waffles on a plate, squeeze some <u>farting</u> syrup onto them, and walk to Mama's room.
                    —Kelly J. Baptist, "The Beans and Rice Chronicles of Isaiah Dunn"

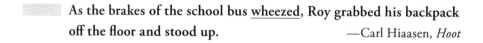   As the brakes of the school bus <u>wheezed</u>, Roy grabbed his backpack
off the floor and stood up.   —Carl Hiaasen, *Hoot*

And somewhere in the distance I could hear the <u>wuff-chuff</u> of an
actual train.   —Stephen King, *11/22/63*

You might also consult Tom Paxton's "The Marvelous Toy" and John Prine's
"Onomatopoeia." Shel Silverstein's poem "Noise Day," Watty Piper's *The Little
Engine That Could,* and Roy Lichtenstein's print of a fighter jet entitled
Whaam! are other good sources. So are games (KerPlunk, for example) and
advertisements (such as Alka-Seltzer's).

WRITING ASSIGNMENTS

At the Gym

In the gym you hear mechanical noises, but what about the people? How do
they sound when they exercise? Ask students to write a sentence employing
onomatopoeia to convey what they hear from the athletes (or would-be athletes) working out. For example:

   Eyes glued to the instructor on the screen, headphones plugged
   into his ears, the sweaty man <u>whooped</u> and <u>chuffed</u> when he
   finished a tough set of reps.

NOTE: Remind students that they are not to identify their classmates, overtly or
covertly, in this exercise.

At the Concert

So much goes on at a concert! The instruments, the singing, audience noise,
and so forth. Play a scene from a concert film, assigning one aspect of sound to
each student or to groups of students. Have them write sentences using onomatopoeia to capture what they hear. Some examples based on the first
Woodstock Festival:

The guitar <u>twanged</u> and <u>screeched</u>, as Jimi Hendrix contorted the national anthem.

<u>Stomping</u>, the crowd <u>squished</u> mud under their feet.

Instead of a concert, substitute a sporting event, a political rally, a parade, or another public event.

In the Factory or on the Farm

Ask students to listen to the sounds they hear in these locations, live if that's possible and desirable, or recorded. Have them write sentences that express the animal or human vocalization, the machines, and other ambient sound. Let them mix standard words (*baa*, *roar*) and their own creations (*tptptpt* or *ooonnnk*, for example).

NOTE: To extend any of these assignments, have students insert their sentences into a scene. Combine sentences from the class or have each student create a separate scene. Short stories or nonfiction narratives are good assignments as well.

SOUND PATTERNS

• •

Some years ago a friend mentioned an audiobook he was "reading." I was startled for a moment; I hadn't thought of listening as reading. Yet hearing the written word, either from someone else or in my own internal voice, *is* reading. Recognizing that fact made me reconsider how I taught sound pattern in my English classes.

Early in my career I discussed sound pattern only in connection with poetry. I'd tap out iambic pentameter and identify the rhyme scheme of a sonnet. Occasionally I'd point out repeated consonant sounds and define that as *alliteration*, which I'd contrast with *assonance*, the repetition of vowel sounds. Over time I realized that identification alone was insufficient and that sound pattern is an essential element of prose, too. So with my students I began to explore how alliteration and assonance link ideas, how a long vowel may emphasize and a short one soothe, how a break in sound pattern draws attention, and much more.

SUGGESTION: To give students a fuller appreciation of "sound effects," pair a sentence or two from this chapter with an especially long sentence and an especially succinct one from Chapter 8. Onomatopoeia and repetition also provide material for lessons on sound.

TEACHING SOUND PATTERNS: A GENERAL PLAN

Introduction (optional)

Select one of these activities to direct students' attention to sound patterns:

- Ask for a show of hands: Who "hears" an internal voice while reading? Discuss the way that silent reading delivers an auditory experience.
- Classroom karaoke: choose a song students aren't likely to know. Play the instrumental track, then the song with lyrics. Do the lyrics match their expectations? If not, what did they expect? Why? A variation of this activity is to present the lyrics first and ask what sort of accompaniment

they imagine (instrument, tempo, volume, etc.) Why? There's no right or wrong answer for either of these activities. The point is to make the class think about words and sound.

Decoding

- Begin by asking a volunteer to read the sentence aloud.
- Before defining unfamiliar words, ask for general impressions of tone, content, purpose, or whatever is relevant. This order prioritizes sound over meaning. Save these responses so you can refer to them during the analysis portion of the lesson, when meaning dominates.

Analysis

- Are there any matching sounds in the sentence? Tell students to ignore spelling as they identify similar sounds.
- Look at the matches. Do those words have anything in common? If so, what?
- Look at the unmatched words. Do those words express opposition or conflict?
- Listen to the rhythm of the sentence. Tap it out, if you can. Does the pattern relate to content?

NOTE: Not every sentence relates rhythm to meaning. But those that do are marvelous. Read *The Little Engine That Could* to hear how the blue engine's self-encouragement mantra ("I think I can") sounds labored, matching her determined progress over the mountain.

TEACHING SOUND PATTERNS: LESSON PLANS

William Butler Yeats, "The Lake Isle of Innisfree"

I will arise and go now, for always night and day
I hear lake water lapping with low sounds by the shore;
While I stand on the roadway, or on the pavements grey,
I hear it in the deep heart's core.

Brief context: The speaker expresses a wish to go to a rural area, the Lake Isle of Innisfree in Ireland.

Extended context: This sentence is the third and last stanza of a twelve-line poem in which the speaker yearns to leave the city for the Lake Isle of Innisfree, located in an area where the poet spent summers as a child. In the first stanza the speaker vows to build "a small cabin," plant beans, and tend bees there. In the second, the speaker imagines himself filled with "peace" that comes "dropping slow" from morning through midnight.

Analysis

With brief context:

• Start with consonants: Which words begin with matching consonant sounds? (true matches: *lake, lapping, low* and *day, deep*; near match: *sounds, shore, stand*)

• Look at the matching words beginning with *l*. Do their meanings connect? How? (all associated with the *water* and the *shore*—natural, soothing, *low sounds*)

• Now examine the *s* words. What's their connection? (connected because they all relate to the speaker; the words don't quite match because they describe different places: the *sounds* of the *lake* are natural; the *shore* is where civilization encroaches, and *stand* is associated with urban *roadway* and *pavements*)

• How about *day* and *deep*? (*day*: part of "night and day," in other words, *always*, which is when the speaker feels a *deep* desire to go to Innisfree)

• Now vowel sounds: start with the long *i*. Which words match? (*arise, night*, several instances of the personal pronoun *I*)

• What's the significance of the matching long *i* sounds? (*I* predominates because the speaker is thinking only of himself and what he will do—*arise*; *night* relates to time and his constant yearning to go to Innisfree)

• Look for matching *a* sounds. Any significant matches? (*always, day, lake, pavements, grey*: the first three relate to the speaker's desire to go to Innisfree, the last two the reason for the desire—to leave drab, urban life)

- How about *o*? Any significant matches? (*go*, *low*—the first expresses the speaker's resolve to leave, the second relates to the destination, a less noisy place)
- The matches are long vowels, not short. What's the effect of this sound pattern? (long vowels last longer and slow the sentence down, reflecting the speaker's desire to slow down)

With extended context:

- Most of the words (37) are single-syllable; only four words have two syllables. What's the effect of so many single syllables? (single-syllable words create an atmosphere of simplicity, and the speaker wants a simple life— beans, bees, peace)
- What about the rhyme and rhythm of the lines? (simple, like a child's chant—speaker's desire is simple and is for simplicity)

SUPPLEMENTAL MATERIAL FOR "THE LAKE ISLE OF INNISFREE"

Grammar

- The first two lines form a compound sentence, two independent clauses joined by the conjunction *for*. The conjunction introduces a reason or explanation for leaving.
- The last two lines, with a dependent and an independent clause, could stand alone as a complete sentence. Yet they're connected to the first two lines by a semicolon. A semicolon both joins and separates. Here, it emphasizes the speaker's unwavering desire to leave the *pavements* and go to Innisfree, expressed in both halves of the sentence. The semicolon also marks the change to city (*roadway*, *pavements*) from the rural references in the first part of the sentence.

Rhetoric

Hear in the deep heart's core is a *metaphor*. As described above, the sentence contains many examples of *alliteration* and *assonance*.

Additional Information and Activities

- William Butler Yeats was part of the "Celtic Revival," a literary movement that rejected traditional English forms. When Yeats wrote "The Lake Isle of Innisfree," Ireland was under British control, which many Irish, including Yeats, resented deeply. Students might research the politics of late nineteenth- and early twentieth-century Ireland for a history/English project.
- For an arts/English project, have students look at examples of visual art, such as traditional Celtic designs. Can they relate what they see to what they hear in Yeats's sentence?
- An audio of Yeats himself reading this poem is available on the internet. In an interview, Yeats explained that he took "a devil of a lot of trouble" getting the poem to sound as he wished it to and that he refused to read it as if it were prose. Definitely worth a listen!

James Thurber, *The Wonderful O*

Somewhere a ponderous tower clock slowly dropped a dozen strokes into the gloom.

Brief context: This sentence, from the beginning of a children's fantasy novel, sets the scene for a meeting between a stranger with a treasure map and a ship captain who hates the letter *o*. The two become partners and travel to an island in search of the treasure. The captain bans anything with an *o* in its name: people may wear *cats* but not *coats*, for example.

Extended context: James Thurber's novel, filled with comic wordplay, makes serious points about power. The captain's dislike of *o* began when his mother became stuck in a porthole. Unable to pull her back inside, he pushed her into the sea. His *edict* (not a *command* because of spelling!) is arbitrary; nevertheless, his crew enforce it brutally. They ban *oranges* and *tomatoes* and *food* in general, as well as *goats* and *horses* and other animals spelled with *o*. They move on to pastimes, professions, and more and more categories. Most residents of the island formerly known as Ooroo (now called *R*) follow the rules as best they can, while the scope of their lives gradually shrinks. Some refuse to give up *hope, love,* and *valor,* and little by little, the rebels regain control, ultimately discovering the treasure the invaders sought: freedom.

Analysis

With brief context:

• Read the sentence aloud and note how many different ways the letter *o* sounds. What's the significance of varied *o* sounds? (illustrates the diversity and flexibility lost by banning the letter)
  • Which words with *o* sound the same? (*ponderous, clock, dropped*)
  • What do those words have in common? (all could refer to time passing slowly and create a sad or ominous mood)
  • What else do you notice about the sounds in the sentence? (repetition of consonant sounds, but with small variations—*s* in *Somewhere, slowly, strokes* and *d* in *dropped, dozen*)
  • What's the significance? (repetition emphasizes unity, variations show individuality; both essential components of a free society)
  • Read the sentence again and listen to the pacing. What do you notice? (impossible to read quickly because of long vowels and clipped consonants; creates a somber mood)
  • Delete the *o* wherever it appears and read the result: *Smewhere a pnderus twer clck slwly drpped a dzen strkes int the glm.* How does it sound? (nonsensical) What's the significance of that change? (absurd rules yield absurd results)

With extended context:

• Can you relate the plot to the pacing of the sentence? (lives slowly diminished, freedom slowly regained)
• Say the island's name before and after the ban. How does the sound relate to meaning? (*Ooroo*—two *oo* sounds resemble a noise made by someone who's eager, *R* is diminished, as the islanders are when *o* is banned; the power to change a name is power over identity)

SUPPLEMENTAL MATERIAL
FOR *THE WONDERFUL O*

Grammar

The sentence is a single independent clause powered by the subject-verb pair, *clock dropped*. This core mirrors the slow, creeping curtailment of citizens' rights to anything spelled with an *o*. Only with unity (the independent clause) can citizens regain freedom.

Rhetoric

As discussed, the sentence contains several examples of *alliteration* and *assonance*.

Additional Information and Activities

- James Thurber was a humorist, cartoonist, and playwright. His imagination in this children's book is matched only by his fascination with wordplay. Students might enjoy reading other works by Thurber ("The Secret Life of Walter Mitty," for example) or looking at some of his cartoons.
- A lipogram is a form of writing that arbitrarily bans a letter. The captain's ban on *o* imposes a lipogram on the island. Students might try to write a sentence lipogram, without *o* or *e* or another vowel. If they struggle, have them try dropping some consonants, which are easier to avoid.
- Although it's a children's story, Thurber's novel is a meditation on justice, freedom, power, and values. A discussion of the book could prompt students to consider how these interconnect and perhaps serve as the basis for a personal essay.

Rosario Morales and Aurora Levins
Morales, "Ending Poem"

I am a late leaf of that ancient tree,
and my roots reach into the soil of two Americas.

Brief context: Rosario Morales and her daughter, Aurora Levins Morales, collaborated on this poem. The speaker is represented as the singular *I* but is actually multiple voices braided together—not just the mother and daughter but their ancestors in Eastern Europe, the Caribbean (specifically Puerto Rico), Africa, and New York City.

Extended context: Rosario Morales was born in New York City to parents who had moved there from Puerto Rico. Her husband's ancestors came from Eastern Europe; after their marriage the couple lived in Puerto Rico, where their daughter Aurora was born. The poem references all aspects of the family's heritage, refusing labels and definitions of ethnicity. In the last lines of the poem, the speakers become "we," a unified "whole."

Analysis

With brief context:

- Which sounds match? (*I* and *my*; *late* and *ancient*; *leaf*, *tree*, and *reach*; *roots* and *reach*; *roots* and *two*)
- How are the matching long *i* sounds related in meaning? (*I* and *my*—the self)
- The matching long *a* sounds? (*late* represents the present, the *leaf* that comes *late* to the tree; *ancient* represents the past; thus the present is connected to the past)
- The long *e* sounds? (a *leaf* grows on a *tree*—connection between the individual and the larger entity, the family tree; ancestry that *reach*[es] into the *soil of two Americas*)
- The *r* sounds? (*roots reach*—both *Americas* nourish the *roots* as well as the speaker; the words connect past and future, with *roots* representing the past and *reach* a stretch into the future)
- The *oo* sound? (*roots* are in *two Americas*—both North and South)
- Italics appear in the original. What do they signify? (varied answers: they may differentiate one author from another or add emphasis to the first portion of the sentence)
- Only three words have more than one syllable: *ancient, into, Americas.*

How do those words relate to each other? (*ancient*—a heritage built over centuries; *into*—a deep connection; *Americas*—on both continents)

With extended context:

- How does this sentence reject ethnic labels and categories? (matching sounds, as well as the syllabic pattern, emphasize an *ancient* heritage and a presence in *two Americas*)
- How does the change to the plural *we* and the declaration of a *whole* identity relate to this sentence? (acceptance of all aspects of identity allows someone to become *whole*)

SUPPLEMENTAL MATERIAL FOR "ENDING POEM"

Grammar

This is a compound sentence, with two independent clauses joined by the conjunction *and*. This structure relates to *two Americas*.

Rhetoric

I am a late leaf is metaphorical, as is the reference to *my roots*.

Additional Information and Activities

- "Ending Poem" is the last piece in a collection of prose and poetry entitled *Getting Home Alive*. The authors explore themes of identity, feminism, and social justice. Seldom is it clear which of the pair wrote a particular piece or line. Does it matter who wrote what? Why or why not?
- Consider heritage, or *roots*. How important is it to understand one's *roots*? What role does one's heritage play?
- The poem appears in many anthologies and is easily available online, should you wish to assign it to your class.
- The authors were members of the Puerto Rican community in New York City and in Puerto Rico itself. They were both activists for political and social change. A history/women's studies/English research project might center on these writers.

MORE SOUND EFFECTS

As you see in the lesson plans above, one sentence often provides more than enough material for several lessons—assonance, alliteration, syllables, rhymes, and so forth. Here are other sentences that can easily be the basis for a sound lesson. I've underlined one aspect to focus on, where that's possible, or mentioned an interesting element after the quotation.

I f<u>ee</u>l the n<u>ee</u>d for sp<u>ee</u>d.

—*Top Gun*

We are all connected; to each other, biolog<u>ically</u>; to the earth, chem<u>ically</u>; to the rest of the universe, atom<u>ically</u>.

—Neil deGrasse Tyson (astrophysicist)

Clear eyes, full hearts, can't lose.

—*Friday Night Lights* (film, television show: pairs of single-syllable words)

<u>F</u>ull <u>f</u>athom <u>f</u>ive thy <u>f</u>ather l<u>ie</u>s;
Of his b<u>o</u>nes are c<u>o</u>ral <u>made</u>;
Those are pearls that were his <u>eye</u>s:
Nothing of him that doth <u>fade</u>,
But doth suffer a <u>s</u>ea-<u>change</u>
Into <u>s</u>omething rich and <u>s</u>trange.

—William Shakespeare, *The Tempest* (Act 1, scene 2)
(alliteration, assonance, rhyme)

Make it so.   —*Star Trek, The Next Generation* (television show, film series: single-syllable words)

So we <u>b</u>eat on, <u>b</u>oats against the current, <u>b</u>orne ceaselessly <u>b</u>ack into the past.   —F. Scott Fitzgerald, *The Great Gatsby*

The only time a man can be br<u>a</u>ve is when he's afr<u>ai</u>d.

—*Game of Thrones* (book and television series)

So it goes.   —Kurt Vonnegut, *Slaughterhouse Five* (single-syllable words)

Make it work.   —Tim Gunn, *Project Runway*

His soul swooned slowly as he heard the snow falling faintly through the universe and faintly falling, like the descent of their last end, upon all the living and the dead.

—James Joyce, "The Dead"

WRITING EXERCISES

Sound in Music

In this chapter I've concentrated on the written word, but song lyrics are, not surprisingly, a great place to search for carefully chosen sounds. Ask students to bring in a sentence from the lyrics of a favorite song, ideally one in which the sound of the words fits the meaning and mood of the song. Then ask them to write a sentence that could substitute for the original lyric. Here's my take on Rachel Platten's "Fight Song" (easily found on the internet, if you'd like to hum along):

I got it right now
and know what's right now
and I will fight now!

As in the original, all the words are single syllables. Instead of repeating *song*, as Platten does, I opted for *now* and retained the sharp *t* sounds to add "a warrior woman" feel.

NOTE: Be sure students read their lyrics aloud. Extra brave students can sing their answers.

Match Making

Challenge students to find words with matching vowel sounds and write a sentence containing as many as possible. Remind them that the same vowel sound may be spelled differently (*dot* and *what*, for example). Here's how an Elvis fan might respond to this assignment:

> **You do a new version of "Blue Suede Shoes" and you'll rue the day you ever heard the tune.**

Rehearing

Ask students to reread something they've already written, aloud if possible. Have them keep the same content but revise the sentence to create a sound pattern. They can choose words that have matching vowel or consonant sounds, manipulate syllables and rhythm, and so forth. The goal is for the sound pattern (the medium) to reinforce what they're saying (the message).

REPETITION

I've read thousands of terrific 250-word essays over the years, each about 500 words long. I've probably expended an entire river of red ink writing "repetitive" in margins, not counting the streamlet I've devoted to deleting multiple exclamation points. (One is enough, people!) And yet.

How can we do without refrains like "London Bridge is falling down, falling down, falling down"? Or the repeated, intensifying events of "There Was an Old Lady Who Swallowed a Fly"? Or Sojourner Truth's insistent question, "Ain't I a woman?" Not to mention the reassuring murmur that "everything's going to be all right."

Effective repetition of sentences is common (see above), but repetition may also appear in a single sentence, where authors employ it to emphasize, unify, or define character. There's no doubt that repetition often comes across as sloppy and insecure, but when this element of style is good, it's very very good. (Notice the repetition there?)

TEACHING REPETITION: A GENERAL PLAN

Introduction (optional)

Select one of these activities to introduce the concept of artistic repetition:

- Play a song with an easily identifiable chorus. Ask students to note which lines are repeated. What's the function of repetition in the song? (reinforce a theme, pleasing or reassuring to hear the same lines and melody again, unifying device)
- Why should you repeat yourself? Why shouldn't you? (varied answers, to which I'll add my own: writers should repeat themselves for artistic effect, but not because they fear they haven't made themselves understood—a common situation for student writers)

Decoding

- The usual procedures for decoding generally apply to sentences with repetitive elements. However, if a word has a different meaning when it's repeated (in a pun, for instance), be sure to note the shift. (For more on word shifts, see Chapter 7.)

- Repetitive sentences can be long, so students may need help untangling the syntax. There's a plus side, though: a lengthy sentence can be a "teachable moment" for punctuation rules, such as commas around nonessential clauses or semicolons separating independent clauses.

Analysis

- Identify the repetitive elements and edit them out. Does the streamlined sentence affect the reader differently? (varied answers)
- Can you identify a reason for repetition? (unify, emphasize, show uncertainty, etc.)
- Is the repetition justified, in your view? (varied answers)

TEACHING REPETITION: LESSON PLANS

Repetitive elements are underlined.

> **William Goldman, *The Princess Bride***
>
> "I'm gonna heave this radio right out the window," I say; "it won't get it, it won't get it, I cannot make it get it."

NOTE: Students may have seen the film based on this book. Consider withholding source information until they've had a chance to react to the sentence.

Brief context: The narrator wants to listen to a football game on the radio but is having trouble tuning in to the broadcast.

Extended context: The sentence appears early in the novel when the narrator, identified as the author himself, recounts the event that led him to write *The Princess Bride*. Sick in bed, the irritable boy wants to listen to the football game (*it*) but the radio (also *it*) can't receive the signal properly. No matter how the narrator twists the dial (this being an analog, not digital system), he *cannot make it get it*. The narrator's father saves the day by reading his son a novel, *The Princess Bride*, as the boy convalesces. Years later the narrator goes to great lengths to secure a copy for his son's birthday. The narrator rereads it—or rather, reads it himself for the first time—and discovers that all those years ago his father omitted unnecessary descriptions and digressions and kept only the exciting parts. The narrator resolves to write the book he once listened to, the result being the version of *The Princess Bride* the reader is reading.

Analysis

With brief context:

- Does *it* have a uniform definition? (no, *it* refers to both the radio and the football game) Does the double meaning make the sentence hard to understand? (not really, though some students may quibble)
- Why use one pronoun to stand in for two different words? (narrator sounds confused and frantic, talking to himself more than to someone else)
- In addition to the word *it*, two expressions repeat (*it won't get it*—twice, *get it*—three times). What's the effect of that repetition? (more frantic, also comic confusion)
- After two exact repetitions (*it won't get it*) the third changes slightly (*I cannot make it get it*). Why change? (increasing emotion, third repetition adds a sense of powerlessness)
- How do the words preceding the repetition (*I'm gonna heave . . . window*) set the scene? (tendency to exaggeration or extreme behavior)
- Suppose the sentence read this way: " 'I'm gonna heave this radio right out the window,' I say, 'because it won't get the football game.' " Which version is better? Why? (varied answers)

With extended context:

- What can you infer about the narrator from this sentence? (irritated, young, in need of distraction and perspective; also sounds like a young child repeating demands as if the repetition could make the result change)
- How may *I cannot make it get it* refer to the novel? (can't make the son *get*

the novel's appeal and importance to the narrator; the narrator can't *get* the book his father once read to him, which is why the narrator rewrites *it*)

SUPPLEMENTAL MATERIAL FOR *THE PRINCESS BRIDE*

Grammar

- The sentence breaks a number of grammar rules. The irregularities add to the character's personality.
- The interrupted quotation is a run-on sentence comprising several independent clauses strung together without conjunctions. This structure gives a sense of the child's demanding urgency.
- The pronoun *it* has two separate antecedents, *radio* and *football game*, neither of which appears in the sentence. Generally, a pronoun requires a clear antecedent. The vague, repeated *it* adds to the comic effect and emphasizes that the child is driven by emotion, not logic.
- The verb in the first clause, *gonna* [going to], is nonstandard. It reinforces that the speaker is a child and that the situation is informal.

Rhetoric

- The repeated use of *it* is an example of *anaphora*, repetition at the beginning of a phrase or clause. However, in anaphora generally more than two repetitions appear.
- *Asyndeton* refers to the elimination of conjunctions (*and*, for instance) to speed up the tempo of the sentence. The last portion of the sentence lacks conjunctions between independent clauses.

Additional Information and Activities

- *The Princess Bride* is a nested narrative, or *frame story*, a literary device that's been popular for millennia. Students might explore other works employing this device, such as Mary Shelley's *Frankenstein*.
- *The Princess Bride* is also a popular film. Compare the opening scene from the film with the presentation in this sentence.
- The narrator is both the sick child and the author shaping the narrative of the sick child, an example of *metafiction*. Discuss what this device adds to the work.

> ### *An Ancient Egyptian Book of the Dead: The Papyrus of Sobekmose*, translated by Paul F. O'Rourke
>
> O Heart that is in the house of hearts, O heart that is in the house of hearts, I have my heart and it is pleased.

Brief context: This is an ancient Egyptian spell to help the deceased safely reach the afterlife.

Extended context: This ancient Egyptian spell comes from a copy of the *Book of the Dead* created for a goldworker named Sobekmose. Such books were thought to guide the deceased to the afterlife. Ancient Egyptians believed that in addition to being a physical organ, the heart was the seat of intelligence and emotions. They further believed that the heart recorded every action taken during a lifetime, and that after death, the heart would be weighed against the feather of Maat, which represented balance and justice. If the scales were equal (not perfect, but enough good deeds to pass the test), the deceased was given access to a full afterlife; if not, the crocodile-headed Ammit, the Devourer of Millions, would eat the heart and the dead person would cease to exist.

Analysis

With brief context:

- Which words repeat? (*heart*, several times; *house of hearts*, twice)
- Given how it's used in the sentence, what can you infer about the *heart*? (it's important; addressed as *O Heart*, as if it had a life of its own)
- Why might the sentence begin with the repeated phrase *O Heart that is in the house of hearts*? (to call for the *Heart's* attention, direct address)
- What can you infer about *the house of hearts*? (perhaps the body itself or a ceremonial place)
- What does *it is pleased* imply? (a *heart* may possibly be displeased)

With extended context:

- What does the sentence tell you about Sobekmose? (he successfully passed the *heart* test—*I have my heart*, so Ammit hasn't eaten it, and *it is pleased*, ready for the afterlife)
- What's the effect of repeating the same words? (chantlike repetition is essential to many rituals; makes the request more insistent; increases solemnity; adds importance)
- How does *O Heart* relate to ancient Egyptian belief? (personifying *Heart* makes sense because the heart is the seat of intelligence and emotions, the essence of a person)

SUPPLEMENTAL MATERIAL FOR
THE BOOK OF THE DEAD

Grammar

Ancient Egyptian writing had no punctuation and often no separation between words. The translator, Egyptologist Paul F. O'Rourke, had to rely on scholarship about burial practices, beliefs, and culture as much as on the hieroglyphs of the original. Here are some thoughts on his rendition of this sentence:

- The first part of the sentence is direct address: *O Heart that is in the house of hearts*. There's no comma after *Heart*, making the location an essential fact, an identifier that has become part of the name.
- The second part consists of two independent clauses joined by the conjunction *and*. Therefore, the ideas expressed by each clause are equally important: that Sobekmose has his *heart* and that *it is pleased*.

Rhetoric

No term directly relates to the repetition seen here. As rendered by the translator, the sentence is a good example of *alliteration*, repetition of a consonant sound, in this case, the *h* of *heart* and *house*. The *heart* is *personified* in this sentence.

Additional Information and Activities

- This sentence can serve as the basis for a history/English research project on ancient Egyptian religious beliefs and burial rituals.
- Hearts continue to be symbols of love. Students might research the origins of Valentine's Day and report their findings to the class.
- Have students write a sentence, modeled on this one, to their brains or to another body part. Obviously, you need to establish some ground rules for this activity—and read everything before it's shared with other students.

Georgia Douglas Johnson, "The Heart of a Woman"

The heart of a woman falls back with the night,
And enters some alien cage in its plight,
And tries to forget it has dreamed of the stars
While it <u>breaks</u>, <u>breaks</u>, <u>breaks</u> on the sheltering bars.

Brief context: This sentence is from a poem written in 1918. It follows a sentence about *the heart of a woman* going *forth with the dawn.*

Extended context: "The Heart of a Woman" has two stanzas, each of which is a complete sentence. In the first stanza, the *heart of a woman* roams "restlessly" over "life's turrets and vales," presumably the highs and lows, during the day. The second stanza, printed above, records its return. When the poem was written, segregation and discrimination by race and sex were legal and widespread.

Analysis

With brief context:

- Which words are repeated? (*breaks, breaks, breaks*)
- Read the sentence aloud. Do you hear a rhythmic pattern? (each line has 11 syllables) How about rhyme? (two couplets, or pairs: *night* and *plight, stars* and *bars*)

- Apart from rhythm, does the repetition have another purpose? (*breaks, breaks, breaks* evokes a bird crashing into bars again and again; a complete break isn't always the result of one forceful blow but may occur after repeated hits)
- What's the significance of *alien cage*? (where *the heart of a woman* dwells at night isn't her home but a prison made by someone else)
- What is the significance of a *heart* that *tries to forget it has dreamed of the stars*? (*tries*, probably doesn't succeed; dreams aren't reality; the reality of the *cage* is harsh)
- How can *bars* be *sheltering*? (the purpose may be to protect but the effect is to imprison)

With extended context:

- Is the fact that this poem is about *the heart of a woman* significant? How? (limitations on women were often justified as "for their own safety")
- This poem was written in 1918. How might it relate to its time period? (limits on women and nonwhites—*alien cages* reflecting an absence of power)

SUPPLEMENTAL MATERIAL FOR "THE HEART OF A WOMAN"

Grammar

- Three verbs (*falls, enters, tries*) have the same subject: *the heart of a woman.*
- The pronoun *it* refers to *the heart of a woman. It* appears twice, with two different verbs (*has dreamed* and *breaks, breaks, breaks*—an archetypal plot sequence).
- Except for *has dreamed*, all the verbs are in present tense; the actions are happening now, or habitually, or both. The present-perfect tense of *has dreamed* connects the past and the present, so the dreams span both periods.
- The first three lines are an independent clause. *While* connects the dependent clause to the independent clause. Thus the effort to forget and the *breaks* are subordinate to the other actions (*falls, enters, tries*).

Rhetoric

Epizeuxis is the repetition of words (*breaks*) in succession within the same sentence.

Additional Information and Activities

- Georgia Douglas Johnson was a writer of the Harlem Renaissance, a flowering of literature, visual arts, and music (not to mention politics and activism) that took place in New York City's Harlem and other Northern cities between the mid-1920s and the 1930s. Consider assigning a research project on this pivotal time period.
- For interdisciplinary work, pair this sentence, or the poem it appears in, with a Harlem Renaissance painting. What are the similarities and differences?

MORE REPETITION

Presented (mostly) without commentary, these sentences are good examples of repetition used effectively.

> Sometimes Sydney seems to be inhabited chiefly by school-children, children kicking pebbles across bridges, children racing fig leaves down the channels of ornamental fountains, children clambering like invading armies all over the Opera House, or mustered in their thousands in the New South Wales gallery.
>
> —Jan Morris, *Contact!*

> I wish, I wish, I wish.
>
> —Misa Sugiura, *This Time Will Be Different* (a daughter, after fighting with her mother, wishing a peaceful interlude could last)

> The rest is the rest of my life.
>
> —Aleksandar Hemon, *The Book of My Lives* (memoir, this sentence about a turning point, emigration from war-torn Sarajevo)

Casting for steelhead is like calling God on the telephone, and it rings and rings and rings, hundreds of rings, a thousand rings, and you listen to each ring as if an answer might come at any moment, but no answer comes, and no answer comes, and then on the 1,001st ring, or the 1,047th ring, God loses his patience and picks up the phone and yells, "WHAT THE HELL ARE YOU CALLING ME FOR?" in a voice the size of the canyon.

> —Ian Frazier, "The Last Days of Stealhead Joe" (*steelhead* are a variety of trout that are particularly difficult to catch)

To each the boulders that have fallen to each.

> —Robert Frost, "Mending Wall"

If you are tired, keep going; if you are scared, keep going; if you are hungry, keep going; if you want to taste freedom, keep going.

> —attributed to Harriet Tubman (abolitionist and "conductor" on the Underground Railroad helping enslaved people escape)

This is the way the world ends, this is the way the world ends, this is the way the world ends—not with a bang but a visitors' center.

> —Robert Macfarlane, *Underland: A Deep Time Journey* (allusion to the last stanza of T. S. Eliot's "The Hollow Men")

WRITING ASSIGNMENTS

Triple Play

Take a cue from Georgia Douglas Johnson and have your class triple up on a word. Here's one example:

Ayesha scooped scooped scooped food into the bowl while her cat Amara pretended to be a poor little kitty who'd last eaten days, not hours, ago.

The above example omits commas, but students can insert them if they wish.

AND

A popular repetition is a list of tasks, either to be done or already completed. In John Green's *Turtles All the Way Down*, one character expresses herself this way:

> Yes, even though I had to close yesterday AND Saturday AND I had this calc stuff that is like reading Sanskrit AND I had to wear the Chuckie costume like twelve separate times.

I imagine students will find it easy to create their own lists, with or without the capitalized *ands*.

Climbing

Have students brainstorm a series of steps toward a goal or an end. With a series of phrases or clauses, each beginning with the same words, have them write the steps. Here's an example:

> Before the first flake fell, before the lawn was covered, before downtown lay under a white, cold blanket, and before the power went out and the batteries in everything died, I was looking forward to a snow day.

The repetitive words that "climb" toward a conclusion make a good argument. Pair students and give them opposing sides on an issue. Have each write a sentence with steps beginning with "for this reason," leading readers to an inescapable conclusion.

Petulance

After they've read the sentence from *The Princess Bride*, ask students to imagine a petulant child (or adult—brats can be any age!). Have them write a repetitive complaint, with the sick child's *it won't get it* as a model. Extra credit: write a scene starring that character.

SIMPLICITY

• •

I have a dog. I like my dog. His name is Rex.

Any small child who wrote these sentences would rightfully take pride in them. They stay on topic and have no spelling or grammar errors. Good for the young writer! Not good for me, though. There's a reason why the youngest students I've taught have reached the two-digit age, the same reason I think educators who work with the under-ten crowd deserve extra pay. If I had to read simple sentences all day long, I'd go crazy. But (there's always a *but*, isn't there?) even I must admit that when I've waded through pages of complex syntax, a stripped-to-the-basics sentence is welcome. Call it a verbal palate cleanser.

Taking a close look at a simple sentence usually requires context. True, a few seem applicable to every area of life, like the slogans on refrigerator magnets. Actually, some simple sentences *are* on refrigerator magnets! It's easy to grasp the appeal: simplicity is a blank screen. Project your own beliefs on it, and voila, the sentence becomes wise, not cryptic. With a bit of context, though, a simple statement reveals its true nature. It can be a coda, the final note that pulls together everything preceding it. It can be an open door, inviting you to take a step inside by making the intimidating feel less so. And at times, a simple sentence is one that breaks the heart. In Wallace Terry's oral history collection, *Bloods*, for instance, a soldier recounts his tour of duty. He concludes by saying that since he's returned home, he reads the Bible once a year looking for an explanation for the horrors he witnessed. He concludes, "I can't find it." Can anyone read that sentence without tears?

This chapter and the next (Excess) function best as a pair. I hope you'll teach lessons from both to your students, so they can gorge and palate-cleanse in their own writing and recognize these techniques in others'.

TEACHING SIMPLICITY: A GENERAL PLAN

Introduction (optional)

Approach the topic of simplicity backward, beginning with an ornate statement and asking students to convey the same idea in fewer words. An example:

ORNATE: It was on that day in February, the 26th of the month, in the year 2020, that he asked her to be his wedded wife.
SIMPLE: He proposed to her on February 26, 2020.

Which do they prefer? Why? I should warn you that sometimes students pick the first version because they see it as more mature. I try to honor their preference while still urging them to think about the merits of simplicity.

Decoding

- Definitions of individual words are generally not an issue in a simple sentence. Connotations, maybe. Be sure both are clear before moving forward.
- Add context as needed so that the meaning of the sentence as a whole is approachable.

Analysis

- Without context, would a reader understand this sentence?
- Imagine people with very different worldviews reading or hearing this sentence. Would their understanding of it match yours? Why or why not?
- Why has the author chosen simplicity? What's gained? What's lost?
- Do you imagine this sentence surrounded by others of similar style and length, or as a counterpoint to longer, more complex sentences? Why?

TEACHING SIMPLICITY: LESSON PLANS

> **Gary D. Schmidt,** *Okay for Now*
>
> **The terrified eye.**

Brief context: In this sentence, a fourteen-year-old boy refers to a drawing of a diving Arctic Tern, a sea bird.

Extended context: The sentence reports the reaction of the main character, Doug Swieteck, to a drawing of an Arctic Tern by John James Audubon.

Doug sees the drawing in the town library and returns often to examine it. He notices that the book the drawing comes from is incomplete and learns that some pages have been sliced out and sold. He decides to track down the pages and return them to the library. It's not an easy task, but then nothing in Doug's life is easy: his father is violent, one older brother is in the army, and the other torments Doug. The family has moved to a small town far from Doug's friends. Plus, they're poor, and Doug can't read. When he looks at the drawing, Doug sees a falling, helpless bird and notes that "there wasn't a single thing in the world that cared at all." But Doug is wrong: the drawing, based on a real work by Audubon, shows a tern diving for prey.

Doug visits the library often; each month a different Audubon drawing is on display. The grumpy-on-the-outside, kind-on-the-inside librarian gives Doug lessons so the boy can sketch the artworks he loves so much. A perceptive teacher notices Doug's struggles and helps him learn to read. Doug gets a job delivering groceries and babysitting children. He seeks out the drawings and finally recovers them all. The novel recounts many other events, some of them dire, but Doug never gives up. The reader is left feeling that Doug is "okay for now," as the title suggests.

Analysis

With brief context:

- Is this a complete sentence? (no, according to traditional grammar rules)
- What's missing? (a complete thought, a verb)
- What's the effect of omitting those elements? (the story isn't complete, the reader must guess what action is taken or if action is possible)
- In what circumstances would a sentence like this make sense? (varied answers: to focus on or heighten the emotion, to show a limited reality, to imply inability to act)

With extended context:

- How does the grammatical structure of the sentence relate to Doug's challenges? (his life is fragmented by family troubles; he at first seems unable to act, and verbs express action)

- Doug is fascinated by *the terrified eye*. Why? (sees himself and his own emotions; eyes are traditionally "windows" into someone's inner life)
- What's the significance of Doug's mistaken interpretation of the drawing? (the bird's not helplessly falling, and neither is Doug—people help Doug, and he takes action also)
- How does the simplicity of the sentence reflect Doug's story? (he takes one step at a time, despite his fear)

SUPPLEMENTAL MATERIAL FOR *OKAY FOR NOW*

Grammar

As mentioned above, this is a sentence fragment: a noun (*eye*), its description (*terrified*), and an article (*the*).

Additional Information and Activities

- Doug's story is set in 1968, when the Vietnam War, the draft, and protests against both affected many American families. The Vietnam War was also the first "televised" war, with graphic images appearing on nightly newscasts. A history/English research assignment might add context to *the terrified eye*.
- Doug's father is violent, as are his older brothers. Doug's mother tries to keep the peace, but often fails. A psychology/English project on domestic violence would also place *the terrified eye* in perspective.
- Doug Swieteck is a minor character in Gary Schmidt's earlier novel, *The Wednesday Wars*. Schmidt has explained that he couldn't let go of the character. If students have read *Okay for Now* or *The Wednesday Wars*, ask them to compare Doug's characterization in each.

> William Blake, *The Marriage of Heaven and Hell*
>
> The bird a nest, the spider a web, man friendship.

Brief context: This line is from a long, philosophical poem.

Extended context: William Blake was a poet, philosopher, and visual artist. For him, those three roles were inseparable. The quoted line is one of a long list of proverbs in the poem, which reflects the author's thoughts on Nature, God, creativity, and many other topics. The book is illuminated: the words, with drawings, were etched on copperplate, with each printed copy hand-tinted by either Blake or his wife, Catherine. The poem was written in the eighteenth century, when the term *man* represented the entire human race.

Analysis

With brief context:

- What three groups appear in this sentence? (1—*the bird a nest*, 2—*the spider a web*, 3—*man friendship*)
- What do the groups have in common? (each names a creature and a supportive structure)
- What point is the poet making about *friendship*? (like the bird's *nest* and the spider's *web*, *friendship* is a home representing comfort and protection; the animals are linked to natural structures, thus *friendship* is natural for *man*)
- What's missing from the sentence? (connective words such as conjunctions, explicit comparisons, verbs)
- What's gained because of the sentence's simplicity? (keeps the focus on the core idea)
- What's lost because of the simplicity? (Blake's meaning may be misinterpreted)

With extended context:

- How does the sentence relate to the illuminated format of Blake's book? (sentence presents images, as does the book)
- After reading this sentence, what do you infer about Blake's philosophy? (connection with Nature, connection with other human beings)

SUPPLEMENTAL MATERIAL FOR *THE MARRIAGE OF HEAVEN AND HELL*

Grammar

The sentence implies but does not state its common verb—most likely, *has*: *the bird* has *a nest*, the spider *has* a web, man *has* friendship.

Rhetoric

- The three portions of Blake's sentence are *parallel*, each beginning with a noun followed by its natural context.
- Because there are three, the term *tricolon* also applies.
- Because the elements are equal in length, this sentence fits the definition of *isocolon*.
- Stringing these ideas together without conjunctions is an example of *asyndeton* or *parataxis*.
- Because Blake hints at but does not explicitly express his point, this sentence employs *paralipsis*.

Additional Information and Activities

- Blake's poem isn't an easy read, in part because he redefines terms such as "hell," which he sees not as a place of punishment but rather a creative, roiling environment. A look at a facsimile edition might inspire an arts/English project.
- A psychology/English research project might focus on the role of friendship in human life.

Herman Melville, "Bartleby the Scrivener"

I would prefer not to.

Brief context: A scrivener—an employee who copies documents—answers requests his employer makes of him with this sentence.

Extended context: In the mid-nineteenth century when the story was written, all copies were handwritten or typeset by printers. Bartleby's employer, an attorney working on Wall Street, employs a number of scriveners, or clerks, to hand-copy legal documents. At first Bartleby is a productive worker. Then he refuses more and more requests and eventually stops working entirely, giving the sentence above as his only response to his employer's requests. The employer indulges Bartleby, shifting the work to other scriveners. He continues to pay Bartleby and, when it's obvious that Bartleby is living in the office, invites him to stay at his home. Again, Bartleby *would prefer not to.* The lawyer moves his office to a different place, and the new occupant has Bartleby arrested and removed. The lawyer visits Bartleby in prison, where he discovers that Bartleby isn't eating. The lawyer sends him food, but Bartleby doesn't eat and dies of starvation.

Analysis

With brief context:

- What tone do you imagine for Bartleby's sentence? Why? (varied answers: defiance, indifference, lack of confidence or weakness)
- What does the verb *would prefer* add to the sentence? (free will)
- The sentence breaks off without saying exactly what Bartleby *would prefer not to* do. Why? (can be read as narrowly focused on the request he refuses but can also be read as a more general rejection of his work, the people around him, or any sort of action)
- In what circumstances is this response to an employer's request appropriate? (varied answers)

With extended context:

- How does the fact that Bartleby never explains his reasoning affect the story? (varied answers: allows readers—and critics!—to project their own interpretations on the character)
- Is the setting, Wall Street, significant? (financial hub, perhaps Bartleby as a symbol of resistance to capitalism)

- Does Bartleby's death relate to this sentence? (cause unclear, but may be that he starves because he *would prefer not to* eat)

SUPPLEMENTAL MATERIAL FOR "BARTLEBY THE SCRIVENER"

Grammar

The sentence is a single clause. The modal verb form, *would*, suggests habitual action, though *would* may also express a conscious, determined attitude.

Additional Information and Activities

- Herman Melville's story is famously intriguing, with multiple and conflicting interpretations. As it's rather short, you might assign it to the class and ask them to formulate a theory of its meaning.
- In the mid-nineteenth century, Wall Street was gaining importance. A history/English project could examine the effects of the financial markets on American life. Was Bartleby joined by others who *would prefer not to* participate?
- Bartleby is sometimes seen as a clinically depressed character. For a psychology/English project, students can research the medical definition of "depressed" and compare it to common usage.

MORE SIMPLICITY

These sentences, presented here without commentary, are good examples of simplicity and may form the basis of lessons modeled on the ones above.

Keep breathing.   —Sophie Tucker (singer and actor, responding to an interviewer's question about the secret of longevity)

Movement never lies.   —Martha Graham (dancer), *Blood Memory*

Regulated hatred.
—D. W. Harding, "Regulated Hatred" (description of Jane Austen)

Mad, bad, and dangerous to know.
>—Lady Caroline Lamb (diary entry about George Gordon, Lord Byron)

Fail better.
>—Samuel Beckett, *Worstward Ho*

Some people are worth melting for.
>—*Frozen* (spoken by Olaf the snowman to Anna)

More matter with less art.
>—William Shakespeare, *Hamlet* (Act 2, scene 2)

Thinking is my fighting.
>—Virginia Woolf (diary entry)

I came, I saw, I conquered.
>—Julius Caesar (on conquering Pontus in 47 BCE)

They lived and laughed and loved and left.
>—James Joyce, *Finnegans Wake*

I want it all.
>—Bea Arthur (as the title character in the 1970s television show *Maude*, on work and family)

The medium is the message.
>—Marshall McLuhan, *Understanding Media*

You're gonna need a bigger boat.
>—*Jaws*

Until death, it is all life.
>—Miguel de Cervantes, *Don Quixote*

Except sometimes. When he felt like it. Out of nowhere.
>—Tommy Orange, *There There* (a character explaining that his father usually won't talk about being Native American)

A carrot is a carrot, and there's nothing more to know.

> —Anton Chekhov (comparing "What's the
> meaning of life?" to "What's a carrot?")

Of all lies, art is the least untrue.

> —Gustave Flaubert (in an 1846 letter)

WRITING EXERCISES

Sometimes I think that simplicity is easier in these tweet-ful days. People are accustomed to pouring a cauldron's worth of thoughts into a thimble-sized message. But simplicity isn't only about length. It's about presenting an idea in pure form. To do so, there must be an actual idea present. Here are some writing prompts to cultivate simplicity.

Microscope

Gary D. Schmidt's sentence, *The terrified eye*, is a good starting point, though you can proceed with this exercise even if you didn't use the first lesson plan in this chapter. Ask students to imagine an emotionally intense moment: a victory celebration, parents watching a child's first step, a moment of grief, and the like. Now ask them to narrow the focus to one participant, and then narrow still more to focus on a physical detail. It can be a body part (a fist striking the air, for instance) or something else (a tear falling onto a letter). Last step: Write a sentence that captures the emotion.

Summing Up

Challenge students to write a sentence that sums up a story or a current event. They can be playful:

Moby-Dick: Ahab tried to get the whale until the whale got him.

or serious:

Fire at Notre Dame: History is burning.

Meme Punch

Have students examine a meme or create one. Give them a photo of, say, a pile of credit cards and ask for a sentence. Some examples:

Buy buy freedom.

Welcome to adulthood.

After you've shown a few responses to the class, but before they discuss the results, ask them to jot down what they think each sentence means. Some readers see the first example as positive: you're free because you can buy things. Others see it as negative: *buy* is a homonym for *bye*, and a pile of credit cards alludes to debt. Discuss the discrepancy and whether clarity and simplicity can coexist. Also discuss whether their responses work without the visual element. Then steer the class to a more general discussion of context.

Honest!

Wading through social waters is so tricky that many of us prefer a raft of words to float on. That's not always bad, but sometimes simple honesty is the better alternative. Example:

SITUATION: George wants to know why his friend Abe didn't tell him about the scholarship Abe won.
ABE: I knew you'd be jealous.

Ouch. But George has learned something important: how he comes across to his friend. That's useful information, simply told. A good follow-up to this assignment is to write a full scene or story expanding on the situation and including the simple sentence.

EXCESS

● ●

"The road of excess leads to the palace of wisdom," wrote William Blake a few centuries ago. I don't agree with Blake's statement when it's applied to life in general, but excess does have its place: in a few—a very few!—sentences. Most are long, but excess is more than word count. It's when idea piles on idea or when a point is made and then hammered at, giving a sense of urgency or inevitability. Excess may also be a host of examples to argue an airtight case or myriad details to take a description into virtual-reality territory. At times, excess can be an unstoppable monologue, revealing anxiety or egotism.

I like to pair a lesson on excess with one on simplicity, the technique I discuss in the previous chapter. In writing, moving from mini to maxi or vice versa creates an interesting rhythmic pattern in a paragraph. In teaching, it's a fine way to demonstrate the versatility of great sentences.

TEACHING EXCESS: A GENERAL PLAN

Introduction (optional)

Create a class sentence. Choose a topic that suits your students' age and mood. It might be "I can't wait to . . ." or "I hate it when . . ." or a series of targeted "I remember" statements. Gather the ideas and, again in partnership with your class, squeeze them all into one sentence. Read the result aloud. How does that single sentence come across? Angry, excited, eager, or something else? Discuss the difference between reading one long sentence and a series of short ones.

Decoding

- Because a sentence characterized by excess can be complicated, you may wish to have your students list the ideas in it.
- Ask them to establish the relationship between ideas on the list. It may be that one item describes another or clarifies a preceding point. Perhaps two or three items establish a pattern and the next item breaks it.
- Before moving on, be sure students grasp the overall meaning.

Analysis

- Are any of the ideas or words in the sentence more important than the others? How do you know? (varied answers)
- When you read the sentence aloud, what tone do you hear? (varied answers)
- Do you see a pattern in the order of ideas? (increasing or decreasing in intensity, chronological, spatial, etc.)
- Look closely at the beginning and the end of the sentence. How are they related? (varied answers)
- Reword the sentence, breaking it into several shorter sentences or deleting anything that doesn't seem crucial. Compare the two versions. How does each affect the reader?

TEACHING EXCESS: LESSON PLANS

T. H. White, *The Sword in the Stone*

There were several boars' tusks and the claws of tigers and libbards mounted in symmetrical patterns, and a big head of Ovis Poli, six live grass snakes in a kind of aquarium, some nests of the solitary wasp nicely set up in a glass cylinder, an ordinary beehive whose inhabitants went in and out of the window unmolested, two young hedgehogs in cotton wool, a pair of badgers which immediately began to cry Yik-Yik-Yik-Yik in loud voices as soon as the magician appeared, twenty boxes which contained stick caterpillars and six of the puss-moth, and even an oleander [moth] that was worth two and six, all feeding on the appropriate leaves, a guncase with all sorts of weapons which would not be invented for half a thousand years, a rob-box ditto, a lovely chest of drawers full of salmon flies which had been tied by Merlyn himself, another chest whose drawers were labelled Mandragora, Mandrake, Old Man's Beard, etc., a bunch of turkey feathers and goose-quills for making pens, an astrolabe, twelve pairs of boots, a dozen purse-nets, three dozen rabbit wires, twelve cork-screws, an ant's nest between two glass plates, ink-bottles of every possible colour from red to violet, darning-needles, a gold medal for being the best scholar at Eton, four or five recorders, a nest of field mice all alive-o, two skulls, plenty of cut glass, Venetian glass, Bristol glass and a bottle of Mastic varnish, some satsuma china and some cloisonne, the fourteenth edition of the Encyclopaedia Britannica (marred as it was by the sensationalism of the popular plates), two paint-boxes (one oil, one water-colour), three gloves of the known geographical world, a few fossils, the stuffed head of a camel leopard, six pismires, some glass retorts with cauldrons, bunsen burners, etc. . .

Brief context: The sentence describes the contents of a room occupied by Merlyn, a wizard.

Extended context: In his 1938 novel, T. H. White reimagines the legend of King Arthur. White's interpretation begins with a young boy called Wart, who lives with a knight, training to become his squire. One day Wart gets lost in a forest, where he encounters the wizard Merlyn, whose home this sentence describes. Merlyn lives backward in time and knows that Wart's destiny is to be king someday. Merlyn's job is to train the boy for his royal role. During lessons, Merlyn sometimes turns Wart into an ant, a hawk, and other creatures, to show Wart the world from various perspectives.

Analysis
With brief context:

- Many of the items in Merlyn's home are unusual. Some are old terms (*libbard* for "leopard"), and some current but rare (*Ovis Poli*, a type of sheep). A few don't appear in the dictionary (*rob-box ditto*). Why choose these words instead of something more readily understandable? (to add a sense of mystery, the exotic, or olden times; to purposely confuse the reader)
- Do you need to know the definition of everything on the list to

understand the overall meaning? (no, the messiness comes across, as does the eclectic nature of Merlyn's possessions)

- Categorize the items. (living animals, preserved specimens, weapons, hunting and fishing implements, plants and herbs, writing and reading material, china and glass, scientific instruments, etc.)
- What sort of person would live here? (varied answers; ask for text-based justification)
- How would a visitor to this room feel? Why? (varied answers: overwhelmed—too many things, curious—odd items, frightened—*weapons, wasps, snakes,* etc.)
- What's the significance of *weapons which would not be invented for half a thousand years*? (magic, altered timeline)
- An *oleander* may be a bush, or a moth that feeds on the *oleander bush.* In this sentence it's the only item assigned a monetary value (*two and six*). Why? (as a moth: emphasizes rarity, the extent of Merlyn's collection; as a leaf: shows careful treatment of his *caterpillars* and *moths*—small creatures often scorned or overlooked, who feed on the *oleander*)
- If this list were shorter, would the sentence's impact on the reader remain the same? What would be gained or lost? (varied answers)

With extended context:

- Wart doesn't know his true identity. How does this sentence reflect that fact? (mysterious items; jumbled and confused collection)
- Do any of the items relate to Wart's training? (yes: weapons; varied creatures and magical items are part of the boy's lessons with Merlyn)

SUPPLEMENTAL MATERIAL FOR
THE SWORD IN THE STONE

Grammar

- Surprising as it may seem, the sentence is one long independent clause, powered by the verb *were.* All the items on the list function as subjects.
- White uses only commas to differentiate one list item from another, even though some items contain commas. Most writers would place

semicolons between items on the list to help the reader group related ideas. White's deviation from the traditional rule echoes Merlyn's odd ways.

Additional Information and Activities

• The Arthurian legends have been a source of inspiration for many writers, artists, and filmmakers. For an arts/English project, have students compare one or two depictions of Merlyn and his surroundings.

• *Harry Potter*'s Dumbledore shares many of Merlyn's qualities. Have students compare J. K. Rowling's description of Dumbledore's office with White's sentence.

• King Arthur most likely never existed, but there are fragments of historical accuracy in the legends. Have students examine the role of myths and legends in shaping a national identity in a project combining psychology with history and language arts.

Toni Cade Bambara, "Raymond's Run"

So I'm strolling down Broadway breathing out and breathing in on counts of seven, which is my lucky number, and here comes Gretchen and her sidekicks: Marie Louise, who used to be a friend of mine when she first moved to Harlem from Baltimore and got beat up by everybody till I took up for her on account of her mother and my mother used to sing in the same choir when they were young girls, but people ain't grateful, so now she hangs out with the new girl Gretchen and talks about me like a dog; and Rosie, who is as fat as I am skinny and has a big mouth where Raymond is concerned and is too stupid to know that there is not a big deal of difference between herself and Raymond and that she can't afford to throw stones.

Brief context: The narrator talks about some girls who live in her neighborhood. Raymond is her brother, whose thinking and planning skills are impaired.

Extended context: Hazel Parker, known as Squeaky, moved to New York City's Harlem sometime before the story takes place. She's a great runner, winning every race she enters. Her family has put her in charge of her older brother, Raymond, whose mental development is equivalent to a toddler's. Squeaky checks on Raymond constantly and defends him whenever anyone speaks disrespectfully to him or about him. At the end of this story Squeaky realizes that Raymond, too, might be a talented runner.

Analysis

With brief context:

- What's the effect of beginning the sentence with *So*? (puts the reader into the middle of a story; could signal a justification or imply a cause/effect structure)
- Which girl does the narrator see as most important? (*Gretchen*, who arrives with *her sidekicks*)
- What is the narrator's attitude toward the girls? How do you know? (negative, each is described as having been ungrateful or disrespectful to Hazel)
- Why can't Rosie *afford to throw stones*? (allusion to the New Testament: Rosie shares some negative qualities with Raymond, about whom she *has a big mouth*)
- Why put all these details into one sentence? (emphasize facts: the girls have a group—*Gretchen and her sidekicks*; emphasize theme: the narrator is in the group in some ways—they live in the same neighborhood and go to the same school)
- How would you characterize the narrator, based on this sentence? (defensive, even defiant; sees herself as wronged—*I took up for her . . . ain't grateful*; has her own eccentricities—*counts of seven . . . lucky number*)

With extended context:

- What does this sentence reveal about Squeaky's relationship with her brother? (she's protective of Raymond—rejects *Rosie* for her *big mouth where*

Raymond is concerned; she also looks down on Raymond—*can't afford to throw stones* implies Rosie and Raymond both have faults)

- Why is the title significant? (Squeaky realizes that Raymond has talent, too, not just impairment)
- How does inserting all this information into one sentence relate to the theme of the story? (run: Squeaky runs, and the sentence feels like a long run; unites Squeaky and the girls: same neighborhood and school and perhaps the same lack of appreciation for Raymond)
- What's the effect of ending the sentence with a reference to Raymond? (discovering his talent is the point of the story, not the neighborhood girls or Squeaky's talents)

Additional Information and Activities

- This story is quite short and easy to read. Consider exploring Squeaky's voice as a first-person narrator, either in this sentence or in the story as a whole.
- The nature of Raymond's cognitive impairment isn't specified, but the story can still be a good basis for a psychology/English project.
- How a group forms and how it treats outsiders is another possible research topic combining psychology and English.

> ### William Shakespeare, *Hamlet* (Act 2, scene 2)
>
> **POLONIUS: . . . Tis true, 'tis pity, / And pity 'tis 'tis true—a foolish figure, / But farewell to it, for I will use no art."**

Brief context: Polonius is a royal advisor; here he has just finished telling Hamlet's mother that her son is mad.

Extended context: Ten lines earlier, Polonius, tangled up in strings of words and digression, reminded himself that "brevity is the soul of wit." He's about to give some bad news to the Queen, Hamlet's mother, but he goes off track, saying that to talk about "what duty is, / Why day is day, night night, and time is time" would only "waste night, day and time." The Queen, angry, demands that he get to the point ("More matter with less art"). He finally says, "Your noble son is mad." He injects still more words into his speech, qualifying his opinion with "Mad call I it." Then he arrives at this line.

Analysis

With brief context:

- Read Polonius's sentence aloud. Does the tone change? Why or why not? (varied answers because this depends on the actor's or director's interpretation; be sure answers are supported by the text and context)
- What's the significance of repeating *'tis true* and *'tis pity*? (varied answers: self-important speaker; anxious, can't bring himself to say what he knows; wants to stay in the spotlight)
- What *foolish figure* is Polonius saying *farewell* to? (most likely a *figure* of speech such as assonance; or a quick aside, referring to the mad Hamlet)
- What *art* is Polonius speaking about? (skilled or imaginative expression)
- Why does Polonius say *farewell to it*? (Queen's displeasure, wants the information more quickly)
- This sentence is relatively short, but it still shows excess. How? Why? (repetition, looping structure—shows uncertainty, silliness, anxiety, or egotism, depending on the interpretation)

With extended context:

- Polonius hasn't followed his own advice ("Brevity is the soul of wit"). Why not? (incapable, needs the spotlight, or simply confused)
- What's another possible meaning of *foolish figure*? (Polonius himself, who dithers and can't impart the information)
- If Polonius truly believes that "brevity is the soul of wit," how would the sentence change? (perhaps not at all, if he can't help himself; the repetition might be removed; the sentence might be deleted entirely, and Polonius would move on to what he believes is the reason for Hamlet's madness)

SUPPLEMENTAL MATERIAL FOR *HAMLET*

Grammar

- The contraction *'tis* is short for *it is*. Thus the subject is implied. Form matches content here, because Hamlet, the subject of Polonius's conversation, is overshadowed by Polonius's remarks.
- In modern times *farewell* usually appears alone, a "goodbye" that stands apart from the sentence. Here *farewell* is a verb, with *it* as an object. Together they form a command: Polonius is ordering himself to say *farewell* to *figure*, or "art," and get to the point.
- The syntax of Polonius's sentence runs in circles. One wonders if that's the way his brain works! It's worth noting, though, that in other scenes he makes far more sense.

Rhetoric

- The short *i* sound creates *assonance*.
- *Anacoluthon* is the interruption of a sentence to begin another thought, disrupting the expected grammatical sequence. Polonius loops around with *And pity 'tis 'tis true* and then veers to *But farewell it*. It's likely the interruption comes from his personality or his mood (or the Queen's!).
- Part of the sentence (*Tis true, 'tis pity, / And pity 'tis 'tis true*) forms a cross, an example of *chiasmus*.

Additional Information and Activities

- Many actors have played Polonius; there's always some comedy, but the focus changes. Some productions highlight Polonius's love for his daughter (whose breakup with Hamlet, at Polonius's direction, is what Polonius believes has brought Hamlet to madness). Others see Polonius as ever angling for political favor. Still others feature a doddering, mentally impaired man. Show the scene (Act 2, scene 2) from a few productions. Which interpretation do students prefer? Why?
- In British English, *will* shows determination. (In American English, *will* tends to be merely a time marker.) Discuss the British meaning of the verb in *I will use no art*.

MORE "EXCESS" SENTENCES

Here's an array of sentences characterized by excess, which serves a different purpose in each.

To show confusion:

And still a moment's strange, incredulous suspense—and then the deluge!—then that mixture of horror, noises, uncertainty (the sound, somewhere back, of a horse's hoofs clattering with speed)—the people burst through chairs and railings, and break them up—there is inextricable confusion and terror—women faint—quite feeble persons fall, and are trampled on—many cries of agony are heard—the broad stage suddenly fills to suffocation with a dense and motley crowd, like some horrible carnival—the audience rush generally upon it, at least the strong men do—the actors and actresses are all there in their play-costumes and painted faces, with mortal fright showing through the rouge—the screams and calls, confused talk—redoubled, trebled—two or three manage to pass up water from the stage to the President's box—others try to clamber up—etc., etc.

—Walt Whitman (speech commemorating the anniversary of Abraham Lincoln's assassination)

To reveal character:

I had a corpse once, worse than this fella, mostly dead he was, and I tickled him and tickled him; I tickled his toes and I tickled his armpits and his ribs and I got a peacock feather and went after his belly button; I worked all day and I worked all night and the following dawn—the following dawn mark me—the corpse said, "I just hate that," and I said, "Hate what?" and he said, "Being tickled; I've come all the way back from the dead to ask you to stop," and I said, "You mean this that I'm doing now with the peacock feather, it bothers you?" and he said, "You couldn't guess how much it bothers me," and of course I just kept on asking him questions about tickling, making him talk back to me, answer me, because, I don't really have time to tell you, once you get a corpse really caught up in conversation, your battle's half over.

> —William Goldman, *The Princess Bride* (character with the power
> to bring the newly dead back to life describes his work)

To create a tone:

I see now how this must have come across to my mother, who was then in the ninth year of a job she'd taken primarily so she could help finance my college education, after years of not having a job so that she'd be free to sew my school clothes, cook my meals, and do laundry for my dad, who for the sake of our family spent eight hours a day watching gauges on a boiler at the filtration plant.

> —Michelle Obama, *Becoming* (mocking her younger self for telling her
> hardworking, self-sacrificing mother that being
> an attorney wasn't fulfilling)

To introduce a topic:

A plate was silently placed in front of me, or rather, a dark brown platform of what looked at first to be sod (actually a mixture of beetroot and mushroom powder with truffle), adorned with bursts of yellow pollen (a compact butter with truffle, root vegetables, and salt), anchored by a crinkled log (potato-starch paper covered in smoked salt, powdered mushroom, and porcini), punctuated by tiny green leaves (fig leaves), and at the bottom a thin layer of mushrooms (button, anchored by a mushroom stock jelly).

> —Maria Konnikova, "Altered Tastes" (writing about innovative food
> and neurogastronomy, the study of the physical
> and mental components of taste)

To emphasize a point:

If you are in love with language, here is how you will read Brian Doyle's posthumous collection of essays: by underlining sentences and double-underlining other sentences; by sometimes shading in the space between the two sets of lines so as to create a kind of

D.I.Y. bolded font; by marking whole astonishing paragraphs with a squiggly line in the margin, and by highlighting many of those squiggle-marked sections with a star to identify the best of the astonishing lines therein; by circling particularly original or apt phrases, like "this blistering perfect terrible world" and "the chalky exhausted shiver of my soul" and "the most arrant glib foolish nonsense and frippery"; and, finally, by dog-earing whole pages, then whole essays, because there is not enough ink in the world to do justice to such annotations, slim as this book is and so full of white space, too.

—Margaret Renkl, "A Memorial of Words" (review of *One Long River of Song: Notes on Wonder* by Brian Doyle)

WRITING EXERCISES

Excess-sentence writing comes with a warning label: punctuation is a challenge. I normally overlook errors until the ideas and syntax are set. Then I teach one concept (semicolons in lists, for instance) and ask students to correct their work. However you handle it, be prepared for errant commas, an overdose of dashes, and even a stray period or two.

Puppy Love

Show a photo of a puppy and ask students to jot down some descriptive words such as *fluffy*, *tiny*, *big-eyed*, and the like. Next go for actions: *sleeping, cuddling, surprised to see his own paws, chasing his tail*, and so on. (I allow *pooping* and *piddling* but not more graphic words: your call!). That done, list some reactions to the puppy: *he got 5481 likes on social media, Mom ordered him off the sofa and then curled up on the floor with him for hours*, and similar statements. Now the hard part: ask students to insert as many items as they can into one sentence. Choose a good basic candidate and let the class work on it together, adding still more. Here's one result:

The big-eyed, fluffy-eared puppy saw his own tail, tried to bite it, fell over his own paws and then stared at me while I took the photo that got 5481 likes on social media.

This exercise works for any interesting photo.

Action!

In many sporting events, dozens of things happen at the same time. An excess of action is perfect for a sentence with excess. Ask for a description of thirty seconds of a hockey or basketball game, or the last minute of one of those competitive cooking or design shows. Video games work for this exercise also. Follow the usual procedure: list the actions and who's doing them and then fashion a sentence containing as many actions as possible.

Character Development

Ask students to select a character and record everything that races through the character's mind in one minute. Some personal details may leak through, so assure students that this prewriting is for their eyes alone. As they write or type, they shouldn't worry about grammar or spelling or punctuation. The goal is to capture as many ideas as possible.

Have them reread what they wrote, looking for one theme or emotion they can expand on. Say, for example, they wrote these words describing the mood outside the classroom door just before an important exam: *hands gripping pencil.*

Ask them to add detail, focused on that moment: *coffee sloshing over Claire's knuckles, "What formula?" clock sounds.* Working from their lists, students now fashion a sentence capturing the pretest mood:

> **Over the loud tick-tock of the clock, Claire heard the word *formulas* and, startled, sloshed coffee over her knuckles as she blurted, "Formulas? We have to know formulas? Which formulas? There are formulas? Why didn't I study formulas? What page are they on?" as she frantically tried to simultaneously wipe her knuckles and rifle through her chem notes.**

The last step (which I've already done in the example above) is to refine punctuation, spelling, and grammar.

CHAPTER 9

CONNECTIONS

FIRST PERSON

. . . .

To Joan Didion, first person is "the act of saying *I*, of imposing oneself upon other people, of saying *listen to me, see it my way, change your mind.*" That's one possibility for first-person point of view, but not the only one. *I* may be internal, a thought that no one else will hear. This point of view also appears in reporting—here's what *I* saw and did—and a challenge: What about you? *I* may be sincere or phony, self-aware or clueless, untrustworthy because of ignorance or bias or intentional deceit. And don't forget the collective form, *we*. Whatever its purpose, first person draws the reader or listener into another's world. When I teach this form, I ask students to determine why the author chose first person and what the sentence reveals or conceals.

TEACHING FIRST PERSON: A GENERAL PLAN

Introduction (optional)

My favorite introductory activity is to distribute "identity" cards. Each has this information on it:

- a name
- occupation (architect, bus driver, student, full-time parent, etc.)
- the situation—just broke a plate, won the lottery, saw a celebrity, and so forth.

Now I ask for a pair of sentences from the first-person point of view. In one, the narrator is reliable. In the other, not. Without making this an acting lesson, I encourage students to read each sentence aloud, putting life into their characters. For example, suppose the card reads "Evan, eighth grader, wants a puppy but his parents don't":

> **RELIABLE NARRATOR:** They didn't budge when I told them Jenna's dog had a litter and that Jenna can't keep all the puppies, but I hope they'll believe my promise to take care of everything, because I really will.
> **UNRELIABLE NARRATOR:** Typical, so typical: they don't want me to have any fun, so they said "no puppy" even though I really want one and the whole thing with the kitten was a long time ago.

After each reading, the class discusses how the narrator or speaker comes across. If time permits, I have them rewrite the sentence in third-person point of view and discuss how its impact changes.

Decoding
- Who's talking or thinking?
- Is the narrator addressing someone else? If so, who?
- What is the narrator or speaker talking about?

Analysis
- What do you know or infer about *I* based on the information in the sentence?
- Is the narrator or speaker trustworthy? How do you know?
- Can you determine the mood or tone? Which words in the sentence tell you that?
- If the sentence were written from third-person point of view, would the effect change? How?

TEACHING FIRST PERSON: LESSON PLANS

> **Raymond Chandler, *The Little Sister***
>
> I killed my cigarette and got another one out and went through all the slow futile face-saving motions of lighting it, getting rid of the match, blowing smoke off to one side, inhaling deeply as though that scrubby little office was a hilltop overlooking the bouncing ocean—all tired clichéd mannerisms of my trade.

Brief context: A private detective pauses as he questions a suspect.

Extended context: Philip Marlowe is the epitome of the "hardboiled detective," a staple of the mystery genre. Written in 1949, *The Little Sister* traces Marlowe's search for a missing man. As he works the case, Marlowe visits seedy hotels and luxurious apartments, uncovering dead bodies, lies, and twisted motives. One evening he drives through Los Angeles, cynically viewing everything as corrupted or fake, chiding himself several times with "You're not human tonight, Marlowe." He eventually discovers the murderer's identity but, as in many of Chandler's Philip Marlowe books, he can't bring the culprit to justice.

Analysis

With brief context:

- What is the narrator doing? (extinguishing and lighting a cigarette, then *inhaling deeply*)
- What does *slow* add to the impression that character makes? (stalling for time, a sense of ritual, deflecting)
- What do you learn about the narrator from this sentence? (cynical—calls his own actions *futile*, *face-saving*, *tired*, and *clichéd*; poor—*scrubby little office*; menacing—*killed* the cigarette)
- What's the significance of the reference to *a hilltop overlooking the bouncing ocean*? (open and natural, opposite of the narrator's reality)

- Is the narrator reliable? How do you know? (probably, given his awareness that he's acting a part)
- If the sentence were changed to third-person point of view, what would be gained or lost? (gained: possibly more trustworthy and objective; lost: intimacy, connection with the character)

With extended context:

- What do the details about the cigarette add to your impression of Marlowe? (danger, lack of hope—*killed, getting rid of*; pretense—*blowing smoke*; perhaps dishonest—*off to one side*)
- What do you learn from Marlowe's thoughts, in the context of the information you're given about the character? (he's afraid of his own cynicism—"You're not human tonight" and angry—*futile* gestures don't lead to justice)
- What does *face-saving* add to the sentence? (he's given up, knows he can't win, acknowledges his pretense)

SUPPLEMENTAL MATERIAL FOR *THE LITTLE SISTER*

Grammar

- The subject, *I*, is attached to three verbs: *killed, got, went.* These three words reflect the arc of a typical crime story.
- A chain of phrases ends the sentence: the first prepositional phrase is *through . . . emotions.* That's followed by another preposition, *of,* which has several objects: *lighting, getting, blowing, inhaling,* all gerunds (verb forms functioning as nouns). The chain suggests that Marlowe's path is set. He can't veer away from *clichéd mannerisms* or subsequent actions in the novel.
- A dependent, or subordinate, clause presents an alternative that doesn't exist: *as though . . . ocean.* What Marlowe truly wants, peace, takes second place to the lifestyle he's chosen.

Rhetoric

The chain of phrases lacks a conjunction, an example of *asyndeton* and a way to convey inevitability.

Additional Information and Activities

- Hardboiled detectives are staples of books, films, and television shows. What's the appeal of these characters? Try a compare/contrast essay or a psychology/English project on this topic.
- In an essay on detective fiction, Chandler wrote: "Down these mean streets a man must go who is not himself mean, who is neither tarnished nor afraid . . . the hero . . . a complete man and a common man and yet an unusual man." Discuss how Marlowe fits this description.
- *The Little Sister* was made into a film and two television programs. Other Chandler works have also been filmed (*The Big Sleep*, *Farewell, My Lovely*, and *The Long Goodbye*, for example). Show a scene from one of the films and have students compare their impression of Marlowe from the sentence and from the scene.

> ### Elisabeth Tova Bailey, *The Sound of a Wild Snail Eating*
>
> **But when I woke the next morning, the snail was back up in the pot, tucked into its shell, asleep beneath a violet leaf.**

Brief context: A bedridden, severely ill woman is given a wild snail, which she places in a potted violet plant.

Extended context: Enduring a debilitating disease, Elisabeth Tova Bailey is surprised one day when a friend brings her a snail from a nearby woodland. Bailey isn't sure the snail will survive, but she spends the day watching it slowly explore its surroundings. The next morning a small square of paper is missing from a letter that rested against the pot; the snail has eaten it. As the weeks go by, Bailey observes the snail's slow, deliberate actions and researches its biology. The snail gets a terrarium to live in, lays eggs, and is eventually returned to the woods. Bailey describes everything, including, as the title suggests, the sound of the wild snail eating. Observing the creature's life inspires Bailey to examine her own. She writes to her doctor, "If life mattered to the snail and the snail mattered to me, it meant something in my life mattered, so I kept on." Though her illness is chronic, Bailey recovers from this bout and returns to her normal life.

Analysis

With brief context:

- What's the effect of beginning the sentence with *But*? (signals surprise or change of direction, implies the narrator hasn't expected to see the snail)
- How does the narrator feel about the snail? How do you know? (intrigued enough to observe closely—*tucked into its shell* and *beneath a violet leaf*)
- What do the snail and the narrator have in common? (both are *tucked into* an enclosed space, the snail in its shell and the narrator in her bed)
- Other than the obvious human/animal divide, how do the narrator and the snail differ? (snail asleep, narrator awake; snail healthy, narrator ill; snail in a large space relative to its size, narrator in a relatively small one, her bed)
- How does first-person narration affect the sentence? (piques personal interest in the animal, entwines the narrator's life with the snail's)

With extended context:

- How does the snail affect the narrator? (awakens her curiosity, invigorates her will to live)
- In what other ways are the narrator and the snail alike? (narrator isn't sure that she and the snail will survive; the snail's slow, deliberate actions mirror the narrator's; both return to ordinary life—the snail to the woods and the narrator to her normal routine)
- Reword the sentence so that it reports the snail's actions without involving *I*. What is lost or gained? (varied answers: adds an authoritative or scientific tone but loses the connection between the ill woman and the animal)

SUPPLEMENTAL MATERIAL FOR *THE SOUND OF A WILD SNAIL EATING*

Grammar

- The sentence contains one independent clause (*the snail was back up in the pot . . . leaf*). This structure emphasizes that the snail has its own life and can live without human intervention.
- The dependent clause, *when I woke the next morning*, modifies the verb *was*. Placing the narrator in the dependent clause underscores the narrator's dependent state.
- Four descriptions follow the verb: *up in the pot, into its shell* (prepositional phrases), *asleep* (adjective), *beneath a violet leaf* (prepositional phrase). The accretion of details reflects the narrator's slow but steady understanding of the snail's habits.

Additional Information and Activities

- The author's close observation of this tiny wild animal is exquisitely reported. Students might observe any animal, either firsthand or on video, and report its actions and environment.
- What is "the sound of a wild snail eating"? This sentence opens the door to a science/English project on snails.
- The author has a mitochondrial disorder, another possible research project combining science and English.

> ## Amy Tan, *The Joy Luck Club*
>
> I went to school, then directly home to learn new chess secrets, cleverly concealed advantages, more escape routes.

Brief context: The narrator, a young girl named Waverly Jong, is a chess champion.

Extended context: Amy Tan's novel traces the lives of four mother/daughter pairs. Waverly's mother, Lindo, believes in "invisible strength," the withholding of crucial information until it can be used to advantage. Waverly adopts this strategy when she learns chess, which she calls "a game of secrets in which one must show and never tell." She also uses it to manipulate her mother, telling Lindo, for example, that she doesn't want to attend a tournament because she may lose, knowing that is a reason her mother will not accept, and Waverly very much wants to attend. After a fight with her mother one day, Waverly runs away, ducking down alleys until she "had nowhere to go" and "no escape routes." In a way, Waverly is playing chess with her mother, who herself has secrets she has not shared with her daughter.

Analysis

With brief context:

- What activities does the narrator take part in? (*school*, learning *new chess secrets*)
- How are those activities related, in the narrator's view? (both involve learning, one required and the other self-motivated)
- What does the narrator's comment about chess reveal about herself? (looks for power through manipulation—*secrets, concealed advantages*; feels trapped—*more escape routes*)
- If this sentence were written about the narrator, instead of from the narrator's point of view, how would the effect on the reader change? (varied answers)

With extended context:

- What do Lindo and Waverly have in common? (both believe in "invisible strength"—*secrets, concealed advantages, escape routes*)
- Who is more successful in the "game" the mother and daughter are playing? (mother, because Waverly has "nowhere to go" and "no escape routes" after the fight)
- What sort of person do you imagine Waverly to be? (varied answers: competitive, intelligent, manipulative, ambitious, rebellious)
- Suppose this sentence were written from the mother's point of view. What would she say? (varied answers)

SUPPLEMENTAL MATERIAL
FOR *THE JOY LUCK CLUB*

Grammar

- The sentence is a single independent clause. It comes from Waverly, who briefly believes that she has independence because of her ability to play chess. Later she realizes her dependence on her mother.
- The conjunction *and* would normally connect *school* to *home*. Here it's implied, giving a sense of urgency about learning chess.

Rhetoric

Omitting the conjunction is an example of *asyndeton*.

Additional Information and Activities

- *The Joy Luck Club* combines two archetypal stories: generational conflict and the immigrant/first-generation experience, which students can follow in the plot arc of a mother/daughter pair or in the novel as a whole. They can research the first topic for a psychology/English project and the second for a history/English study.
- Multiple narrators in fiction often offer conflicting points of view, demonstrating how characters misunderstand one another. Discuss this aspect of fiction and whether it matches students' life experiences.
- Waverly is a chess prodigy and, like all prodigies, she receives rewards for her achievements but endures pressure to succeed. Students can read about real-life prodigies to evaluate the accuracy of Amy Tan's portrayal of Waverly.

MORE FIRST-PERSON SENTENCES

If you have a vehement cold, you must take no notice of it; if your nose-membranes feel a great irritation, you must hold your breath; if a sneeze still insists upon making its way, you must oppose it, by keeping your teeth grinding together; if the violence of the

repulse breaks some blood-vessel, you must break a blood-vessel—
but not sneeze.

—Fanny Burney (1875 letter to her mother, advising her of
the etiquette of meeting a member of the royal family)

Monday morning was the worst possible time to have an
existential crisis, I decided on a Monday morning, while having an
existential crisis.

—Riley Redgate, *Noteworthy* (comment from the narrator, a high school
junior in an arts school realizing she's not succeeding in musical theater)

IF I DIDN'T LIKE YOU SO MUCH I WOULD HAVE MADE
YOU MY EX-BEST FRIEND 4-EVER BY NOW.

—Paula Danziger and Ann M. Martin, *P.S. Longer Letter Later* (communication
from a twelve-year-old to a friend who moved away)

We tried to pass it [a football] and throw it and kick it and we
couldn't do it, and it was very discouraging for him and for
me—almost, we almost quit—and finally we had a nice enough
neighbor come over and put some air in it, and what a difference!

—Bob Uecker, Baseball Hall of Fame induction speech (player and broadcaster,
about his immigrant father's attempt to play football with him)

I never asked for anything before you can look it up.

—child's letter to God (asking for a pony, date unknown)

This failure could scarcely have been more predictable or less
ambiguous (I simply did not have the grades), but I was unnerved
by it; I had somehow thought myself a kind of academic
Raskolnikov, curiously exempt from the cause-effect relationships
which hampered others.

—Joan Didion, "On Self-Respect" (on not being
elected to Phi Beta Kappa in college)

I might have only one match / but I can make an explosion.

> —Rachel Platten, "Fight Song"

Let me just say for the record that I think middle school is the dumbest idea ever invented.

> —Jeff Kinney, *Diary of a Wimpy Kid* (novel about a seventh grader)

I'm sick and tired of being sick and tired.

> —Fannie Lou Hamer, gravestone inscription
> (civil rights activist, 1917–1977)

I was listening for a sound—a sound a friend had told me I'd never hear—the ringing bells of Santa's sleigh.

> —Chris Van Allsburg, *The Polar Express* (children's
> book about a little boy on Christmas Eve)

Don't you tell me what you think I can be.

> —Imagine Dragons, "Believer"

I have two homelands: Cuba and the night.

> — José Martí, "Two Homelands"

WRITING ASSIGNMENTS

There, Not There

Have students report an event they witnessed, providing a "I am there" perspective:

I winced when the batter swung hard, about a half inch too high, and covered my ears so I wouldn't hear the deafening cheers of the opposing fans.

What changes if this event is reported by a nonattendee, as in this version:

> **Those rooting for the batter couldn't have been pleased that the swing was a half inch too high and that opposing fans cheered loudly.**

It's worth noting that one is not necessarily better than the other, just different, and that's the key point of the discussion.

I, Um . . .

Having read many, many college admission essays, I know that it's hard for some students to talk about themselves. First person can be a challenge because most of us are conditioned to avoid bragging, and those who aren't prefer to sound as if they were humble. Yet application statements, for college or anything else, require a solid, first-person presentation.

The key to writing in first person is to be specific. To make this point, ask for one general and one specific statement conveying the same idea. Sample response:

> GENERAL: I am a hard worker and a great help to others.
> SPECIFIC: On Saturdays, before I sit down to four or five hours of homework, I coach a children's T-ball team from nine until noon and then pick up groceries for a homebound neighbor.

Students immediately see the advantage of the second version and begin to apply this technique in all sorts of writing.

Trust No One

Okay, I don't actually recommend withdrawal of trust. I do recommend cultivating students' critical eye by asking for two sentences, one from a reliable and another from an unreliable narrator. Remind them to insert clues about what the narrator or speaker really knows (the reliable version) and what desires, assumptions, or bias have infiltrated the statement (unreliable).

A sample response:

RELIABLE: I had left my physics homework and my history paper until the last minutes, so I bought ready-made cupcakes for the bake sale.

UNRELIABLE: Yeah, I had lot of homework but I'm totally committed to the bake sale and made these cupcakes myself and even put them in a box that my mother was about to recycle because my little brother had eaten every last crumb in it.

SECOND PERSON

•••

With apologies to *Star Wars*, no one needs to wish that "the force be with *you*." It's already there. *You*—second-person point of view—is powerful because when someone talks to *you*, *you* tend to listen. Thus second person is a common choice for speeches, as well as for how-to and self-help works. Conversely, in fiction and poetry, *you* is powerful precisely because it's unexpected. In some works, second person establishes a connection between author and audience. In others, *you* represents a divided self—the inner voice of recrimination ("*you* shouldn't have done that") or motivation ("*you* can do it"). *You* may also be the voice of memory and dreams, in which *you* recounts what happened in the past or in an unreal world.

In teaching second-person point of view, I like to mix the obvious (a sentence from a speech) with the unusual (one from a story). The latter requires a little more context than other types of sentences, but the extra effort pays off when students discover the force that is always with *you*.

TEACHING SECOND PERSON: A GENERAL PLAN
Introduction (optional)
Ask students when they use *you*. First-round answers tend to be obvious: to speak directly to someone, to give commands, and so forth. Push a little harder: has anyone ever employed *you* for an internal pep talk or scolding? To tell a story? Make a list of reasons why second person, *you*, may be a good choice.

Decoding
- Who is speaking or writing? *You* or someone else?
- If it's someone else, who is it?
- What else do you know about the identity of *you*?

Analysis
- If *you* is both speaker and audience, why is *you* talking to *you*?
- If someone else is speaking or writing to *you*, what's the purpose?

- Compare *you* to possible alternatives, such as *I/we* or a proper name. Discuss the impact of *you* on reader or audience reaction.
- *You* is nongendered and may be either singular or plural. Do those qualities affect its role in the sentence? How?

TEACHING SECOND PERSON: LESSON PLANS

> **Kermit the Frog, 1996 commencement address at Southampton College**
>
> You are no longer tadpoles. The time has come to drop your tails and leave this swamp.

Brief context: Kermit the Frog is a muppet created by Jim Henson. A tadpole is a baby frog with a tail, living in water. At maturity, the tadpole sheds its tail, grows legs, and begins to live on land.

Extended context: Southampton College was known for its marine science program, never more so than when the school selected Kermit the Frog as its commencement speaker. Among other remarks, Kermit told graduates, "You are not just saving the environment, you are saving the homes and lives of so many of my relatives." Kermit also confessed that he hadn't known "there was such a thing as 'Amphibious' letters" despite his work with the alphabet for many years on *Sesame Street*.

Analysis

With brief context:

- Technically, Kermit's remarks are two sentences. How are they related to each other? (second sentence expands on the first)
- What does the first sentence imply? (graduates are now reaching maturity)
- What's the significance of *drop your tails*? (leave childhood behind, grow up)

- What's the *swamp*? (college life)
- Why use this imagery instead of speaking directly about maturity? (relates to Kermit's identity as a frog; comic effect)
- What's the impact of second person? (a command, more personal, less abstract)
- Why not use first-person plural, *we*? (different species, different stages in life)

With extended context:

- *Drop your tails* is a metaphor. What do graduates *drop*? (varied answers: college way of life, community of friends and classmates, perhaps financial dependence on parents)
- In what way is *leave this swamp* related to the future? (graduates will be out in the world, pursuing environmental science; some may literally save the *swamp*)
- What do the graduates (*you*) and Kermit have in common? (both receive degrees, both are dependent on and concerned about the environment)
- Is Kermit serious? If so, why make jokes? (yes, the reference to the environment and to wildlife is an important message; humor keeps attention and makes the point gently)

SUPPLEMENTAL MATERIAL FOR KERMIT'S COMMENCEMENT ADDRESS

Grammar

These are two separate sentences, punctuated in print with periods. They could be combined into one sentence with a semicolon (because they're closely related) or a colon (because the second explains the first).

Rhetoric

Kermit's comment is an example of *metaphor*, perhaps even *extended metaphor* because he continues the *tadpole* image in the second sentence.

Additional Information and Activities

- *The Muppet Show* and *Sesame Street* may be familiar to your students. If not, they can watch clips and discuss how closely Kermit's comment meshes with his character in those shows.

- Traditionally, commencement speakers employ second person in order to advise graduates. Kermit mixes first- and second-person remarks, alternately speaking of himself and speaking to *you*, the students. Discuss the effectiveness of this format in formal speeches (addresses). Compare it to third-person comments or first-person plural, both of which Kermit could have chosen for his speech.

- This sentence can serve as the basis of a biology/English research project on the life cycle of a frog in nature and in literature (or commencement speeches).

> ### Margaret Atwood, "Bread"
>
> There's no doubt that you can see the bread, you can even smell it, it smells like yeast, and it looks solid enough, solid as your own arm.

Brief context: The essay begins by asking the reader to "imagine a piece of bread."

Extended context: *You* begin in your own kitchen, then move in your imagination to a starving country, then to a prison. Next *you* hear of two sisters, one wealthy and one poor. Last, *you* are back in your kitchen where the bread floats above the table. *You* move your hand around the bread, checking for wires, but you don't touch it to see whether it's real. The story ends with "You don't want to know, imagine that."

Analysis

With brief context:

- What do *you* know about *the bread*? (what it looks like, how it smells, where it is)

- What don't *you* know about *the bread*? (how it feels; whether it's *solid* or just *looks solid enough*)
- How does *the bread* relate to *you*? (*solid as your own arm*—*you* connected to *the bread* or to an image of it)
- What does *There's no doubt* add to the sentence? (brings up the issue of *doubt*, appearance/reality theme)
- Several statements run together in this sentence, with some repetition (*smell it, smells like yeast, looks solid enough, solid as your own arm*). What effect does this pattern have? (anxious mood, almost like *you* are trying to convince yourself or checking the accuracy of your perception)
- What sort of *bread* do you imagine when you read this sentence? Why? (varied answers)
- What sort of person is the *you* of the sentence? How do you know? (varied answers)
- Suppose that *the bread* were presented without referring to *you* or to *your own arm*? How would the story be different? (less personal, reader less involved and less conscious of the process of reading about *bread*)

With extended context:

- How does placing *the bread* in several different settings change the meaning? (the subject is perception, truth, and imagination; brings up the idea that value is relative—the bread means more to the poor and starving than to the wealthy)
- What's the significance of the story's ending? (stories and imagination are more important than a reality check; people like their illusions)
- The story asks *you* to imagine. What does that add to the meaning? (references the power of the writer to transport readers to a different reality)
- Can the same effect be achieved without *you*? (varied answers: less personal, less conscious of the way fiction requires reader participation, etc.)

SUPPLEMENTAL MATERIAL FOR "BREAD"

- Margaret Atwood's many novels show that she can easily transport readers into an alternate reality. In "Bread," she makes the process conscious by specifically asking *you* to imagine. Discuss the relationship between author and reader. What's required from each?

- Atwood's most famous novel, *The Handmaid's Tale*, has been adapted for film. Discuss whether a viewer's experience differs from a reader's.
- Human beings eat a variety of food, but *bread* carries extra significance, even appearing in prayers, religious rites, and sacred texts. Students might research the cultural significance of bread and discuss how Atwood's essay would change if it were based on a different food.

> ### Ernest Hemingway, "The Clark's Fork Valley, Wyoming"
>
> You could ride in the morning, or sit in front of the cabin, lazy in the sun, and look across the valley where the hay was cut so the meadows were cropped brown and smooth to the line of quaking aspens along the river, now turning yellow in the fall.

Brief context: The author describes his extended visits to Wyoming, where he hunted and fished, taught his children to ride, and wrote.

Extended context: Ernest Hemingway's article on Clark's Fork Valley was printed in *Vogue* magazine in 1939. The idyllic life he describes encompasses moments of danger: another sentence mentions a "big grizzly" who tore open the cabin every time the occupants were away and a ride with "the snow blowing so you could not see." *You* feels great admiration for nature, at one point thinking of all the animals that "you . . . refused to shoot" and ending the article calling the area "a good country."

Analysis

With brief context:

- What is *you* doing? (riding, sitting, relaxing, observing the landscape)
- What sort of area is *you* in? How do you know? (rural, perhaps wilderness, distant from where *hay was cut*)

- What does *could* add to the sentence? (lots of choices, free will, no commitments or obligations, ability to do many things or nothing)
- What time period does the sentence cover? (the past—indicated by past-tense verbs *could, was cut, were chopped*; *now* could be the present but also a moment in a past autumn when *you* remembers the summer)
- Who is *you* talking to? (the reader; himself—calling up memories, a form of internal dialogue)
- What does second person add to the sentence? (evaluation, distancing the present state of mind from the memories of past experiences)

With extended context:

- Why does the writer think about animals "you . . . refused to shoot"? (sense of power—could have killed but didn't; respect for nature, including wild animals)
- What does "a good country" mean in relation to this sentence? (fertile and unspoiled nature, freedom)

SUPPLEMENTAL MATERIAL FOR "THE CLARK'S FORK VALLEY, WYOMING"

Grammar

- The sentence is anchored by its subject (*you*) and the verbs attached to it: *could ride, sit,* and *look*. This is the core of the independent clause, emphasizing the freedom *you* has in Wyoming.
- A long dependent clause modifies *valley* (*where . . . fall*). Because the descriptions of the valley appear in a dependent clause, the role of *you* is even more dominant. Adding to this impression is that the verb forms in the dependent clause are passive (*was cut, were cropped*). The human role, represented by *you*, is dominant over nature.

Additional Information and Activities

- Ernest Hemingway is famous for idealizing a certain vision of life— hunting, drinking, taking every action to its extreme. Discuss the consequences of living this sort of life.

- How do students define "a good country"? Ask them to justify their answers and to listen to others' views.
- An internet search for the title of this article directs you to several sites describing Hemingway's time in Wyoming. It might be interesting to ask students how the image of the writer they formed after reading this sentence changes (or not) with additional information. This exercise develops media literacy, especially when paired with a discussion of persona.

MORE SECOND-PERSON SENTENCES

Commands

These three are inspiring: the first for the vocation it celebrates, the second for the beauty of nature it presents, and the last for the approach to life it advocates.

> **Lift your voices**
> **Until you've patched every hole in a child's broken sky.**
> > —Donovan Livingston, 2016 commencement speech
> > at the Harvard Graduate School of Education

> **Picture a scarlet macaw: a fierce, full meter of royal red feathers head to tail, a soldier's rainbow-colored epaulets, a skeptic's eye staring out from a naked white face, a beak that takes no prisoners.**
> > —Barbara Kingsolver and Steven Hopp, "Seeing Scarlet" essay

> **Stare, pry, listen, eavesdrop—die knowing something.**
> > —Walker Evans, photo caption

Commentary

The first sentence comes from an essay that, in alternating sections, analyzes drug policy and an account of the narrator's attempts to help *you*, an uncle struggling with mental illness and drug addiction. The policy discussion is written in third person, the personal narrative in second person. The second sentence is a set of definitions.

> You want to be in charge of your own money. . . . For a year, at least, you manage all right.   —Sarah Resnik, "H."

> If you describe things as better than they are, you are considered to be a romantic; if you describe things as worse than they are, you will be called a realist; and if you describe things exactly as they are, you will be thought of as a satirist.
>
> —Quentin Crisp, *The Naked Civil Servant*

Fiction with a Self-Help Twist

The narrator of this sentence is a teenager who gets up at four every morning during his summer vacation because he loves basketball and needs a ride to the court. His silent father drops him off on his way to work. At first, everyone ignores the narrator, who gradually realizes that the best player has been teaching him without words—just as his father has.

> But over time you'll begin to see the power of his silence. And surprisingly, it will remind you of your old man's silence.
>
> —Matt de la Peña, "How to Transform an Everyday, Ordinary Hoop Court into a Place of Higher Learning and You at the Podium"

Jamaica Kincaid's short story, "Girl," is one long sentence of instruction/command, presumably from a mother to a daughter, with an occasional protest in first person from the daughter. A portion of the mother's remarks:

> Wash the white clothes on Monday and put them on the stone heap; wash the color clothes on Tuesday and put them on the clothesline to dry; don't walk bare-headed in the hot sun; cook pumpkin fritters in very hot sweet oil . . .

The advice above is practical, but sometimes the mother criticizes the daughter's interactions with men. Here, of course, is where the daughter's objections appear.

Science Fiction

Modeled on the popular "choose-your-own-adventure" series, the story in which this sentence appears gives *you* a chance to escape a deadly infection:

> **You run down a long, metal hallway to the Medical Clinic, grateful for the artificially generated gravity that defies the laws of physics and yet is surprisingly common in fictional space stations.**
> —Caroline M. Yoachim, "Welcome to the Medical Clinic at the Interplanetary Relay Station | Hours Since the Last Patient Death: 0"

With wry humor, the author sends *you* on many paths until *you* realize there is no escape.

Nonfiction

Of migrant workers in California during the Great Depression, John Steinbeck writes:

> **You can see a little of dirty rags and scrap iron, of houses built of weeds, of flattened cans or of paper.**
> —John Steinbeck, "The Squatters' Camp"

Only later does the author realize that "these are homes."

Here's a sentence from an article on neuroscientific devices that may be possible someday:

> **Consider what you could do with a chip in your head that linked directly to the Internet: Within milliseconds, you could retrieve just about any piece of information.**
> —Maria Konnikova, "Hacking the Brain"

This sentence comes from an article on the microbes inhabiting the human body, which account for 90 percent of the cells:

> **You are mostly not you.**
> —Brendan Buhler, "The Teeming Metropolis of You"

Following this sentence is another: "In other words, it's looking increasingly likely that it's not so much that you are mostly not you as that you are also the slime sloshing around your innards."

In this sentence the author remembers her mother's return after a weekend away:

> **You jump out your side, my mother in happy red lipstick and red earrings, pushing back your dark hair from the shoulder of your white sleeveless blouse, turning so your red skirt swirls like a rose with the perfect promise of *you* emerging from the center.**
>
> —Barbara Kingsolver, "Letter to My Mother"

At the age of three, when this happened, the author resented her mother's enjoyment of time away from her. Only when she became a mother herself did she reevaluate this memory, recognizing that her mother was happy to be reunited with her child.

In this one, hyperbole meets helicopter-parenting:

> **Your adolescent's weekly allowance is the size of the gross national product of Burkina Faso, a small, poverty-stricken African country neither you nor your adolescent had ever heard of until recently, when you both spent several days working on a social studies report about it.** —Nora Ephron, *I Feel Bad About My Neck*

WRITING EXERCISES

Advice

Have your students give advice, as Kermit does, to those about to graduate. Depending on the maturity level of the class, sometimes I ask for bad advice (adolescents love this one) or good advice (nonteenagers). Typical responses:

> **When you have a problem, avoid it at all costs! (teenager)**

> **Don't go in the street without a grown-up. (four-year-old)**

Split Personality

Second person often reflects the thoughts of a single person. There's conflict, encouragement, or worry. Ask students to write a sentence in second person, identifying why the self is divided:

> **SITUATION:** Abdur is helping his sister study for her math final, but his friends are organizing a soccer game and want him, their best goalie, to play.
> **SENTENCE:** You can't let her fail the test, and if you go, your team might not win anyway, but maybe you can hurry her through the decimal chapter because she knows that already.
>
> **SITUATION:** The first day of camp.
> **SENTENCE:** You got this, girl, you're going to make a lot of friends, you know, you always do.

Personal Change

Challenge students to take a first- or third-person sentence and change it to second person. I like to do this with sentences from science, history, and math textbooks. For example:

> **ORIGINAL, FROM A MATH TEXT:** The area of a triangle is equal to one half of the base multiplied by the height.
> **REVISION:** To find the area of a triangle, you multiply the base times the height and divide by two.

After they've written, discuss which sentences are more effective. Why?

NOTE: There's no right or wrong answer here, because both work. The goal of the lesson is simply to examine the effect of second person.

QUESTIONS

• •

Any questions? How many times have you said those words when you've finished a topic, only to see an ocean of hands waving, all eager to ask you what you just said—twice! Very clearly! With everything but an orchestra and fireworks backing you up!

That's the bad side of questions, but the good side makes our profession the wonderful one it is: Who doesn't love a question showing that (a) students are engaged by the topic and (b) they want to know more? No need to come up with your own answer, as I've set you on the path to the one I want. That's what a rhetorical question does.

Because rhetorical questions engage the listener or reader, they're valuable tools for writers. So are nonrhetorical questions, which keep the reader reading (or the listener listening) to find out the answer. They assist with characterization, too. Just think about how much "Is this going to be on the test?" tells you about the questioner.

TEACHING QUESTIONS: A GENERAL PLAN

Given that questions are woven tightly into everyday life, it's easy to overlook their nuances. Your job is to focus students' attention on what they might otherwise overlook.

Introduction (optional)

Select one of these activities to introduce the concept of a question as a valuable tool:

- Put one student on the spot by asking, "How do you feel when someone asks you a question?" Assuming you selected a student with a sense of humor (the ideal choice for this activity), you'll get an amusing response or, in some cases, a nonresponse. Either way, you can point out that the question accomplished one goal: drawing the student's interest. It's an easy segue from that moment to examining the sentence.
- Ask students to write down one question they want answered and one

they don't. Assure them—and keep your promise!—that you won't ask them to share their responses. Instead, ask them how they felt writing the questions. Tell them to imagine, but not share, what their response would be if someone *did* see what they wrote. Now they're ready for a discussion of the power of questions, both answered and unanswered.

Decoding

- As always, go over the vocabulary in the sentence and have them render the question in their own words.
- Who's asking? To whom?

Analysis

- What answer do you expect? or What other questions might follow this one? or What sort of situation would give rise to this question?
- Does the author or speaker expect an answer? (You may have to help students distinguish a real question from a rhetorical one.)
- If no answer is needed, why ask? (engage the reader/listener, introduce an argument, steer the audience to the conclusion the author wants)

TEACHING QUESTIONS: LESSON PLANS

> ### Emily Flake, "Parent as a Verb: Sleep Training"
>
> **But what is parenting if not an exercise in eating your own words?**

Brief context: This sentence is from a comic strip about a mother's changing attitude toward her child's sleep habits.

Extended context: *Parent as a Verb* is a recurring comic strip written and drawn by Emily Flake. In this installment, a mother admits that her five-year-old daughter won't sleep alone. One panel flashes back to pregnancy, when the woman explains that there won't be any "hippie communal-bed" nonsense. Her plan to enforce strict rules falls apart when, around age two, the child engages in "absolutely psychotic barf-crying if left alone in her room for two seconds." Successive panels show other parents admitting that their kids can't sleep alone, images of the remains of a mother curled around her child in the ruins of Pompeii, and current threats (nuclear war, environmental catastrophe).

Analysis

With brief context:

- What does *eating your own words* mean? (being forced to admit you were wrong)
- In the context of this sentence, what does *an exercise* mean? (customary practice)
- The sentence includes *But* and *if not.* How do those words affect the meaning of the question? (imply that other possibilities have been ruled out)
- Reword the sentence: "Isn't parenting an exercise in eating your own words?" Does that version affect the reader differently? (still sounds like an excuse, but more neutral than the original)
- Does this question call for an answer? (no, it's rhetorical)
- Why make it a question? (attempt to make the reader complicit, joining in the mother's justification for not being strict about her child's sleep habits)

With extended context:

- How have the mother's beliefs changed? (her original stance is a strong one, but she crumbles when her child resists)
- Why include Pompeii? (show universal instinct to protect your children)
- Why depict contemporary threats? (justify the need for protection now)
- Consider the way the child's crying is described. What does that add to the piece? (comic exaggeration but also a sense of what the parents faced)

SUPPLEMENTAL MATERIAL FOR "PARENT AS A VERB: SLEEP TRAINING"

Grammar

- The strictest grammarians frown on beginning a sentence with a conjunction such as *But*. But nearly everyone does so, including Shakespeare (and me).
- *But* and *if not* form a double negative, expressing a positive, that *parenting* is *an exercise in eating your own words*.

Rhetoric

The sentence is a *rhetorical question* designed to elicit a predetermined answer—in this case, "yes, that's what parenting is."

Additional Information and Activities

- Emily Flake's comic strip is very funny, and students might enjoy seeing more. The entire installment can be found on *The New Yorker* website.
- Those interested in Emily Flake's work can check her website, www .emilyflake.com._
- Budding artists can draw a cartoon or a comic strip based on a rhetorical question of their own. Stick-figures-only students can write the captions for photographs they took or found on the internet or elsewhere.

Sy Montgomery, "Deep Intellect"

Many times I have stood mesmerized by an aquarium tank, wondering, as I stared into the horizontal pupils of an octopus's large, prominent eyes, if she was staring back at me—and if so, what was she thinking?

Brief context: The sentence describes the author's encounter with an octopus in an aquarium.

Extended context: The author visits the octopus, Athena, several times and interviews scientists who work with her. He discusses the strong intelligence of the animal, citing numerous scientific studies, and describes Athena's measured approach to meeting him. First she tentatively explores his arms, then calmly accepts his presence. When he returns another day, she clearly remembers him. Throughout the article, the author questions scientists at the aquarium, and himself, about Athena's thought processes.

Analysis

With brief context:

- Have students identify the questions in this sentence. (*if she was staring back at me* and *what was she thinking?*)
- Why are the questions in this order? (first is physical, what the animal is doing; the second is more speculative)
- The questions appear at the end of the sentence, which starts out with a statement of fact (*Many times . . . at me*). If the questions were in a separate sentence, would they have the same effect on the reader? (varied answers; some may point out that starting with a fact and asking a question about it is the way scientists begin research)
- Many words in the sentence deal with the animal's *eyes*. Why attach the question to that aspect of the octopus instead of, for example, the arms? (eyes are "windows of the soul," perceived as revealing mood or character)

With extended context:

- The author asks many questions. Why not simply state what he learns from the answers? (scientists ask questions and try to answer them)
- Given the information about the octopus's intelligence and her acceptance of the author, what would a possible answer be to the question in this sentence? (yes, she's staring back; she's probably thinking about the author)

SUPPLEMENTAL MATERIAL FOR "DEEP INTELLECT"

Grammar

- The sentence starts with an independent clause (*Many times I have stood mesmerized by an aquarium tank*). The clause continues with a participial phrase beginning with *wondering*. With this structure, the author starts with his own body (*I have stood*) and moves to his mood (*mesmerized*) and thoughts (*wondering*). In the same way, the questions begin with the octopus's body (*if she was staring back at me*, a dependent clause describing *wondering*) and move to the animal's mind (*if so, what was she thinking?* another dependent clause).
- The verb *have stood* is in present-perfect tense, which connects the past and present. The author *stood mesmerized* in the past and continues to do so.
- The dash sets off the most important question, which goes to the main point of the article: research into the thinking process and intelligence of an octopus.

Rhetoric

This sentence asks two questions that are speculative, but not rhetorical. The author really wants an answer, and in the article he gives evidence pointing to possible answers.

Additional Information and Activities

- This sentence is a great starting point for a science/language arts unit. Students may consult the website of the New England Aquarium, the home of the octopus in this sentence.
- Sy Montgomery attempts to see the animal as an animal. Has he succeeded? Has he anthropomorphized Athena? Discuss the tendency to attribute human qualities to nonhuman animals.

Shawn Mendes, "In My Blood"

Does it ever?

Brief context: This question comes just after the singer asks for reassurance that "it gets better."

Extended context: The title of the song refers to the singer's innate persistence. The song expresses anxiety so extreme that the singer wants to give up, but he won't, because it isn't his nature to do so. The singer asks for help and considers several remedies for his emotional overload: drinking, sex, and prescribed medication. He ends the list with the question above.

Analysis

With brief context:

- What are some possible meanings of *it*? (current physical or mental state or situation)
- Why ask such a question? (hoping for an answer that will bolster confidence and calm fear; to signal that he needs help)
- What mood might the question portray? (varied answers, such as fear, unhappiness, desperation)
- Is there any optimism in this question? (yes, or there would be no reason to ask it)

With extended context, add these points:

- Why leave *it* undefined? (allusion to a common expression of reassurance; to make the question apply to more than one emotion or situation)
- Is persistence innate, as the title implies? (varied answers)
- Of the remedies the singer considers, how would you rank this one? (varied answers)
- How would the meaning change if this question were an exclamation? (*Does it ever* can be an emphatic *yes*, as in "Does that clue have any significance? *Does it ever!*)

SUPPLEMENTAL MATERIAL FOR "IN MY BLOOD"

Grammar

It's not easy to determine where one sentence ends and another begins because each line begins with a capital letter, a convention of written lyrics. The question may stand alone, as I present it, or it may be attached to the preceding line: "Keep telling me that it gets better." In the latter case, the sentence begins as an *imperative* (command) and moves to *interrogative* (question). Such a sequence shows more insecurity and greater need.

Rhetoric

This question seeks a real answer, so it's not *rhetorical.*

Additional Information and Activities

- This sentence can be a starting point for a psychology/English/music project. Students can listen to the song, analyze the emotions it expresses, and discuss how the content matches the sound.
- How does creative expression (music, writing, visual arts, etc.) relate to emotional expression? This is a good discussion question and may also be the basis of a research project.

MORE QUESTIONS

Some questions need a bit of context to turn them into a lesson. I've provided that for the first bunch in this section. Others easily stand alone, and that's how you'll find them here.

> **What brought her to say that: "We are in the hands of the Lord"?
> she wondered.**   —Virginia Woolf, *To the Lighthouse*

This question comes from the thoughts of Mrs. Ramsay, who, in a rare moment of solitude, first thinks *We are in the hands of the Lord* and then questions herself, because she doesn't believe in a divine, guiding presence. The mother of a large family and wife of a demanding husband, Mrs. Ramsay is attuned to others and is not given to introspection. In this scene, she's musing about her family and glances through the window at the lighthouse, a physical structure that some scholars see as a symbol of God or death.

The whole meal? On your first day?
—Elizabeth Acevedo, With the Fire on High

The protagonist of Elizabeth Acevedo's novel, Emoni Santiago, is a talented chef, a teenaged mom, and an indifferent student until she enrolls in a culinary class at her high school. The demanding teacher earns her respect, and when the class goes to Spain to intern with food industry professionals, Emoni is placed with a chef who tasks her with creating the day's "special." These two questions come from a classmate Emoni calls "Pretty Leslie," initially presented as a hustler but eventually revealed as someone who aspires to be the first in her family to graduate from high school and attend college. Leslie's questions reveal her jealousy and ambition, as she was allowed to do far less on the first day of her internship.

Can nature be ironic?   —Samira Ahmed, *Internment*

Samira Ahmed's question highlights the theme of her novel *Internment*, which is set in the near future but inspired by the internment of Japanese Americans during World War II. The protagonist, Layla, is a Muslim and an American citizen. She and her family are sent to a camp in the California desert, in accordance with the "Exclusion" laws that have first taken away her parents' jobs and then Layla's right to attend school. She asks this question after observing: "A liquid blue sky stands out against the snow-tipped peaks of the Sierra Nevada. And the sun gleams. Too bright, almost." The beauty of the physical, natural world contrasts sharply with the ugly impulse in human nature to fear and exclude those perceived as different.

Would one tell them so soon the whole truth, that one must be ready at all hours, and always, that the ideas in their shimmering forms, in spite of all our conscious discipline, will come when they will, and on the swift upheaval of their wings—disorderly, reckless; as unmanageable, sometimes, as passion?
—Mary Oliver, "Of Power and Time"

Poet and essayist Mary Oliver asks this question of herself, in relation to *them*, those who wish to write. She personifies *ideas*, which have *shimmering forms* and are *unmanageable*, not subject to *conscious discipline*. The implications for writers are serious: forget plans and systems, Oliver implies, because imagination will strike whenever, and however, it wants.

> **Who's there?**   —William Shakespeare, *Hamlet* (Act 1, scene 1)

The first line of this famous play comes from an ordinary guard, Bernardo, stationed outside the royal castle in Denmark to watch for intruders. His question is answered by Francisco, another guard arriving for duty. The question, however, applies to much more than this ordinary encounter. The title character of the play agonizes for five acts about his father's murder, his mother's swift remarriage to his uncle (the murderer), and his own inability to avenge his father. He calls himself a "rogue and peasant slave" but also proudly announces himself as "Hamlet the Dane." Intricate in his psychology, Hamlet analyzes himself constantly and draws the audience (and a raft of literary scholars) into the process. "Who's there?" is the question Hamlet asks about himself and attempts to answer.

> **When I was in the Navy—you believe me in the Navy? I used
> to get seasick on the ferry—the people on the ferry used to say,
> "You're going to protect us? You're going to war?"**
> —Phil Rizzuto, Hall of Fame speech

Phil Rizzuto's questions reveal his character more than any explanation I can give, but I'll give one anyway: he was a Yankee baseball player (1941–56) and broadcaster—(1957–96), legendary for his enthusiastic playing and his looping syntax and frequent non sequiturs. This quotation comes from the speech he gave when he was inducted into the Baseball Hall of Fame. The *ferry* is the Staten Island Ferry, as motionless a boat as ever there was.

Now for those that need no explanation:

> **Why should the humble broom have become the one object legally
> allowed as a means of wizarding transport? Why did we in the
> West not adopt the carpet so beloved of our Eastern brethren? Why**

didn't we choose to produce flying barrels, flying armchairs, flying bathtubs—why brooms?"   —J. K. Rowling, *Quidditch through the Ages*

When I heard "Humpty Dumpty sat on a wall," I thought, "Did he fall or was he pushed?"   —P. D. James (mystery writer)

"Does genius burn, Jo?"   —Louisa May Alcott, *Good Wives*

WRITING ASSIGNMENTS

Who/How Are You?

Have students select a character from a work they're reading or from a film or show they like. Ask them to create a question that shows something about the character's state of mind or personality. For example:

> CHARACTER: nervous student taking a test
> QUESTION: When you say "define these words," do you mean we should define them?

Sad but true fact: This question is a direct quote from an anxious young man I taught many years ago. I'm glad to report that he eventually calmed down.

NOTE: This exercise can be completed quickly, but you can also ask students to write a scene based on the question. That's a longer project, but worthwhile.

Double Up

Shawn Mendes manages to double up on meaning in one short question. Can your students do the same? Have them create a question with a second possible interpretation. For instance:

> MOTHER, SPEAKING TO SON: Do you have time to take out the garbage?
> FIRST MEANING: Are you free now to do a chore?
> SECOND MEANING: Did you forget, yet again, that this is the one thing I ask . . .

I could add a third meaning here, which isn't a question at all: "Take out the garbage, now." That's what I mean when I say this to my own offspring.

No Answer Required

Give students a chance to pose rhetorical questions, such as this one:

> **Do you want to wait in line at the Department of Motor Vehicles for hours, or would you like to download the DMV app?**

To check the effectiveness of their efforts, have the class write quick answers to the question before the author explains the intended response.

NOTE: The "DMV app" exists only in my imagination, as far as I know.

Philosophy 101

Life's big questions are fodder for eager minds, and I assume that description applies to students in your class. Ask them to write a question, or several questions, about life as they experience it. What do they really want to know? If the schedule permits, expand this exercise by having them write an essay responding to their own question.

CHAPTER 10
COMPARISONS

CONTRADICTION

. . . .

Legendary baseball manager and language mangler Casey Stengel once remarked, "I've made up my mind both ways." Because I've spent most of my career teaching adolescents, Stengel's comment makes perfect sense to me. Sure, it can be frustrating to deal with someone who simultaneously sits on both sides of the fence, as young people often do. But it can also be inspiring. Instead of closing doors, teenagers tend to leave them open—or to break through walls when no door exists.

A taste for contradiction isn't limited to one age group, of course. Contradiction acknowledges complexity, recognizing that much of life doesn't fit a binary framework. Consider the opening sentence of Charles Dickens's *A Tale of Two Cities*: "It was the best of times, it was the worst of times. . . ." More than a century after he wrote it, Dickens's sentence frequently reflects today's news. Casey Stengel's remark, too, encapsulates a kernel of truth: most decisions are fraught with indecision, and few are irreversible.

Writers, adolescent or not, exploit the power of contradiction in figurative language, psychological portraits, and philosophical speculation. Guide your students to look for contradiction in what they're reading and, where warranted, to employ it in their writing.

TEACHING CONTRADICTION: A GENERAL PLAN
Introduction (optional)
To introduce the concept of contradiction, select one activity:

- Discuss the common expression *mixed feelings*. What does it mean? Have they ever experienced *mixed feelings*? (Out of respect for privacy, don't ask for details.) Is it possible to have an *un*mixed feeling? Why or why not?
- Show the class a surrealist painting. My favorite for this exercise is entitled *Not to Be Reproduced*, a René Magritte painting of a man looking into a mirror and seeing his own back, an image that contradicts the laws of physics. Discuss how Magritte's painting may convey a psychological truth—that when we look at ourselves, we see our past.

Decoding

- After they decode the sentence, ask students to identify the contradictory aspect.
- Is the contradiction meant to be taken literally? Figuratively? How do you know?

Analysis

- What does this stylistic device add to the sentence? If students struggle with this point, have them restate the sentence so that it expresses the same meaning without contradictions. For example, the Dickens sentence I quote above may be reworded as "Some wonderful things happened, but there were extreme drawbacks, too." Discuss what's lost in the change from contradictory to straightforward expression.
- In the context of the sentence, why has the writer or speaker employed contradiction? What's the goal?
- If the contradictory expression is a simile or a metaphor, have students explore both the literal and the figurative aspects, as each adds meaning and nuance to the sentence.

TEACHING CONTRADICTION: LESSON PLANS

Henry David Thoreau, *Walden*

I have a great deal of company in my house; especially in the morning, when nobody calls.

Brief context: The narrator lives alone in a cabin he built near Walden Pond in Massachusetts in the nineteenth century.

Extended context: Henry David Thoreau was a transcendentalist, adhering to a philosophy that emerged in the early nineteenth century. Transcendentalists see human nature, and nature in general, as innately good but vulnerable to corruption by society. They prize solitude and self-reliance. Thoreau kept few possessions in his one-room cabin and spent his days growing his own food and observing the natural world. Following this sentence, Thoreau asks whether a bird in the pond or the pond itself is lonely. He notes that the sun is alone, as is a leaf. After a series of similar comparisons, Thoreau declares that he is "no more lonely than the Mill Brook . . . or the north star . . . or the first spider in a new house."

Analysis

With brief context:

- Discuss the meaning of *nobody calls.* (no visits from people)
- What does *a great deal of company* mean? (not alone)
- Can both statements be true? (yes, if the *company* isn't human or if the narrator's company is his own thoughts)
- Why express this idea as a contradiction? (challenge readers' assumption of what *a great deal of company* is)

With extended context:

- How does *a great deal* reflect Thoreau's philosophy? (he's in nature, which transcendentalists venerate as *great*)
- How does Thoreau's sentence as a whole fit with his philosophy? (he's fortunate, with *a great deal* as measured by nature's standards, not by society's)
- Why isn't Thoreau lonely? (nature and his own thoughts are sufficient company)
- Why *especially in the morning*? (*when nobody calls*, he can appreciate

nature more fully; society, in the form of visitors, is distracting and potentially a bad influence)

SUPPLEMENTAL MATERIAL FOR *WALDEN*

Grammar

- The sentence has one independent clause; *I have* is the subject-verb pair.
- Two descriptions modify the verb: *especially in the morning*, which explains when *I have a great deal of company* and *when nobody calls*, which explains why *I have a great deal of company.*
- A semicolon normally joins two independent clauses or separates items in a list when at least one item contains a comma. The semicolon in this sentence plays neither role. Instead, it sets off the contradictory statement. The reader expects to see a list of visitors and receives a different message: *nobody calls.*

Rhetoric

Thoreau's statement is an *oxymoron*, a seeming self-contradiction.

Additional Information and Activities

- Thoreau's sentence lends itself to interdisciplinary and multidisciplinary projects: History/English: What was happening in the early nineteenth century that led Thoreau to seek simplicity? Psychology/English: Is solitude the same as loneliness? Science/English: Thoreau treasured the environment and tried to live in harmony with nature. Is that possible now? How do Thoreau's ideas connect to today's environmental movement?
- *Walden* is a series of essays loosely based on Thoreau's experience at Walden Pond but compressed and edited. Does that matter? Students might discuss and perhaps write an essay about the difference between reporting (journalism) and interpreting (essay, memoir, autobiography).
- The transcendentalists—Thoreau, Emerson, Alcott, Fuller, and others—are an interesting group. Have students research the lives and literary works of one or more authors.

> ### Susan Glaspell, "His Smile"
>
> A new town was only the same town in a different place, and all of it was a world she was as out of as if it were passing before her in a picture.

Brief context: *She* is a woman who has traveled to *a new town*, to see a film in which her late husband, Howie, appears in the background of one scene.

Extended context: The story is set in the early twentieth century, when watching movies at home was impossible. *She* has gone to several theaters to see the film. Her goal is to reconnect with Howie, if only for the few moments he's on screen. But the film's run is ending, so this will be her last chance to see him. Grieving, she thinks about Howie and all the ways in which he tried to help people. She watches him on the screen as he loosens a dog's too-tight collar. Just before the camera moves on, she sees Howie smile. The widow realizes that although she can no longer feel close to Howie by watching the film, she can feel close to him by taking care of others. As the story ends, she eases a sleeping child in the seat next to her into a more comfortable position.

Analysis

With brief context:

- How can a *new town* be *the same town*? (similar size and appearance, no distinguishing features)
- How is *in a different place* significant? (the physical location has changed, as has her life situation)
- Why employ this contradiction? (to show uninterest, detachment)
- What's the significance of *a world she was as out of as if it were passing before her*? (the town doesn't matter, only that the film is being shown there; she has little interest in life)
- Why does the author specify *in a picture*? (she's there to see *a picture*—a film)

With extended context:

- How is the *world . . . passing before her*? (uninterested in anything; immersed in grief)
- What's the significance of *in a picture*? (Howie isn't there, only his *picture*)
- How is contradiction relevant to the widow's situation? (what's real feels unreal; for most of the story, what's unreal matters most)
- How does the last showing of the film change her? (she moves away from the unreal and reconnects with reality by helping the child)

SUPPLEMENTAL MATERIAL FOR "HIS SMILE"

Grammar

- The sentence comprises two independent clauses, linked by both a semicolon and the conjunction *and*. In modern usage, either would be sufficient. Perhaps Glaspell agreed with Abraham Lincoln, who professed "great respect" for the semicolon and wrote, "With educated people, I suppose, punctuation is a matter of rule; with me it is a matter of feeling."
- The pronoun *it* has no clear antecedent. Glaspell most likely left *all of it* purposely vague because to the widow, everything but Howie's moment on the screen is vague background.
- The verb *were* is subjunctive, because the *world* isn't *passing before her in a picture.*

Additional Information and Activities

- "His Smile" is told in third person limited, from the widow's point of view. The reader knows only her perceptions of others, with no objective narrator to guide them. Discuss how accurate her assessment of the intentions and actions of other characters is.
- Glaspell is considered a feminist writer, so her work might form the basis of a women's studies/English research project. Or, you might ask students to write an argumentative essay supporting their definition of "feminist writer."

Her tongue's attached in the middle and flaps at both ends.

Brief context: This is a comment about a woman who's been making up stories about a town resident.

Extended context: This humorous story takes place in a small town, where the narrator spends summers with his grandmother. When an elderly man named "Shotgun" Cheatham dies, no one seems to know his legal name. An out-of-town newspaper sends a reporter, who hears many made-up stories, especially from Effie Wilcox, the woman whose tongue is described in this sentence. The insult to Effie comes from Grandma, who knows the real story of Shotgun's name: at the age of ten, he tried to shoot quail with a shotgun and killed a cow instead. If he'd been aiming for the cow, the grandmother adds, "she'd have died of old age eventually." Grandma fabricates an elaborate lie for the reporter about Shotgun's service in the Civil War and eventually scares off the visitor by convincing him that Shotgun is rising from the dead.

Analysis
With brief context:

- What does the *tongue* represent? (Effie's comments)
- The description contradicts reality; it's anatomically impossible to have a tongue that's *attached in the middle and flaps at both ends*. What does Grandma really mean? (what Effie says is impossible; Effie lies)
- Why does Grandma say this? (she knows the real story, Effie makes one up)
- Many mouth-centered expressions refer to speaking more than one should: "loose-tongued," "loose-lipped," and "loose-mouthed." How do those meanings relate to this sentence? (Effie speaks unwisely and is not to be trusted)

With extended context:

- A common expression is "to speak out of both sides of your mouth"— that is, "to declare contradictory positions." How does this expression relate to the sentence? (townspeople want to keep the reporter's interest but also resent his intrusion)
- What does the contradiction add to the sentence? (humor, sense of Grandma's creativity and enjoyment of mischief)
- What sort of character is Grandma? How do you know (doesn't mind exaggerating—the description of Effie's tongue—and playing tricks—the "rising" of Shotgun's corpse)

SUPPLEMENTAL MATERIAL FOR "SHOTGUN CHEATHAM'S LAST NIGHT ABOVE GROUND"

Grammar

This straightforward sentence is one independent clause with a compound verb (*is attached*, *flaps*).

Rhetoric

Hyperbole, or comic exaggeration, applies here.

Additional Information and Activities

- "Shotgun Cheatham's Last Night Above Ground" is an easy read and very funny. Consider assigning the whole story, which comes from Richard Peck's collection entitled *Past Perfect, Present Tense*.
- Exaggerated speech adds humor to stories by Mark Twain, Flannery O'Connor, and Zora Neale Hurston, among others. Have students compare Peck's sentence with one from another author who employs a similar technique.
- The gullible visitor is a stock character. Assign Saki's "The Open Window" and the entire Shotgun Cheatham story. Have students compare the young man in Saki's story and the reporter in Peck's. Possible essay question: Why do residents feel antipathy for visitors? Why do visitors believe impossible or contradictory statements?

MORE CONTRADICTIONS

A few extra examples, with minimal commentary:

> **If he flew them he was crazy and didn't have to; but if he didn't want to he was sane and had to.**   —Joseph Heller, *Catch-22*

He is a pilot; *them* refers to combat missions. The title phrase of Joseph Heller's novel of World War II refers to the rule that excuses pilots from flying if they're insane but judges them sane for asking to be excused. The phrase *catch-22* appears several times in Heller's novel and in ordinary life, whenever bureaucratic nonsense triumphs over common sense or someone is caught in an impossible, contradictory situation.

> **I don't care to belong to any social organization that will accept me as a member.**
> —Groucho Marx, "Letter of Resignation to the Friars Club"

Reminiscent of Heller's *Catch-22*, Groucho Marx's statement contradicts itself in an absurd fashion. With this sentence Groucho Marx resigned from the Friars Club, whose members are comedians and celebrities, because his application was accepted.

> **I'm all in favour of free expression provided it's kept rigidly under control.**   —Alan Bennett, *Forty Years On*

Alan Bennett's 1968 play is set in a British school, where students are putting on a play about the time period between the end of World War I and the first years of World War II. As the play-within-a-play proceeds, the retiring headmaster comments on changes in society. His sentence perfectly represents the character: stuffy, upholding arbitrary "standards," oblivious to his own contradictions.

> **I cannot speak well enough to be unintelligible.**
> —Jane Austen, *Northanger Abbey*

The narrator, Catherine Morland, is a naïve young woman sent to the English resort of Bath with a neighbor from her rural village. Catherine has little experience of the world but has read a great many gothic novels, a genre rife with odd events, mysterious characters, and hidden evil. Catherine is more mystified by the social scene, as her sentence illustrates. Many of the people she meets lie or equivocate; she says what she means. The sentence is a perfectly serious statement from Catherine: she literally does not know how to be "unintelligible" and play verbal games.

> **Here were two teams that had made a career of failure and had enjoyed staggering success at it.**
> —*The Red Smith Reader*, edited by Dave Anderson

Red Smith, sports reporter, writes about a football game between Harvard and Yale, two universities known for their intellectual accomplishments (in a good way) and, as Smith points out, for their athletic accomplishments (in a bad way).

> **We go down to see what is unseen, unseeable—we go in search of illumination that can be found only in the dark.**
> —Will Hunt, *Underground*

Will Hunt's exploration of tunnels, catacombs, sewers, and abandoned mines is the subject of this nonfiction book. Hunt introduces the reader to underground enthusiasts, who range from archaeologists to physicists to cave hunters and simple tourists. Here he ponders why people are drawn to the underground. The contradictions in this sentence—*to see what is unseen, unseeable* and *illumination that can be found only in the dark*—make sense on the psychological level. Only when the distractions of normal life are removed can we turn inward and focus on usually hidden aspects of ourselves.

WRITING ASSIGNMENTS

Contradictory Mergers

A merged term (portmanteau) combines parts of two existing words to form a third. Add a dash of contradiction, and you have a *portmandiction* or a *contra-*

manteau or . . . a contradictory merger. A few already exist: *slacktivist* combines "slacker" and "activist" to name those who feel passionately about an issue enough to sit on the sofa and yell at the television on which a *dramedy* (comedy plus drama) is playing. Ask students to join antonyms and then to write a sentence containing their creation.

When?

Have you ever given a positive answer that's really a negative, such as in this exchange?

> STUDENT: May I have another assignment? This one is boring.
> ME: Of course! Just tunnel under the floor and crack the safe in which I keep the interesting assignments.

This assignment is more fun when students pair up, one creating the request and the other the "yes of course" reply.

What Do You Know?

Life lessons that are stated in a sentence often emerge as contradictions, a tendency that undoubtedly says something about life. Ask students to write something they believe to be true, with a contradictory twist. Two examples, the first from Vita Sackville-West and the second from Malcolm Forbes:

> **I have come to the conclusion after many years of sometimes sad experience that you cannot come to any conclusion at all.**

> **Let your children go if you want to keep them.**

If you wish, have students write essays in which their contradictory sentences serve as thesis statements.

Opposites Attract

Select some antonym pairs (*apathy* and *interest*, *love* and *hate*, *cruelty* and *kindness*, and so forth). Or, allow students to choose their own pair. Challenge them to create a character in which both qualities combine and to write a descriptive sentence. They don't have to use the words, but the sentence should display contradictory qualities. Here's a sample response for *lazy* and *active*:

> **Julia took great pride in her fitness plan, which, if she ever got off her sofa and tried it, would do wonders for her cardiovascular system.**

Extra credit: Write a scene featuring the character.

CREATIVE COMPARISONS

More than once I've overheard this sort of conversation between two students:

> **STUDENT ONE:** That concert! The guitar was like . . .
> **STUDENT TWO** (nodding): Totally.

Huh? As they retreat to their phone screens, satisfied that they've communicated, I wonder whether they're able to tap into a collective imagination beyond my grasp, or, in less hopeful moments, whether language is doomed.

Maybe it is, but I'm an English teacher and I'm not going down without a fight. I require a complete simile ("The guitar sounded like Mount Rushmore yelling") or an apt metaphor ("Every chord was a feather on my ear"). An occasional allusion would be nice, too ("The song started out *Game of Thrones* and morphed into *Mr. Rogers*"). Actually, any creative comparison, even an analogy, would be better than word fragments. Because #clarity.

Just kidding with that last bit, but not kidding at all about the importance of imagination squeezed into words. That's what this chapter is about.

NOTE: Chapter 7 tackles descriptive details and vivid verbs. Mix and match sentences from those sections for like, better communication, you know?

TEACHING CREATIVE COMPARISONS: A GENERAL PLAN

Introduction (optional)

Most likely students are already familiar with creative comparisons, whether or not they've had formal lessons on the topic. But everyone's skills improve with a little extra attention. Try this:

- Ask for a volunteer to sit looking away from the class. Show everyone else an object: a teddy bear, a hat, a scarf, a photo of a celebrity . . . whatever.
- One by one, have students describe the object by relating it to something

else. No literal descriptions allowed! Let's say you've chosen a scarf. The first student says, "It's a snake without muscles." The next adds, "It's like a warm bath on a cold day."

- After each description, the volunteer takes a guess, continuing until the object is identified.
- Debrief for a moment: Which descriptions are most helpful? Why?

Decoding

- After they've decoded the literal meaning of the sentence, have students identify the creative comparisons.
- Explore the connotations of the creative comparison as a whole.
- Focus on individual words in the comparison. What feelings or ideas do those words bring to mind?

Analysis

- What does the creative comparison add to the sentence?
- How about the individual words in the comparison? Do they affect meaning? How?
- If the comparison were literal, what would be lost?

TEACHING CREATIVE COMPARISONS: LESSON PLANS

An Na, *A Step from Heaven*

This drink bites the inside of my mouth and throat like swallowing tiny fish bones.

Brief context: The narrator, a child whose family recently immigrated to the United States from Korea, tastes her first soda.

Extended context: In An Na's novel, the narrator doesn't want to leave Korea. While displaying her worn, rough hands, the narrator's mother tells her that if the family goes to America, the narrator will grow up to be "better than a fisherman's wife." In Korea, the father of the family owned a fishing boat. In

America, he works as a janitor. The father is sometimes violent toward his wife and insists on unquestioning obedience from his daughter. After the sentence above, the narrator says that she wants to "push the drink away" but "cannot show bad manners."

Analysis

With brief context:

- Does the child like the soda? How do you know? (she doesn't like it—*bites, swallowing fish bones*)
  - What does the verb *bites* suggest? (pain, being eaten, harm)
  - What does the phrase *swallowing tiny fish bones* suggest to you? (discomfort, not bad enough to do real damage but a series of small wounds, indigestion)
  - If the word *swallowing* were removed, how would the sentence change? (*swallowing* is what the child does, so with this word she participates in an action that hurts her; without *swallowing*, the soda inflicts damage)
  - What does *tiny* add to the sentence? (the narrator is a child, *tiny* and powerless)

With extended context:

- How does *bite* reflect the family dynamic? (father insists on unquestioning obedience, so the child must be silent and drink the soda, even though it hurts her mouth—figuratively, her ability to speak up for herself is hurt)
  - Why include *inside of*? (emphasizes silence and the closed dynamic of this family)
  - How does *swallowing tiny fish bones* relate to the family's history? (father owned a fishing boat in Korea but he's *tiny* in America; he must *swallow* or accept a lesser status; the narrator is *tiny* and powerless)

SUPPLEMENTAL MATERIAL
FOR *A STEP FROM HEAVEN*

Grammar

The sentence is one independent clause, with *drink bites* as the subject-verb pair and *inside* as direct object, modified by *of my mouth*.

Rhetoric

The phrase *like swallowing tiny fish bones* is a *simile*, a direct comparison.

Additional Information and Activities

- Many immigrant stories feature an encounter with an unfamiliar food. Discuss the cultural and psychological significance of food and drink with the class or assign it as a research project.
- The sentence reflects a child's point of view. Discuss the effect of that perspective on the author's options and the readers' reaction.
- An Na's novel depicts, with little detail but unmistakable impact, the dynamic of family violence. Students can research this topic for a psychology/English project.
- *A Step from Heaven* may be a good class text. It's a quick read with simple vocabulary, but the topic is complex and worthy of discussion. The novel neither idealizes nor demonizes immigrants and ends on a relatively positive note. Spoiler alert: the narrator eventually breaks her silence and one day calls the police to report her father's violence. He returns to Korea after his arrest, and the mother and children create a good life for themselves in America.

> ### John Donne, "A Valediction Forbidding Mourning"
>
> Our two souls therefore, which are one,
> Though I must go, endure not yet
> A breach, but an expansion,
> Like gold to airy thinness beat.

Brief context: A husband, about to take a long trip, tells his wife not to be sad.

Extended context: John Donne wrote this poem to his pregnant wife shortly before he left England for a long trip abroad. The speaker forbids "mourning" and asks for "no noise, / no tear floods." Their love is more than a physical bond, the speaker claims, because he and his beloved are connected spiritually and therefore "[c]are less, eyes, lips, and hands to miss." In other stanzas the speaker elevates their relationship above that of other couples, which he calls "sublunary" (literally, "beneath the moon" or "inferior").

Analysis

With brief context:

- Which words form a comparison? (*Like gold to airy thinness beat*)
- What does that image bring to mind? (something beautiful, valuable, durable, able to be shaped)
- How does that image relate to the rest of the sentence? (*two souls . . . are one*—beautiful and valuable relationship; they will be apart physically—the relationship will take a different "shape" but endure)
- What does *airy* bring to mind? (healthy, natural, intangible)
- How do those associations relate to the rest of the sentence? (their souls are intangible but real, the couple has a natural, healthy bond)
- What does *beat* bring to mind? (heartbeat; also pain or punishment)
- How do those associations relate to the rest of the sentence? (the parting will be painful, but their love will withstand the separation—no *breach*)

With extended context:

- The comparison refers to a physical substance, *gold*. How is *gold* related to the speaker's point? (their bond is more valuable than most couples'; *gold* isn't brittle and can be beaten without a *breach*, or break; gold doesn't decay)
- How does *airy thinness* relate to the speaker's message? (despite their physical separation, an intangible—*airy*—bond connects them; their bond will be stretched to *thinness* but will still exist)
- What does the word *beat* add to the sentence? (despite "forbidding

mourning" there will be pain; also adds physical aspect—they may "care less" but they will miss being together physically)

- What is the effect of the image as a whole? (varied answers: mix of sadness and hope; their love has both physical and spiritual aspects; the speaker and his wife will be separated but their bond is better than the norm, durable)

SUPPLEMENTAL MATERIAL FOR "A VALEDICTION FORBIDDING MOURNING"

Grammar

- *Our two souls endure not yet a break but an expansion*—independent clause, stating the main idea.
- *which are one, Though I must go*—two dependent clauses, the first modifying *two souls* and the second modifying *are*. Though they are dependent clauses, they convey important information: the souls' unity.
- *Like gold to airy thinness beat*—two prepositional phrases. The first, *Like gold*, modifies *expansion*. The second, *to airy thinness beat*, modifies *gold*. This "chain" of descriptions underscores the link between the couple.

Rhetoric

Like gold to airy thinness beat is a *simile*, a direct comparison.

Additional Information and Activities

- John Donne (1572–1631) was one of the most important metaphysical poets, a group that favored unusual metaphors and extended metaphors, or *conceits*. Students might read other poems by Donne ("Death Be Not Proud," for example) or compare his work to that of other metaphysical poets such as Andrew Marvell or George Herbert.
- "A Valediction Forbidding Mourning" devotes three stanzas to an extended metaphor comparing the couple to a compass, a hinged instrument with one fixed foot and another that revolves around it. Compasses are sometimes used in math or art classes to draw circles. Students can explore the math/art aspects of the poem.

> ### Elizabeth Kolbert, "Greenland Is Melting"
>
> **This is 400 million Olympic swimming pools' worth of water, enough to fill a single pool the size of New York State to a depth of 23 feet.**

Brief context: *This* is the amount of water that melted in four years from the ice sheet that covers much of Greenland.

Extended context: Just prior to this sentence the author explains that "more than a trillion tons of ice have been lost [melted]" in the preceding four years. The author describes the ice sheet in several ways: it's two miles deep in spots, so large that it "creates its own weather," and so heavy that it crushes the bedrock beneath. The top layer of snow fell in the last two years but under that are layers that froze when "Washington crossed the Delaware" and, deeper still, when "Hannibal crossed the Alps." The lowest layer of ice is about 115,000 years old. The article describes scientific research conducted in Greenland, focusing on the effect of climate change on Greenland's glaciers.

Analysis

With brief context:

- What does the sentence tell the reader about *This*, the water from melted ice? (how much there is)
- What words generally describe a quantity of water? (gallons or liters for volume, feet or meters or fathoms for depth, tons or pounds for weight)
- What words does the author use to describe the water? (*400 million Olympic swimming pools' worth of water, enough to fill a single pool the size of New York State to a depth of 23 feet*)
- What are some advantages of specifying *swimming pools* and *New York State*? (brings the information closer to readers' reality, provides a point of reference)
- Which is more effective? (varied answers)

With extended context:

• How does this sentence reflect the author's technique elsewhere in the article? (uses other concrete references—Washington, Hannibal)
• What other techniques does the author use to describe the ice sheet? (statistics—"two miles" and "115,000 years"; startling facts—"creates its own weather" and "crushes the bedrock")
• Which type of description is most effective? Why? (varied answers)

SUPPLEMENTAL MATERIAL FOR "GREENLAND IS MELTING"

Grammar

• The antecedent of the pronoun *This* appears in the previous sentence: "more than a trillion tons of ice" that melted.
• The two descriptions (*400 million . . . water* and *enough . . . 23 feet*) are presented as appositives.
• The apostrophe doesn't show possession in the usual sense of ownership, but it does create a relationship between the amount of water and *worth*.

Additional Information and Activities

• Elizabeth Kolbert's article makes a strong case that we have a climate emergency, yet the article is not just a set of alarming facts. Instead, she describes the scientists working there and small moments that humanize their endeavors, such as the first oral doctoral defense ever conducted atop the ice sheet. Consider assigning the whole article or a science/ English research project focused on field studies.
• The specific scientific project the author observes is the East Greenland Ice-Core Project. Students might research ice cores—what can be learned from them, how they're obtained, and so forth. Presenting the information creatively, as Kolbert does, can be a class project. Divide the group and assign types of descriptions: dates or events in history, statistics, small details, etc. Discuss the advantages and disadvantages of each technique.

NOTE: You may wish to include similes, metaphors, and other figures of speech, combining lessons in this chapter with some from the section on descriptive details.

- The article is written from the first-person point of view. Kolbert participates in some of the events she describes. Discuss how the author's participation may influence what's reported and how the reporting is received.

MORE CREATIVE COMPARISONS

This is such a rich topic that it's hard not to add more examples. I'll try to restrain myself. Here are a few more, grouped by type.

Allusions

An *allusion* creates a comparison by bringing a completely different world into the sentence. That's great, unless it's an alien world! In discussing allusions, alert your students to the fact that what may be perfectly clear to one generation (yours, for example) may befuddle another (theirs) and vice versa. A few examples:

> **He's slim and youthful, with crinkly Paul Rudd eyes and a jovial, laid-back air.**
> —Chris Colin, "This Sand Is Your Sand" (*Paul Rudd eyes* resemble those of the actor; the title alludes to Woody Guthrie's "This Land Is Your Land")

> **George Gershwin is Sullivan-Gilberting with his own brother, Ira.**
> —Ring Lardner (the Gershwin brothers were a superstar songwriting team of the Jazz Age; *Sullivan-Gilberting* is an allusion to another musical team, Arthur Sullivan and W. S. Gilbert, more commonly referred to as "Gilbert and Sullivan")

> **Call me whatever.**
> —Christopher Buckley, "My Year at Sea" (author's memoir of his gap year; allusion to the first line of *Moby-Dick*)

It is not just Mowgli who was raised by a couple of wolves; any child is raised by a couple of grown-ups.
>   —Randall Jarrell, essay (*Mowgli* alludes to Rudyard Kipling's *The Jungle Book*; implies that a *child* and *grown-ups* belong to different species)

Every great man nowadays has his disciples, and it is always Judas who writes the biography.
>   —Oscar Wilde, interview (*Judas* alludes to the disciple who betrays Jesus)

Analogies

Analogies, as Elizabeth Kolbert's sentence illustrates, help readers grasp information. Science is a good hunting ground for these comparisons:

The visual models are striking: our planet is like a giant beach ball completely surrounded by a dense layer of M&M's (the debris in low Earth orbit), and also by sparser concentric circles of M&M's (the debris at other altitudes, such as geostationary orbit, mostly used for telecommunications).
>   —Ceridwen Dovey, "Dr. Space Junk Unearths the Cultural Landscape of the Cosmos" (nonfiction article about debris in orbit)

It [the ocean] is also the home of living things so small that your two hands might scoop up as many of them as there are stars in the Milky Way.
>   —Rachel Carson, "Undersea" (reference to diatoms, single-celled creatures that play a crucial role in the marine ecosystem)

Similes and Metaphors

I am lonesome so regular it's like a job I gotta report to every day.
>   —Alice Childress, *Rainbow Jordan*

Wraiths only scare people, centaurs only awe people, and unicorns, aside from some healing properties in their horns, akin to the antibiotics in frog skins, only attract virgins—which, power-wise, puts them at the same level as boy bands.
>   —Kathryn Schulz, "Fantastic Beasts and How to Rank Them"

"So?" Logan asked, looking at him as if he'd said fish sticks were best when made out of people.

—Anne Ursu, "Max Swings for the Fences"

Playing "bop" is like playing Scrabble with all the vowels missing.

—Duke Ellington (in an interview)

The mall is a zoo, if the zoo forgot to build cages.

—Tim Federle, "Secret Samantha"

I am the sole author of the dictionary that defines me.

—Zadie Smith, *NW*

Some of us [office workers] had new Macs, some had high-powered notebooks, and some unfortunate souls had to pedal furiously under their desks to keep a spark running through their extinct models.   —Joshua Ferris, *Then We Came to the End*

Truth is a letter from courage.

—Zora Neale Hurston, *Dust Tracks on a Road*

WRITING ASSIGNMENTS

Creative comparison assignments work best when there's an element of play. Send your students into a sandbox of words with these exercises.

Animals

In *The Sympathizer*, Viet Thanh Nguyen's narrator is a North Vietnamese spy working as an aide to an unsuspecting South Vietnamese general. He describes a moment when he's nearly caught:

An X-ray of my skull would have shown a hamster running furiously in an exercise wheel, trying to generate ideas.

Ask students to choose an animal to describe their thought processes in a specific situation: just before an exam, just after, when it's time for lunch, and so forth.

Equivalencies

Elizabeth Kolbert's sentence about melted ice is strikingly vivid, and not solely because the phenomenon she's describing is dramatic. Ask students to convey one bit of information in a relatable way. They may employ an analogy, as Kolbert does, or a different technique. Here's one possible response:

> FACT: A curtain six-and-a-half-feet high and twenty-feet long separates men and women during religious services.
> SENTENCE: The men and women prayed together, separated by a curtain just high enough to prevent their seeing each other.

Instead of measurements, the details about the curtain reveal both its size and its purpose.

Object Lessons

Challenge students to creatively compare two objects, people, events, or something else. For example, how does a tomato relate to a student about to take an exam?

> My face red from the strain of keeping my nerves under control,
> I was an overripe tomato when I entered the classroom, but soon
> knowledge was dripping out of my pen.

NEGATIVITY

Negativity garners few positive ratings. That's a shame, because a writer who exploits its power can produce a five-star sentence. Negativity can soften (calling an eighty-year-old "not young," for example) or emphasize ("Never is when you can skip homework!"). A negative statement can also undermine an assumption, double up to create a colloquial tone, and define by exclusion.

TEACHING NEGATIVITY: A GENERAL PLAN

Introduction (optional)

Depending on the age of your students, *no* may be their favorite word, especially when talking to an authority figure. Move them beyond knee-jerk rebellion into a thoughtful consideration of negativity with this activity: Give them a simple positive statement: "He's interesting," "we're prepared," or something similar. Have them flip it to the negative: "He's not boring," "we're not unprepared." Compare the positive and negative versions. Does the effect on the reader or listener differ? How?

Decoding

- In addition to the usual decoding, help students unravel double negatives, if any are present. Which are emphatic ("didn't do nothing") and which are reversals in formal English ("not unkind")?
- In a negative definition, what's excluded or presented as a contrast?
- If a character is involved, have students identify the speaker and topic.

Analysis

- Does the negative in the sentence downplay or emphasize?
- Is the statement literal? Ironic? Humble or falsely humble? Ask students to support their opinions.
- Explore connotation and tone, with special attention to the negative element.
- Flip the sentence from negative to positive. Explore the difference.

- What does a negative comment from a speaker, narrator, or author reveal about personality and attitude?

TEACHING NEGATIVITY: LESSON PLANS

In these sentences, the negative elements are underlined.

> ### Richard Powers, *The Overstory*
>
> There are <u>no</u> individuals in a forest, <u>no</u> separable events.

Brief context: A statement about a forest from a scientist who has studied the ecosystem.

Extended context: In Richard Powers's novel, trees form a collective character that's related to nine human characters, all interacting with trees, and sometimes with each other, in surprising ways. The sentence comes from Patricia Westerford, a scientist writing a book (within Powers's book) about trees. Westerford is fictional, but her character presents accurate information drawn from research on how trees function within the ecosystem they inhabit. Surrounding this sentence are details about trees to support the negative statement. Two examples: Fungi in the soil tap into tree roots for sugar and grow into a sort of underground cable system, "trading networks of goods, services, and information" from tree to tree across miles of forest. Some species, such as oak and hickory, "synchronize their nut production to baffle the animals that feed on them."

Analysis

With brief context:

- What *individuals* does the sentence refer to? (trees, other vegetation)
- What might be some examples of *separable events*? (a tree dies or is cut down, an animal or a species arrives or goes extinct, the amount of rainfall changes, a fire breaks out, etc.)

- What are the consequences of *no individuals*? (what appears to happen to one tree or plant happens to all; interdependence between trees and other vegetation and animals, possibly with human beings as well)
- What are the consequences of *no separable events*? (can't dismiss one fire, dry period, or flood as an anomaly; one event is tied to another in a cause/effect relationship; long-term arc of events)
- What's the effect of saying *no individuals* and *no separable events* instead of "collective organism," "chain of consequences," or something similar? (starts with the assumption of individuality and contradicts it)
- The sentence is quite simple in structure and word choice. How does that simplicity affect readers' reaction? (no wiggle room for different opinion, stark statement of fact)

With extended context:

- How does knowing that there are "nine human characters" interacting with trees affect your perception of the sentence? (raises the question of human individuality, emphasizes interconnection, implies that human fate is connected to that of the forest)
- What's the significance of having this statement come from Westerford? (authority confers legitimacy; not impressions but scientific facts)
- What do the two examples add to your understanding of the sentence? (varied answers such as "convince skeptics," "show relationships between trees," "reveal complexity," "personification of fungi and other vegetation," etc.)

SUPPLEMENTAL MATERIAL FOR *THE OVERSTORY*

Grammar

- The sentence is a single independent clause. This construction mirrors the meaning: only one creature (the forest) is present.
- In a *there are* construction, the subject comes after the verb. In this sentence, *individuals* and *events* are subjects of the verb *are*.
- The subjects are modified, or described, by *no* and *in the forest*.

Rhetoric

The temptation is to call this sentence a *hyperbole*, or exaggeration, but Powers inserts so much science into his novel that I, for one, see it as realistic.

Additional Information and Activities

- This sentence is a good base for a science/English collaboration on trees and the forest ecosystem. *The Hidden Life of Trees: What They Feel, How They Communicate* by Peter Wohlleben is a nonfiction book that presents the research supporting Powers's sentence.
- A history or current events/English project is also possible. *Overstory: Zero: Real Life in Timber Country* by Robert Leo Heilman is a nonfiction account of the lives of loggers, environmental activists, millworkers, and many others whose work relates to the forest. Students might compare a sentence from this book with Powers's sentence.

Robert Lipsyte, *Yellow Flag*

But he <u>wasn't</u> sure if he <u>wasn't</u> sure.

Brief context: This sentence follows a young man's statement that he's "not sure" about his plans.

Extended context: The sentence describes Kyle Hildebrand, a teenager whose family has been involved in stock-car racing for generations. The family's hopes to attract sponsors, which they desperately need, rest on Kyle's brother, Kris. Kyle's passion is music; he plays the trumpet in a school band. When Kris is injured, Kyle takes his place in a race. His success increases the pressure to join the family business and leave his music behind. Complicating the situation is that Kyle enjoys racing. Asked whether he'll choose racing and, by implication, put his music aside, Kyle answers, "I'm not sure." This sentence follows.

Analysis

With brief context:

- What's the meaning of the repeated negative? (doubles the uncertainty emphasizes how hard the choice is)
- In what sort of situation would a writer begin a sentence with *but*? (to qualify the preceding statement, to raise an objection)
- What do you imagine comes before this sentence? ("I'm not sure" or a similar statement)
- What state of mind is *he* in? (doesn't know what he thinks/feels, doesn't want to face his decision yet)

With extended context:

- Kyle is torn between his family's business and his own interests. How does this sentence reflect that? (indecisive, even about his own indecision)
- Why might Kyle be *not sure he wasn't sure*? (consequences of his decision to the family and to himself, fearful of reactions to his decision)

SUPPLEMENTAL MATERIAL FOR *YELLOW FLAG*

Grammar

- By the strictest definition, this isn't a complete sentence, because it begins with a conjunction. The "fragment" echoes Kyle's situation; his decision is incomplete, and his future path unclear.
- The double negative here hints at a positive statement that reverses the apparent meaning. Kyle considers changing his often-expressed preference for music.
- The subordinate conjunction *if* leaves the door open to possibility but also hints at consequences (*if/then*). Replacing *if* with *that* would convey greater certainty. Lipsyte layers much doubt into this short sentence.

Rhetoric

Antistrophe is the repetition of words or phrases at the end of clauses. In this sentence, *wasn't sure* is an example of antistrophe.

Additional Information and Activities

- A fast-paced novel for young adults, *Yellow Flag* could be the basis for an English/sports research project into NASCAR racing or the business of sports in general.
- The protagonist feels pressure from his family and peers to move in opposite directions: a good basis for a psychology/English project or discussion.
- Lipsyte's novel might open the door to other literary works that focus on the conflict between family expectations and personal preference, such as *Romeo and Juliet* and *Great Expectations*.

Dylan Thomas, from a letter

I'm a freak user of words, <u>not</u> a poet.

Brief context: This sentence comes from a letter that Dylan Thomas, author of many poems, wrote to a friend.

Extended context: Dylan Thomas may have denied being a poet, but few people would agree, given that he is the author of several acclaimed books of poetry and a play written in verse. His sentence is from a long letter in which he writes, "I shall have nothing to send you. The old fertile days are gone, and now a poem is the hardest and the most thankless act of creation." In other words, writer's block.

Thomas describes his struggles, telling the recipient of his letter that if he wrote "My dead upon the orbit of the rose," "dead" would not mean "dead," "orbit" would not mean "orbit," and "rose" would "most certainly not mean 'rose.'" His judgment: "They are not the words that express what I want to express; they are the only words I can find that come near to expressing a half."

Analysis

With brief context:

• In the context of this sentence, what's the meaning of *freak*? (several definitions apply: "capricious," "enthusiastic," "unusual")

• Examine any definitions of *freak* students have offered. What are the implications for the sentence? ("capricious"—done on a whim, not seriously; "enthusiastic"—not necessarily talented, just eager; "unusual"—working or writing in an uncommon way)

• What do those definitions say about Thomas and his definition of *a poet*? (varied answers)

• What about *user*? How does that word choice affect the sentence? (neutral; doesn't imply an identity, as *poet* does)

• What does Thomas imply about being a *poet*? (varied answers—something to aspire to, someone more serious or capable than he is, poetry as a vocation, not a hobby or a job)

With extended context:

• The additional quotations show that Thomas is struggling to write. How does that information relate to his statement that he is *not a poet*? (can't claim that title without writing; disparages his ability and his work)

• Thomas says the words he writes "come near to expressing a half" of what he wants to say. What are the consequences of that fact or belief? (frustration, dissatisfaction)

• Why does Thomas write that "dead," "orbit," and "rose" don't mean "dead," "orbit," and "rose"? (words differ from what they name)

• Why is "rose" in a special category? (varied answers—perhaps because it's a tangible object and the other two words, as used in Thomas's letter, are more abstract)

• Moving beyond writer's block, what else is Thomas discussing? (the nature of art, poet as an identity, the distinction between words and reality)

SUPPLEMENTAL MATERIAL FOR DYLAN THOMAS

Grammar

- *Freak* is generally a noun, but in this sentence it's used as an adjective and is less important than the noun it describes, *user*. This construction hints at exploitation; Thomas *uses* words (and perhaps his public). He's not *a poet*.
- The phrase *not a poet* defines *freak user of words* by exclusion. It functions as a negative appositive of *freak user*.

Rhetoric

Hyperbole comes to mind, because Thomas's statement is over the top (as was his life). However, it's a stretch to apply this label to Thomas's sentence.

Additional Information and Activities

- Poets meditating on poetry and writers writing about writing (both common occurrences!) are fruitful areas to explore. The Poetry Foundation website is a good starting point.
- If you've given your students extended context, you might show them René Magritte's painting *The Treachery of Images* in which a pipe hovers over the French words for "This is not a pipe" ("Ceci n'est pas une pipe"). Magritte's painting and Thomas's comments compare art to reality.

MORE NEGATIVITY

Below each sentence is the "extended context" information, which you can edit down to the basics if you wish. The negative words are underlined.

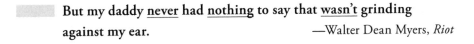

> But my daddy <u>never</u> had <u>nothing</u> to say that <u>wasn't</u> grinding
> against my ear.   —Walter Dean Myers, *Riot*

Written as a screenplay, Walter Dean Myers's *Riot* presents historical events: the 1863 draft riots in New York City, one of the worst episodes of civil unrest in American history. The sentence comes from a minor character, Josh Lancaster, a seventeen-year-old Union soldier. In this scene Lancaster is talking with another teenage recruit, who asks Josh whether he joined the army to escape from his father. Lancaster doesn't answer but later tells Claire, another character in the scene, that he's in the army because he believes "in God and my country and in all people being free." Beyond family troubles, Lancaster's sentence reveals his lack of education. When he hears that Claire knows how to read and write, he says that he wants to go back to school after the war. The three negatives of Lancaster's sentence are confusing, but the meaning—that his *daddy* was always *grinding* against his son—is clear. The sentence encapsulates Myers's themes: his characters are often perplexed by the situation they're in, as the Civil War has been *grinding* away the bonds between citizens.

> If you asked the kids and teachers at Lincoln Elementary School to make three lists—all the really bad kids, all the really smart kids, and all the really good kids—Nick Allen would <u>not</u> be on any of them.
> —Andrew Clements, *Frindle*

Nick, as Andrew Clements notes in the next sentence of his novel, "deserved a list of his own." Fond of practical jokes, Nick tries to confound his language arts teacher who "*loved* the dictionary" (author's italics) by referring to his pen as a "frindle," a word Nick coined. He convinces first his class and then others to use the word, to the teacher's dismay. What's interesting about Clements's sentence is that it asserts Nick's unique personality by excluding him from three categories. He's not *really bad*; he just likes to joke around. He's not *really smart*; he invests little energy into his schoolwork. Nor is he *really good*; the jokes are frivolous and initially intended to defy his teacher. In the end (spoiler alert!), Nick achieves success, with *frindle* in the dictionary and his own career soaring.

> If that's what you think, you <u>don't</u> know Mama.
> —Mildred D. Taylor, *Roll of Thunder, Hear My Cry*

In this sentence Stacey, a young boy, quickly shuts down another student's assertion that Stacey has advance information about a test because his mother is their teacher. *Mama* is a principled woman and will not give her son an unfair advantage. Nor will she remain quiet in the face of injustice. She organizes a boycott of a local store after the owners burn an African American man for a perceived offense. *Mama* and her family know that they are risking their lives by protesting injustice. Taylor based her novel on incidents in her own family's history in Mississippi during the Jim Crow era. The sentence refers to one small incident (a school exam), addresses one character (Stacey's friend T.J.), and sheds light on one character (*Mama*). It implicitly refutes the belief that, under sufficient pressure, those who fight for equal rights will give up: *If that's what you think you don't Mama* or the strength of her principles.

SOME SHORT TAKES

These negative sentences are comprehensible, and teachable, without context.

> Studying the data, Seager [Sara Seager, astronomer studying other planets] supported the discovery and agreed that it might boast a life-sustaining—or at least <u>non-life-threatening</u>—surface temperature.
> —Chris Jones, "The Woman Who Might Find Us Another Earth"

> I was <u>not</u> afraid: <u>not</u> near my house, <u>not</u> on the other side of campus, <u>not</u> even in the bleak brick-and-mud Taigu village alleys scattered with trash and piles of used coal pellets.
> —Elizabeth Lindsey Rogers, "One Person Means Alone"

> I think I may boast myself to be, with all possible vanity, the most <u>unlearned</u> and <u>uninformed</u> female who ever dared to be an authoress.   —Jane Austen (from a letter)

> Discretion is <u>not</u> the better part of biography.
> —Lytton Strachey (from a letter)

> Sir, they [newspapers] are the most villainous—licentious—abominable—infernal—<u>Not</u> that I ever read them—<u>No</u>—I make it a rule <u>never</u> to look into a newspaper.
> —Richard Brinsley Sheridan, *The Critic*

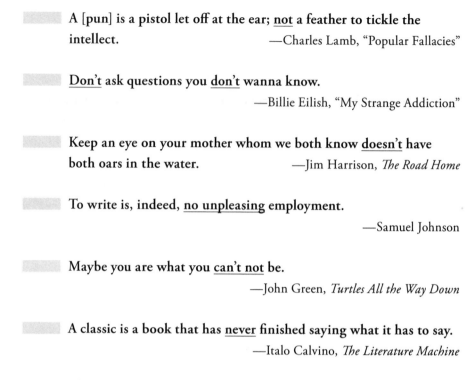

A [pun] is a pistol let off at the ear; <u>not</u> a feather to tickle the intellect.   —Charles Lamb, "Popular Fallacies"

<u>Don't</u> ask questions you <u>don't</u> wanna know.
                                    —Billie Eilish, "My Strange Addiction"

Keep an eye on your mother whom we both know <u>doesn't</u> have both oars in the water.   —Jim Harrison, *The Road Home*

To write is, indeed, <u>no unpleasing</u> employment.
                                    —Samuel Johnson

Maybe you are what you <u>can't not</u> be.
                                    —John Green, *Turtles All the Way Down*

A classic is a book that has <u>never</u> finished saying what it has to say.
                                    —Italo Calvino, *The Literature Machine*

These songs also provide some great negative sentences: "Satisfaction" by the Rolling Stones, "Two Outta Three Ain't Bad" by Meatloaf, and "The Rising" By Bruce Springsteen.

WRITING ASSIGNMENTS

A few additional activities, for in-class or long-term work:

Protest Song

Have your students identify a cause they believe in and imagine that they're organizing a rally to promote their views. (They can choose something trivial, like better cafeteria food, or something more significant.) Given a choice of any singer in the world, living or dead, who would they want to perform at the rally? Ask them to formulate a negative expression for their answer. Here's an example:

I won't say no to Billie Eilish, because there's no societal norm she's unwilling to break.

Now have them rule someone out, again in a negative statement:

Thumbs down on that guy my sister listens to all the time, because if he's performing no one but my sister will go.

Street Lingo

Ask students to create a character who avoids formal English at all costs. Have them write some double-negative lines for the character. An example:

"Not gonna go to detention no more," muttered Bobby as he pretended to search for his phone, scurrying off to detention as soon as his friends left.

If you wish, have them embed their characters in a scene.

Double Double

Review Robert Lipsyte's sentence from *Yellow Flag* and ask students to write sentences that repeat a negative. Here's one possible response:

I don't know anything about algebra; I don't even know what I don't know about algebra!

Another possible model, this one from Tommy Orange's novel *There There*:

We'd been over there to celebrate not celebrating Thanksgiving.

Not Untrapped

The double-negative construction can be great, as you see in these sentences from Shakespeare and Larry McMurtry (in that order, not that I need to tell you which is which!):

Let him fly far, / Not in this land shall he remain uncaught.
—*King Lear* (Act 2, scene 1)

I have known cowboys broken in body and twisted in spirit, bruised by debt, failure, loneliness, disease, and most of the other afflictions of man, but I have seldom known one who did not consider himself phenomenally blessed to have been a cowboy, or one who would not cancel half the miseries of existence by dwelling on the horses he had ridden, the comrades he had ridden them with, and the manly time he had had.
—"Take My Saddle from the Wall"

Ask students to write a double negative of their own, with positive intentions. Just remind them not to overdo this rhetorical device. If they go overboard, let George Orwell scold them with his example of overwrought negativity:

A not unblack dog was chasing a not unsmall rabbit across a not ungreen field.

That ought to do it!

SYNESTHESIA

· ·

The number four is slippery and yellow. A pretzel tastes like whistling, and a marble sculpture smells like cheese. Welcome to the world of synesthesia, where what's picked up by one sense is processed as if it were another. A small percentage of the population are true synesthetes, each with a unique way of processing sensory input. But it's likely that all of us have some elements of synesthesia hardwired into our brains. That's why "clear as a bell" and "bitter cold" are clichés.

I'm sure you discourage students from using clichés and encourage them to explore figurative language—images, many of them synesthetic, that add texture and originality to writing. By going further, teaching students to consciously identify synesthesia and exploit its potential, you improve students' ability to discern layers of meaning and to write more vividly.

TEACHING SYNESTHESIA: A GENERAL PLAN

Introduction (optional)

This activity introduces the concept of synesthesia: Ask students to assign colors to each day of the week and then explain their choices. The connotations associated with the color will emerge, and so, most likely, will sensory crossovers. That opens the door to the concept of synesthesia and how it affects meaning.

Decoding

- Which words refer to sensory information?
- What do those words do? (generally, describe or compare)
- Which senses are involved?
- Which words entwine or cross more than one sense?

Analysis

- Have students free-associate to the synesthetic word(s). What do those associations add to the sentence?

- Examine the role of the synesthetic expression in the sentence? What's the effect on meaning?
- Synesthesia and figurative language go together like iron and magnets. Identify figures of speech (similes, metaphors, personification, etc.). Discuss what they add to the meaning of the sentence.

TEACHING SYNESTHESIA: LESSON PLANS

In these sentences, the synesthetic elements are underlined.

> Jonathan Auxier, *Sweep: The Story of a Girl and Her Monster*
>
> Nan would count to fifty; Charlie would <u>count to purple</u>.

Brief context: Nan is a young girl, and Charlie is the magical creature assigned to guard her.

Extended context: Jonathan Auxier's novel entwines Jewish folklore with British history. Nan Sparrow is an eleven-year-old girl who earns her living as a chimney sweep in Victorian London. Auxier portrays the perils of that life with historical accuracy. Nan was once protected by an adult she calls the Sweep; when he dies he leaves her a lump of charcoal, which, at a dangerous moment, becomes a living creature, whom Nan names Charlie. He's a golem, a magical creature who protects the Jewish community in some stories and causes problems in other tales. Auxier's golem is childlike, and Nan takes on a parental role, teaching Charlie language and many other basic skills. When they watch fireworks from the roof of the abandoned building where they live, Charlie remarks that the sounds of fireworks are "painting the air."

Analysis

With brief context:

- What surprises you in this sentence? (*purple*)
- What do you associate with *purple*? (varied answers)
- Why would Charlie count in colors? (magic, childlike, doesn't know numbers, thinks differently from Nan)
- The sentence says *would count*. How does the word *would* affect the meaning? (habitual action in the past, implies that this activity happened on a regular basis, which in turn implies a relationship between the two)

With extended context:

- What does Charlie's identity as a golem tell you about Nan? (he's her protector, so she's potentially in danger)
- The statement about Nan precedes the statement about Charlie. Why? (Nan's older than he is; she's more important in the relationship because it's his job to protect her)
- Discuss Charlie's observation of firework sounds *painting the air.* How does that add to your understanding of his character? (child's expression, doesn't separate sound and sight, creative)
- Discuss the subtitle. Does Charlie appear to be a *monster*? Why or why not? (varied answers)

SUPPLEMENTAL MATERIAL FOR *SWEEP: THE STORY OF A GIRL AND HER MONSTER*

Grammar

- The sentence consists of two independent clauses connected by a semicolon.
- Both clauses follow the same pattern: subject, verb, prepositional phrase.
- A balanced structure implies an equal relationship. The content, though, doesn't. Counting *to purple* breaks the rules of math. Consider exploring this disjunction (equal, unequal relationship) with the class.

Rhetoric

The two clauses are *parallel*, with balanced grammatical patterns.

Additional Information and Activities

- *Sweep* is an excellent text for a history/English study. Without child labor laws and a protective social net, orphaned or abandoned children in Victorian England lived difficult, often short lives.
- The monster-who's-not-a-monster story is not uncommon. Mary Shelley's *Frankenstein* and Isaac Bashevis Singer's *The Golem* are just two examples. Students might explore the definition of *monster* and relate it to the image the sentence presents.
- The golem is a magical, protective element. What draws people to imagine such characters? Students might research the concept of *golem* in Jewish tradition and compare it to protective creatures from other religions.

H.D. (Hilda Doolittle), "Sea Rose"

Can the spice-rose / <u>drip</u> such acrid <u>fragrance</u> / <u>hardened</u> in a leaf?

Brief context: This question comes from a short poem comparing a spice-rose—a delicate, full-petaled flower—with a sea rose that the poet describes as "harsh," "thin," and "stunted."

Extended context: Hilda Doolittle, more commonly known as H.D., wrote imagist poetry, a genre that emerged in the early twentieth century and relies on images to convey meaning. A sea rose, as its name implies, grows near the coast. The title plant is "caught in the drift," first carried along by the water and then washed up on the shore. Living in "harsh" circumstances, the sea rose is "marred" and "spare of leaf." Yet it's "more precious" than the large bloom of the spice-rose, the kind of delicate flower you'd expect to see in a decorative arrangement.

Analysis

With brief context:

- After decoding, turn students' attention to *acrid fragrance*. What sort of smell is that? (unpleasant, irritating to the nose, corrosive)
- What does *acrid fragrance* do, according to the sentence? (*drip*) Is that the usual action of a *fragrance*? (no, a gas—the *fragrance*—doesn't *drip*)
- What's *hardened* in the sentence? (*fragrance*) Is that realistic? (the source of a *fragrance* can harden—sap or resin, for example—but not *fragrance* itself)
- Why express this impossibility? (impossible for the *spice-rose* to be like a sea rose)
- What ideas do you associate with *leaf*? (life, growth, natural cycle)
- What's the effect of putting *acrid fragrance*, *hardened*, and *leaf* together? (enduring "harsh" conditions leads to growth; also, implication that the natural cycle is hard)

With extended context:

- Is this a real question? (no, it's rhetorical)
- The sea rose is described as less than beautiful. Why? (accuracy, realism, beauty of imperfection, challenge to traditional standards of perfection/beauty)
- What's the significance of the flower's being *caught in the drift*? (not in control, carried along by natural forces from the sea to the shore, power of unchained nature)
- Why might the sea rose be *more precious*? (its ability to survive "harsh" conditions and a precarious situation)

SUPPLEMENTAL MATERIAL FOR "SEA ROSE"

Grammar

The question is a single independent clause in which the subject *spice-rose* pairs with the verb *can drip*. The direct object is *fragrance*, which is described by the adjective *acrid* and the participial phrase *hardened in a leaf*.

Rhetoric

The sentence is a *rhetorical question*; H.D. clearly expects a negative reply.

Additional Information and Activities

- Imagist poetry was prominent in the early twentieth century. Famous imagists include Ezra Pound, William Carlos Williams, Amy Lowell, and H.D. Students can select an image from a different poem and compare it to the "Sea Rose."

- Roses are traditional Valentine's Day gifts that, in stereotyped gender roles, a male lover presents to his female beloved. The poem refers to "single on a stem," reinforcing the link to Valentine's Day. Roses are also associated with feminine beauty. H.D.'s poem refutes a common image of beauty as delicate and perfect. A good discussion might focus on the argument made by feminists that a single definition of beauty is both unrealistic and unfair.

Norton Juster, *The Phantom Tollbooth*

Milo nibbled carefully at the letter and discovered that it was quite sweet and delicious—just the way you'd expect an A to taste.

Brief context: Milo, during a fantastic journey, eats the letter A, which has been offered to him at a market.

Extended context: *The Phantom Tollbooth* describes what happens when a bored little boy, Milo, receives a mysterious present, the tollbooth of the title. His journey is one long wordplay: the "watchdog" is a canine whose body is a clock, a "spelling bee" is a buzzing insect that spells aloud, and a "light meal" is nothing but shining beams. This sentence comes from Milo's visit to a market where all sorts of words are for sale. Milo samples an A at the "DO IT YOURSELF" stall, where the vendor gobbles a G and an R while their juices "drip down his chin." The C is "crunchy," but X tastes "like a trunkful of stale air," which, the vendor explains, is why so few people use that letter. Milo eventually rescues two princesses, Rhyme and Reason, and returns them to their rightful place in the kingdom of Wisdom.

Analysis

With brief context:

- What senses do you associate with the letter A? (sight and hearing)
- Which sense is associated with A in this sentence? (taste)
- How does A taste? (*sweet, delicious*)
- What does the verb *nibbled carefully* bring to mind? (small bites, perhaps motivated by caution or courtesy)
- What about the verb *discovered*? What's the effect of that choice on the reader? (implies that Milo is surprised, as the reader may be; links Milo's experience with the reader's)
- How does the sentence change after the dash? (instead of surprise, this part settles into what *you'd expect*; the unusual is now normal; *you* connects the reader to *Milo*, making his experience more universal)

With extended context, add these points:

- The A tastes good and the X doesn't. What point is the author making, in a humorous way? (gravitate to what we enjoy and avoid the unpleasant)
- Milo is eating the letter at a stall called "DO IT YOURSELF." What does that tell you about the scene? (buyers create their own words from letters; other stalls sell complete words)
- Compare this sentence to the "watchdog," "spelling bee," and "light meal." How does it match or differ? (match: imaginative, fantastical; differ: dog, tree, and meal are literal interpretations of common expressions but the letter's taste is synesthetic)
- What point is the author making about wisdom? ("rhyme" and "reason" are necessary there; these words represent pattern and order, which are also needed for wisdom to flourish)

SUPPLEMENTAL MATERIAL FOR
THE PHANTOM TOLLBOOTH

Grammar

- Everything preceding the dash is one independent clause, with *Milo* as the subject paired with a compound verb, *nibbled* and *discovered*.
- A noun clause (*that it was quite sweet and delicious*) is the direct object of *discovered*. Within the noun clause, *was* is a linking verb completed by the subject complements *sweet* and *delicious*.
- The words following the dash function as an appositive to *sweet and delicious*. The core word in the appositive is *way*, which is modified by an adjective clause, *you'd expect an A to taste*.

Rhetoric

Assigning taste to a letter is an example of *synesthesia*.

Additional Information and Activities

- Norton Juster's *The Phantom Tollbooth* is filled with synesthesia. An additional example: the orchestra conductor coaxes color, not sound, from his musicians, playing the day in with increasingly intense, multicolored light. To increase students' appreciation of wordplay, assign the whole text.
- The audio version of the novel brings still another sense into the mix. Consider playing a few minutes in class.

MORE SYNESTHESIA

The examples of synesthesia are underlined.

A billion or so <u>flavors</u>, none of them quite the same, and a <u>sky</u> to slowly suck on.   —Markus Zusak, *The Book Thief*

She had been cooking and the house <u>smelled of sentiment</u>, a rich aroma of beef broth and star anise I can only describe as the

bouquet of love and tenderness, all the more striking because
Madame had never cooked before coming to this country.
                                —Viet Thanh Nguyen, *The Sympathizer*

Little could be heard over the squawking of the Diricawls, the
moaning of the Augureys and the relentless, piercing song of the
Fwoopers.   —J. K. Rowling, *Fantastic Beasts and Where to Find Them*

"I'm the pitcher," Molly said, each word an ice cube slipped down
the back of Max's pants.   —Anne Ursu, "Max Swings for the Fences"

It [the sound of parents fighting] sits in my chest, hitting, hitting
my heart until my eyes bleed water from the sea.
                                        —An Na, *A Step from Heaven*

As my grandfather went, arm over arm, his heart making sour little
shudders against his ribs, he kept listening for a sound, the sound
of the tiger, the sound of anything but his own feet and lungs.
                                        —Téa Obreht, *The Tiger's Wife*

The voice is a second face.
                        —Gérard Bauer, *Carnets d'un voyageur Traque*

Language most shows a man: Speak, that I may see thee.
                                —Ben Jonson, *Timber; or Discoveries*

The words of his mouth were smoother than butter, but war was
in his heart: his words were softer than oil, yet were they drawn
swords.   —Psalm 55, King James Bible

To find more synesthesia, listen to Taylor Swift's song "Red," which attaches
color to emotions, or consult *Like Water for Chocolate* by Laura Esquivel,
which mixes emotions and taste. Robert Hayden, in his poem "Those Winter
Sundays," employs synesthesia in nearly every line to describe a parent-
child relationship.

WRITING ASSIGNMENTS

Choose any sentence in this chapter as a model, or randomly assign two senses and ask students to write a sentence that braids them together. More possible tasks are below.

Paint Swatching

Gather a handful of paint samples. Remove or obscure the assigned names of the colors and distribute the cards to the students. Have them write a sentence or a paragraph describing how each color smells, sounds, and feels (tactile or emotional). To extend the lesson, ask them to explain their reasoning.

Music to My Eyes

Select a wordless audio track: I've found that Rossini's *William Tell* Overture, Rimsky-Korsakov's *Scheherazade*, and Miles Davis's album *Kind of Blue* work well. I'd avoid something closely associated with a film; it's hard not to see a giant shark when you listen to the opening notes of *Jaws*. Play a few minutes of the work while students jot down what they see, smell, and sense tactilely. Have them fashion one of those impressions into a descriptive sentence.

Art Swap

Show an abstract painting (a work by Rothko, Pollock, Krasner, Frankenthaler, or other artist). What does the painting sound like? How does the image smell? Feel? Cross as many senses as possible.

TIME MARKERS

• •

About two months into my first year of teaching, a high school senior asked me how people danced when I was young. I was twenty-two, she eighteen, but the years didn't matter to her. She was measuring time by the chasm that lay between us as teacher and student.

And she was on to something. We English teachers spend a lot of class time on time, explaining the function of verb tenses and helping students select the right one for whatever they're trying to say. In the real world, though, time is not just on the clock: it's events, life stages, and changing perspectives. The beauty of words, and of great sentences, is that they're unbound by natural law. A sentence can flick through centuries, see into the future, and take readers back to infancy or ahead to old age. A study of how time works in a sentence, either through verb tense or in another way, is a path to creativity and, perhaps, to insight.

TEACHING TIME: A GENERAL PLAN

Introduction (optional)

Time, as in "there's never enough" or "are we there yet?" is a universal, 24/7 thrum in our lives. That means it's easy to overlook how writers shape time references. Focus your students' attention on creative time references with this activity: Challenge them to select a decade and convey it with three, nontime references: *Kennedy*, *hippies*, and *Vietnam* for the 1960s, for example. This exercise, of course, requires some knowledge of history and thus is better for older students. With younger, less historically informed kids, narrow the time frame to a season, such as *unsharpened pencils*, *blank notebooks*, and *alarm clocks* for back-to-school month.

Decoding

- Which words refer to time?
- What time period do those words refer to? (depending on the sentence: past, present, future; span of time; stage of life; historical era)
- Does the sentence refer to more than one time period? If so, which ones?

Analysis

- Is the time period clearly stated or is it implied?
- Why has the author chosen to state or to imply the time?
- Is time an important factor in the sentence or just an extra detail?
- If there's a change in perspective ("had I but known," for example) why is the change important?
- Check for figurative language—allusions such as those I list in the first introductory exercise, or similes and metaphors. What does figurative language add to the sentence? If that element were removed and a date inserted, what would the sentence gain or lose?

TEACHING TIME: LESSON PLANS

J. K. Rowling, *Fantastic Beasts and Where to Find Them* by Newt Scamander

I look back across the years to the seven-year-old wizard who spent hours in his bedroom dismembering Horklumps and I envy him the journeys to come: from darkest jungle to brightest desert, from mountain peak to marshy bog, that grubby Horklump-encrusted boy would track, as he grew up, the beasts described in the following pages.

Brief context: This sentence comes from the introduction to a textbook on magical animals assigned to students at Hogwarts.

Extended context: J. K. Rowling's fertile imagination gave rise to the Harry Potter books, and to the "Potterverse" she created within them. Newt Scamander, the supposed author of the textbook *Fantastic Beasts and Where to Find Them*, is a character in a spin-off of that series. *Fantastic Beasts and Where to Find Them* is a single-volume encyclopedia of information about the title characters: their appearance, food preferences, potential danger to wizards, habitat, and so forth. Scamander's introduction recounts the wizards' debate over the definition of "beast" and briefly refers, in this sentence, to the author's childhood and career.

Analysis

With brief context:

- Identify the time clues in this sentence. (*look back across the years, hours, seven-year-old, to come, would track, grew up*)
- What time periods does this sentence reference? (present, when Scamander is writing: *I look back*; distant past—Scamander's childhood: *seven-year-old wizard*; more recent past: *journeys to come* that Scamander took throughout his career)
- Does the sentence say anything about the future? (not from the point of view of the author as he writes, but when the author remembers himself at seven, he mentions *journeys* he will take)
- What do the time references tell you about the author? (now older, reflecting on his past and the origins of his career in "magizoology")

With extended context:

- What perspective has Newt Scamander gained over the years? How do you know? (sees himself as fortunate to have gone on *journeys . . . from darkest jungle to brightest desert, from mountain peak to marshy bog*— he feels *envy* because his younger self will have a chance to go on those journeys, implies regret that he's past that stage of life but proud of his accomplishments)
- What does the book represent to Scamander? How do you know? (sum total of what he's learned—an encyclopedia; pride in his accomplishments conveyed by his description of his *journeys*)

SUPPLEMENTAL MATERIAL FOR *FANTASTIC BEASTS AND WHERE TO FIND THEM*

Grammar

- The clauses in this sentence entwine, much as the narrator's past and present entwine.
- The sentence comprises three independent clauses: (1) *I look back across the years to the seven-year-old wizard* (2) *I envy him the journeys to come* (3) *that grubby Horklump-encrusted boy would track . . . the beasts described in the following pages.* The first two independent clauses are in the present tense, with a first-person point of view, because Scamander is thinking about what he's done and what he's learned. The third clause inserts the narrator into the past, looking forward to what he now knows will happen. Scamander is looking at his younger self, so he adopts third-person point of view in this clause.
- Within those independent clauses are two dependent clauses. The first, *who spent hours in his bedroom dismembering Horklumps*, describes *wizard*; the second, *as he grew up*, describes *would track*. Both dependent clauses situate the activities they describe in specific time periods, childhood and early adulthood.
- A participial phrase, *described in these pages*, modifies *beasts*. This construction puts the spotlight on *beasts*. If it were revised to *I describe*, the narrator would be more important than the *beasts*—the opposite of the way Scamander sees himself.
- A string of prepositional phrases (*from darkest jungle to brightest desert, from mountain peak to marshy bog*) trace where the author *would track*. They precede the subject (*that grubby, Horklump-encrusted boy*) because the journeys are more important to Scamander than he himself is.

Additional Information and Activities

- Rowling parodies the stuffy tone of old textbooks and memoirs, as well as the nostalgic tone of an older person looking back at youth. Students might enjoy comparing Rowling's parody with introductions to a late nineteenth- or early twentieth-century text. A good online source is Project Gutenberg.

- Fantastic beasts have roamed the human imagination for centuries, and they're fun to research. Students might select a beast from the Harry Potter series or elsewhere and report on it to the class.
- A psychology/English project can examine why so many people believe in supernatural creatures.

> ## Jane Austen, *Mansfield Park*
>
> I only entreat everybody to believe that exactly at the time when it was quite natural that it should be so, and not a week earlier, Edmund did cease to care about Miss Crawford, and became as anxious to marry Fanny as Fanny herself could desire.

Brief context: This sentence describes a happy ending when Edmund realizes that Fanny, not Miss Crawford, is his true love.

Extended context: Despite the ladylike gowns and surface politeness of her novels, Jane Austen was a vicious writer who delighted in skewering the foolish, dishonest, or hypocritical. Happiness bored her, and so, as this sentence indicates, did happy endings. For hundreds of pages Fanny has been pining over Edmund, a young man about to become a minister whose romantic attention has been directed to Miss Crawford. Fanny has a solid moral foundation to guide her behavior, but Miss Crawford does not. Edmund finally understands that Miss Crawford would not be a good life partner and proposes to Fanny, who accepts.

Analysis

With brief context:

- What are the time markers in this sentence? (*exactly at the time, not a week earlier*)
- How much time elapses between Edmund's attraction to Miss Crawford ends and his attraction to Fanny begins? (impossible to know)

- How does Austen characterize the moment when Edmund realizes that he loves Fanny? (*when it was quite natural*)
- Why doesn't Austen specify the time period? (each person's love is unique, as is each relationship)
- How does Austen's vagueness affect the reader? (varied answers: some frustrated, others pleased that their views shape the story)

With extended context:

- How does this sentence reflect Austen's lack of interest in happy endings? (no buildup to or description of the proposal)
- Why might Edmund's feelings have changed? (aspiring to the ministry, presumably values morality)
- What gender roles does this sentence reflect? (the man must actively ask, the woman passively wait)

SUPPLEMENTAL MATERIAL FOR *MANSFIELD PARK*

Grammar

- The first-person point of view, directly from the author, is unusual, as the rest of the novel is told from the third-person point of view.
- The clarifier *and not a week earlier* is set off by commas. That's the punctuation format for nonessential information that can be lifted out of the sentence without changing the meaning. Austen's making a point about what is *quite natural*: the amount of time doesn't matter, because nature—in this case, human nature—will proceed at its own pace.
- The verb *did cease* adds an emphatic note to the sentence. Had Austen substituted *ceased*, readers would still understand what happened. Adding *did* makes the sentence resemble an argument along the lines of "I know you think he didn't but he did!" The first verb in the sentence, *entreat*, has a similar tone. Austen begs for belief that true love will prevail *exactly* when it should.

Additional Information and Activities

- Austen's novels have been adapted for film and television many times. For an arts/English project, students might watch the final Edmund-loves-Fanny scene and compare the text to what they see.
- In her other novels, Austen's female protagonist (and often the male love interest) must grow and change before reaching a happy ending. In *Mansfield Park*, though, Fanny is a steady center. Discuss the relative merits of static and dynamic characters.

Renée Watson, "Half a Moon"

As soon as I see her, my heart vibrates and my mind replays ages seven and eight and nine and ten, and eleven and twelve and all the years without my dad, because the girl on the bus sitting on a seat by herself is my dad's daughter.

Brief context: The narrator's father and mother are divorced; the father has another daughter whom the narrator knows of and, in this scene, sees for the first time.

Extended context: The narrator is a camp counselor. She believes that her father left the family because of his relationship with another woman, who became pregnant. The narrator blames her half-sister for her father's absence from her life. In this sentence, the two are on the way to camp, the narrator as a counselor and her *dad's daughter* as a camper. Told by a wise adult that there is no such thing as a "half-sister," just as there is no such thing as "half a moon," the narrator comes to accept the girl as a family member.

Analysis

With brief context:

- What are the time markers in this sentence? (*soon as, ages seven and eight and nine and ten, and eleven and twelve and all the years*)

- Why does the narrator specify *as soon as*? (to convey an immediate, instinctive reaction; a sense that she's surprised and overwhelmed)
- What does the list of years signify? (time without the father)
- Why count out each year? (gives the impression that the years passed slowly, each weighing heavily on the narrator)
- One comma appears in the list, separating *eleven and twelve and all the years* from the preceding four years. Why? (varied answers: much changes at eleven—nearly a teenager, onset of puberty, beginning of middle school)

With extended context:

- What else does the list of years reveal about the narrator's feelings? (blames her sister, the list sounds like an indictment, each year a crime)
- How does the title relate to this sentence? (moon cycles measure time, the narrator counts years without the father)
- Why "half a moon"? (the entire moon exists, even the parts that are not visible at a particular time; the sisters exist, even though they aren't in each other's lives until camp begins)

MORE TIME

As the lesson plans illustrate, time may be expressed specifically or kept deliberately vague. It may also be the subject of the sentence: the nature or meaning of time itself. In this section are a few additional sentences, with comments where needed, that work well in lessons structured like those above.

> If I am to speak for ten minutes, I need a week for preparation; if fifteen minutes, three days; if half an hour, two days; if an hour, I am ready now.
>
> —Woodrow Wilson (president of the United States, 1913–21)

> Life seemed to be an educator's practical joke in which you spent the first half learning and the second half learning that everything you learned in the first half was wrong.
>
> —Russell Baker, "Back to the Dump"

At this age she has chin-to-chest disease, but even so you can see
how riveting are her dewy green eyes.

> —Gish Jen, *Mona in the Promised Land* (referring to a middle-schooler)

Even while a thing is in the act of coming into existence, some part
of it has already ceased to be.   —Marcus Aurelius, *Meditations*

"It's everything I do," Ms. Sikes said.
Did.   —Frances Robles, "They Paid Nearly a Half Million in Ransom"
> (newspaper article about the custodian of records for Lake
> City, Florida, whose electronic records were
> encrypted and held for ransom)

Nothing's so beautiful as the memory of it.

> —Charles Wright, "A Journal of the Year of the Ox"

The time not to become a father is eighteen years before a war.

> —E. B. White

It is the time you have wasted for your rose that makes your rose so
important.   —Antoine de Saint-Exupéry, *The Little Prince*

But most of what we saw foretold the future. Automobiles and
airships and moving pictures.

> —Richard Peck, "The Electric Summer"

At the time I first realized I might be fictional, my weekdays
were spent at a publicly funded institution on the north side of
Indianapolis called White River High School, where I was required
to eat lunch at a particular time—between 12:37 p.m. and 1:14
p.m.—by forces so much larger than myself that I couldn't even
begin to identify them.

> —John Green, *Turtles All the Way Down* (narrator has obsessive-
> compulsive thoughts, in this sentence about being
> nothing more than a vehicle for microbes)

I sit beside the fire and think
Of people long ago
And people that will see a world
That I shall never know.
>   —J. R. R. Tolkien, *The Lord of the Rings* (from a song that
>   Bilbo Baggins sings, looking back over his life)

My evening visitors, if they cannot see the clock, should be able to
find the time on my face.
>   —Ralph Waldo Emerson (1842 journal entry)

She was a handsome woman of 45 and would remain so for many
years.   —Anita Brookner, *Hotel du Lac*

"It's never o'clock," he said.
>   —Will Hunt, *Underground* (comment from a researcher in a cave far below
>   the surface of the earth, with constant temperature and complete darkness)

West said he had to pursue "what's-the-earliest-date-by-which-you-
can't-prove-you-won't-be-finished" scheduling in this case.
>   —Tracy Kidder, *The Soul of a New Machine* (refers to computer pioneer Tom
>   West, pushing his team to create an advanced computer very quickly)

WRITING ASSIGNMENTS

Apart from modeling, try these assignments. In all of them, time is more
than a deadline.

Stages of Life

The exercise has a double benefit: not only will students practice inserting time
markers, but they will also learn the power of allusions. Ask for three nontime
references to a stage of life, such as *finger painting, a bicycle with training
wheels*, and *bedtime stories* for childhood. Fair warning: This exercise may elicit
stereotypes. Prepare for a discussion of why stereotypes exist and what effect
they may have on the group they're applied to.

Split Screen

A popular television drama hops back and forth in time, showing the same characters at different moments in their lives: a scene featuring parents with a toddler, for example, might suddenly shift to that child, all grown up, dealing with his own kids. Challenge students to express two moments of one life in a single sentence. An example:

> **Lucy, checking her phone every two minutes, waited for her blind date at a restaurant around the corner from the nursery school their son would walk into seven years later, head turned for a reassuring glimpse of Mommy and Daddy.**

Extra credit: Have them fashion a fully developed story based on their sentence.

Definitions

What is time, exactly? Don't let them rest on a dictionary definition. Instead, ask them to think about what time means in their life. In *The Glass Menagerie*, for instance, Tennessee Williams defines time as "the longest distance between two places." What's their take?

The Songs of Time

A fair number of songs concern time. A few suggestions:

"The Times They Are A-Changin'" (Bob Dylan)
"Time After Time" (Cyndi Lauper)
"It's Time" (Imagine Dragons)
"Take Your Time" (Sam Hunt)
"Sign of the Time" (Harry Styles)
"As Time Goes By" (Dooley Wilson)
"Cat's in the Cradle" (Harry Chapin)

Play one of these, or ask students to bring in their favorite time songs. How is time expressed in the song? Can they write an extra sentence for the song? Tell them not to worry, initially, about rhyme and rhythm. Start with the concept. Later, if they wish, they can revise their sentences to suit the music.

CONTRAST

• •

When I pull socks from my drawer, I can't tell navy blue from black until I hold the two next to each other. Contrast enhances my perception. As with socks, so too with writing, whether the contrasting elements have billboard-sized differences or atomic-level variations. Perhaps the best quality of contrast is its versatility. It may define, as in Arthur Ashe's declaration that true hero-ism is "not the urge to surpass all others at whatever cost, but the urge to serve others at whatever cost," which contrasts *surpass* and *serve.* Contrast also describes, as in Robert Benchley's observation that in America there are "two classes of travel . . . first class and with children." Contrast establishes relative importance: The first person on the moon, astronaut Neil Armstrong, took "one small step for a man" and "one giant leap for mankind." Moreover, con-trast may warn, as it does in Andrew Young's statement: "People who think education is expensive have never counted the cost of ignorance."

Students most likely have written compare/contrast essays, so the concept needs little introduction. The true potential of contrast, though, may not be as obvious until they take a closer look.

TEACHING CONTRAST: A GENERAL PLAN

Introduction (optional)

This is my favorite activity to begin a study of contrast:

- Go shopping for small edibles. I use blueberries and grapes, but other combinations also work.
- Stash the grapes where they won't be seen. Drop a blueberry on each desk. Ask for a list of descriptive words or phrases. When students are finished, they can eat the blueberry or throw it in the compost bin.
- Now distribute the grapes, one per student. Ask for another list of descriptions. This time, don't let them eat or discard the grape when they've completed their lists.
- Last "course": place a new blueberry next to each grape. Have students reread their lists and add anything they missed the first time.

- Have their lists grown longer? Most often, the answer is yes, because now they're contrasting the two.
- Full disclosure: I have fallen flat on my face with the exercise at times. But when it works, it works really well. And when it fails, I explain what I thought would happen. Either way, I've focused their attention on contrast. Plus, they like the snack.

Decoding

- After the usual vocabulary and syntax explication, have students identify contrasting elements.
- Is the contrast implied or stated directly? Ask them to restate the contrast in their own words.

Analysis

- Is one element of the contrast more important than the other? How do you know?
- What's the purpose of the contrast? How do you know?
- Have students reword the sentence to make the same point, but without contrast. How does the effect on the reader change? Which version do they prefer?

TEACHING CONTRAST: LESSON PLANS

> ### Clayton E. Wheat, "West Point Cadet Prayer"
>
> **Make us to choose the harder right instead of the easier wrong, and never to be content with a half truth when the whole can be won.**

Brief context: This sentence appears on a plaque at the United States Military Academy at West Point, New York.

Extended context: Embodying the values of the institution ("Duty • Honor • Country"), the West Point Cadet prayer is nondenominational but acknowledges a higher power. In other sentences, the prayer asks for greater "admiration for honest dealing and clean thinking" and continuing hatred for "hypocrisy and pretense." The prayer also seeks "courage that is born of loyalty to all that is noble and worthy, that scorns to compromise with vice and injustice." Further, it asks for loyalty, cheerfulness, and "new opportunities of service."

Analysis

With brief context:

- The first contrast in this sentence is between *the harder right* and *the easier wrong*. Why not simply *right* and *wrong*? (intensifies the contrast, implies that choosing what is *right* leads to difficult experiences; issues a challenge)
- What's the significance of the second contrast between *half truth* and *the whole* [that] *can be won*? (another challenge: to go the distance; also, *the whole* must *be won*—implies that it's a fight)
- How does this contrast relate to the military? (future soldiers will face difficulties and must not give up)

With extended context:

- How does this contrast relate to the values of West Point? (duty and honor: ethical behavior instead of the easy way out; giving one's all, not accepting less than full truth)
- How does this contrast relate to the rest of the prayer? (same values; similar to the contrast between *noble and worthy* and *vice and injustice*)

SUPPLEMENTAL MATERIAL FOR "WEST POINT CADET PRAYER"

Grammar

- The sentence is imperative (*Make us*).
- In the second infinitive phrase (*never to be content . . . won*) the verb is passive (*can be won*). This structure emphasizes the goal (the *whole* truth) over the individual.

Rhetoric

- The contrasted elements are *parallel*.
- Because they're opposites, the contrasted elements are an example of *antithesis*.

Additional Information and Activities

- The entire prayer can be found at the West Point website. Discuss how the prayer is unified both in theme and in structure.
- Chapel attendance was mandatory at West Point until the 1970s, when it became optional. At least one lawsuit, *Anderson v. Laird* (D.C. Cir. 1972), challenged the obligatory recital of this prayer as a violation of the First Amendment (freedom of religion). You may wish to assign a research project on church/state separation.

> Clementine Hunter, quoted in Shelby R. Gilley,
> *Painting by Heart*
>
> **Cotton's right there for you to pull off the stalk, but to paint, you got to sweat your mind.**

Brief context: The person who said this was an acclaimed artist who picked cotton for many years to support herself.

Extended context: Clementine Hunter (1886–1988) lived her entire, very long life in Louisiana, not far from where her grandparents had once been enslaved. Hunter had little formal education. From an early age she worked in the fields, picking cotton on a plantation owned by a patron of the arts. Many writers and visual artists visited; one artist gave Hunter leftover materials. She immediately began to paint on every surface she could find: the walls of her house, discarded boxes, a window shade, and so forth. Her work depicts African American life in the early twentieth century: fieldwork, community gatherings, weddings, funerals, and the like. Sold for as little as 25 cents at first, her paintings soon caught the attention of curators and were exhibited in museums and galleries. Today she is considered one of the most important American folk artists. To paint a picture, she said, "it has to come in my head."

Analysis

With brief context:

- What elements are contrasted? (picking cotton, painting)
- How are they different, as depicted in this sentence? (one is physical, one mental)
- Which one is harder, according to the speaker? (painting, because it isn't *right there*; you have to *sweat your mind* to paint)
- What's the significance of *sweat your mind*? (most people associate *sweat* with physical labor, but Hunter associates it with creativity; emphasizes the effort that painting entails)

With extended context:

- Why is Clementine Hunter uniquely qualified to make this statement? (she's done both)
- How does this sentence relate to her approach to painting? (the picture "has to come in my head")
- How does the sentence relate to Hunter's life? (lack of formal education shows in her language; her point of view was shaped by direct experience with fieldwork and art)

SUPPLEMENTAL MATERIAL FOR CLEMENTINE HUNTER

Grammar

- This compound sentence has two clauses joined by the conjunction *but*.
- The subject of the first clause is *Cotton*, combined with the contracted verb *is*. In the second clause, the subject is *you*. Normally, *you* pairs with *have*, but Hunter uses the more colloquial form, *got*.
- There are two infinitive phrases: *To pull off the stalk* modifies *right there*; *to paint* is the object of the implied preposition, *in order to*.

Additional Information and Activities

- This sentence might be the basis for a history/English research project on African American rural life in the early twentieth century. An arts/English project might explore folk art.
- Clementine Hunter's sentence is vivid and unconventional. Discuss the role and limitations of standard English. What's gained when you break a rule? Anything lost? When is each appropriate?

> ### Jane Austen, *Sense and Sensibility*
>
> **Seven years would be insufficient to make some people acquainted with each other, and seven days are more than enough for others.**

Brief context: This is a comment from a young woman who has accepted an expensive gift from a man she's known only for a short while.

Extended context: The character who says this is Marianne Dashwood, who exhibits the "sensibility" of the title. The term, which refers to extreme emotional reactions, became popular in Jane Austen's time. To those who admired the concept, sensibility was a hallmark of an open mind, characteristic of a person receptive to beauty and keyed in to others' emotions. Marianne's sentence is a reply to her sister, Eleanor Dashwood, the "sense" of the title. Eleanor thinks, and sometimes overthinks, every situation. The siblings are protagonists of Austen's novel, which, like all her novels, deals with the romantic attachments and marriage prospects of the characters.

Analysis

With brief context:

- What's the contrast in this sentence? (*Seven years, seven days*)
- Why these time periods? What do they add to the sentence? (extremes: one quite long and one very short)
- How does contrast reveal the speaker's point? (people can know each

other for a very long time without forming a relationship, but in the right circumstances, they may quickly become close)

- Why does the character say this? (to defend her acceptance of the gift—it's not from a stranger)

With extended context:

- What can you infer about the character from this sentence? (comfortable with extremes, relies on emotions instead of numbers)
- Without the contrast, what would Marianne say to her sister? ("Time doesn't matter," "love at first sight," "numbers are irrelevant when it comes to emotions," and so forth)
- What does the contrast add? (shows Marianne's tendency to exaggerate; creation of two groups: "some people" and "others")

SUPPLEMENTAL MATERIAL FOR *SENSE AND SENSIBILITY*

Grammar

The sentence has two independent clauses joined by the conjunction *and*. Fittingly, the clause referring to *seven years* is longer than the one referring to *seven days*.

Additional Information and Activities

- Austen's novel has been adapted for television and film several times. A comparison of the scene in the book and its representation on screen would contrast the two media (a good fit for this topic).
- In Austen's time, sensibility was associated with a weak nervous system. A common belief was that those with sensibility were prone to fainting and hysteria. A psychology/English project might focus on the relationship between physical symptoms and emotions. A project focused on stereotypes of women may also arise from this sentence.
- Spoiler alert: Eleanor has to become more emotional and Marianne less so before each is ready to form a mature relationship. In other words, the protagonists contrast with one another. If the class reads the entire novel,

students can trace the evolution of the sisters and perhaps infer Austen's attitude toward sensibility.

MORE CONTRASTS

A few more, fairly self-explanatory contrasts:

Dogs have masters, cats have staff.
—internet meme (note: Some substitute "human companions" for "masters.")

I did not just fall in love, I made a parachute jump.
—Zora Neale Hurston, *Dust Tracks on a Road*

Teaching is not a lost art, but regard for it is a lost tradition.
—Jacques Barzun (educator and historian, in an interview)

It doesn't matter who my father was; it matters who I remembered he was. —Anne Sexton, *A Small Journal*

It's not the man, it's the plan. —Ossie Davis (actor and activist, 1971 speech to the Congressional Black Caucus)

Your skull was not made to put ideas in, it was made to throw potatoes at. —Mark Twain, (unsent response to a letter of complaint)

The tyrant dies and his rule is over; the martyr dies and his rule begins. —Søren Kierkegaard (philosopher)

There is only eighteen inches between a pat on the back and a kick in the seat of the pants.
—Hattie McDaniel (actor, in an interview)

What a man must know, a boy must learn.
—*The Lookouts* (comic book series)

Some say the world will end in fire,
Some say in ice.   —Robert Frost, "Fire and Ice"

You can cage the singer but not the song.
                        —Harry Belafonte (singer and activist, in an interview)

I come to bury Caesar, not to praise him.
                        —Shakespeare, *Julius Caesar* (Act 3, scene 2)

WRITING ASSIGNMENTS

Am / Was

Nothing's more interesting to kids—actually, to all of us— than their own lives. To encourage contrast, ask students to think about themselves five years ago and now. How have they changed? They should generate a private list of contrasting personality traits, habits, activities, likes/dislikes, or goals. They select some and plug them into this structure:

_____ used to be _____ but now _____

Encourage them to go beyond the literal level. Perhaps someone used to lack confidence but now isn't afraid to speak up, as in this sentence:

I used to whisper, but now I brass-band everything.

NOTE: If you or your students have concerns about privacy, they can write about fictional characters.

Is / Isn't

A dictionary definition is useful but oh so ordinary. Try contrast, instead. Have the class brainstorm some abstract qualities: responsibility, leadership, failure, hope, maturity, and so on. Challenge them to create a contrasting definition, one that states what the quality is as well as what it isn't, moving beyond the literal level. A possible response:

> Maturity doesn't mean you've walked down every path but instead that you know you don't have to walk down every path.

A variation of this exercise deals with closely related concepts, highlighting the contrast. An example:

> To patriots, everything that affects their country matters, but to nationalists, only their country matters.

Subtleties

It's easy to contrast an elephant and a mouse, but what about two elephants? Or two mice? There's no perfect match, even when two people, things, or places appear identical. Even clones differ, once life and time change them. This exercise directs students' attention to small variations, the tiny contrasting elements that confer uniqueness.

I like to start with clothing: a pair of shoes or gloves, for example. Have students look closely at the items and write a sentence showing how they differ. For example:

> You can tell that my gloves have been through a lot of snowball fights recently, with a tear in the left (my throwing arm) and some salt stains in the right, where I store ammunition.

I sometimes assign this exercise for two of Andy Warhol's "identical" paintings: his portraits of Marilyn Monroe or Campbell's soup cans, for example. I show the images and ask for a sentence contrasting two versions of the same subject. If students examine the images carefully, they see variations in tint or line.

APPENDIX A

THEMES

I've sorted the sentences into broad themes, based on either the content of the sentence or the work it's drawn from. The author and the first three words of the sentence appear; search the index by author name to locate the sentence in the text. Asterisks (*) indicate sentences I've used successfully with younger students.

ART/CREATIVITY

Adler, Mortimer. "In the case"
*Alcott, Louisa May. "Does genius burn"
*Alter, Alexandra. "Jim Kay's favorite"
Atwood, Margaret. "There's no doubt"
*Austen, Jane. "I think I"
*Belafonte, Harry. "You can cage"
*Bennett, Alan. "I'm all in"
*Binchy, Maeve. "I don't have"
*Calvino, Italo. "A classic is"
Chandler, Raymond. "I killed my"
Connolly, Cyril. "Better to write"
*Cummings, E. E. "[an artist] is"
*Ellington, Duke. "Playing 'bop' is"
*Ellison, Ralph.
    "Shoes, a coat"
    "So don't worry"
*Evans, Walker. "Stare, pry, listen"

Fateman, Johanna. "If it slams"
*Flaubert, Gustave. "Of all lies"
Godden, Rumer. "As she [Madame]"
Graves, Robert. "If there's no"
Harwood, Ronald. "To carry on"
*Henderson, Leah. "As I balloon"
*Hunter, Clementine. "Cotton's right there"
*Johnson, Samuel. "To write is"
*Jonson, Ben. "Language most shows"
Lamb, Charles. "A [pun] is"
Leon, Donna. "I have long"
*McLuhan, Marshall. "The medium is"
Oliver, Mary. "Would one tell"
Percy, Walker.
    "But for writers"
    "The total freedom"
Renkl, Margaret. "If you are"
Shakespeare, William.

337

"More matter with"
"Tis true, 'tis"

ART/CREATIVITY *cont.*

*Soloski, Alexis. "Nancy Drew, the"
Southey, Robert. "The arts babblative"
Strachey, Lytton. "Discretion is not"
Thomas, Dylan. "I'm a freak"
*Van Gogh, Vincent. "First I dream"

CAREERS

Barzun, Jacques. "Teaching is not"
*Cummings, E. E. "[an artist] is"
*Ellison, Ralph.
    "Shoes, a coat"
    "So don't worry"
*Evans, Walker. "Stare, pry, listen"
Ferris, Josh. "Some of us"
Graves, Robert. "If there's no"
*Hunter, Clementine. "Cotton's right
    there"
*James, P. D. "When I heard"
*Johnson, Samuel. "To write is"
Jones, Chris. "Studying the data"
Kidder, Tracy. "West said he"
*Livingston, Donovan. "Lift your voices"
McMurtry, Larry. "I have known"
Obama, Michelle. "I see now"
Percy, Walker.
    "But for writers"
    "The total freedom"
Sheridan, Richard Brinsley. "Sir, they
    [newspapers] are"
*Van Gogh, Vincent. "First I dream"

ETHICS/LAW/RELIGION/PHILOSOPHY

*Anonymous child. "I never asked"
Aurelius, Marcus. "Even while a"

*Barnhill, Kelly. "It's a terrible"
*Boyne, John. "What kind of"
Cervantes, Miguel de. "Until death, it"
Colin, Chris. "I thought that"
De Vries, Peter. "We're not primarily"
Dickinson, Emily. "Some things that "
Godden, Rumer. "As she [Madame]"
Graves, Robert. "If there's no"
*Hurston, Zora Neale. "Truth is a"
Jackson, Shirley. "The people of"
Kagan, Elena. "Like the binoculars"
*King, Martin Luther, Jr. "With this
    faith"
*Lao Tsu. "For one gains"
Leland, John. "Instead, there is"
*Macmillan, Harold. "Jaw-jaw is"
*Papyrus of Sobekmose. "O Heart that"
*Robeson, Paul. "To be free"
*Saint-Exupéry, Antoine de. "It is the"
*Steffens, Lincoln. "Morality is moral"
*Stewart, Potter. "Swift justice
    demands"
Tyson, Neil deGrasse. "We are all"
Vowell, Sarah. "Our good ship"
*Wheat, Clayton. "Make us to"
Woolf, Virginia. "What brought her"
Wright, Charles. "Nothing's so
    beautiful"

FAMILY RELATIONSHIPS

*Baptist, Kelly J. "Then I put"
*Boyne, John. "What kind of"
Brinkley, Jamel. "But his life"
*Cline-Ransome, Lesa. "Every day I"
Danticat, Edwidge. "My Madonna
    cried"
*De la Peña, Matt. "But over time"
De Vries, Peter. "The value of"
*Ellison, Ralph. "Shoes, a coat"

Ephron, Nora. "Your adolescent's weekly"
Flake, Emily. "But what is"
*Green, John. "Getting Harold's engine"
*Harrison, Jim. "Keep an eye"
*Hiaasen, Carl. "His mother caught"
Howe, Tina. "You then proceeded"
Jarrell, Randall. "It is not"
Kincaid, Jamaica. "Wash the white"
Kingsolver, Barbara. "You jump out"
Lardner, Ring. "George Gershwin is"
McLaughlin, Mignon. "The young are"
*Myers, Walter Dean. "But my daddy"
*Na, An. "It sits in"
Obama, Michelle. "I see now"
Obreht, Téa. "As my grandfather"
O'Gieblyn, Meghan. "Once she returned"
Orange, Tommy. "Except sometimes. When"
Resnik, Sarah. "You want to"
*Salinger, J. D. "If you really"
*Satrapi, Marjane. "The harder I"
Sexton, Anne. "It doesn't matter"
Shakespeare, William. "Full fathom five"
*Sugiura, Misa. "I wish, I"
Tan, Amy. "I went to"
*Taylor, Mildred D. "If that's what"
*Trillin, Calvin. "Blackstone declined to"
*Watson, Renée.
    "As soon as"
    "The dining hall"
*White, E. B.
    "So every morning"
    "The time not"

*Acevedo, Elizabeth. "The whole meal?"

*Auxier, Jonathan. "Nan would count"
*Bambara, Toni Cade. "So I'm strolling"
*Blake, William. "The bird a"
*Childress, Alice. "I am lonesome"
*Clements, Andrew. "If you asked"
*Danziger, Paula, and Ann M. Martin. "IF I DIDN'T"
De Vries, Peter. "We're not primarily"
*Emerson, Ralph Waldo. "My evening visitors"
Forster, E. M. "Only connect"
*Frozen. "Some people are"
Glaspell, Susan. "A new town"
*Henderson, Leah. "As I balloon"
Lamb, Caroline. "Mad, bad, and"
*Magoon, Kekla. "To be close"
*Marx, Groucho. "I don't care"
Thoreau, Henry David. "I have a"
*Tolkien, J. R. R. "I sit beside"
*Ursu, Anne.
    "I'm the pitcher"
    "'So?' Logan asked"
Wilde, Oscar. "Every great man"

*Anonymous child. "I never asked"
*Baker, Russell. "Life seemed to"
*Bambara, Toni Cade. "So I'm strolling"
Didion, Joan. "This failure could"
*Emerson, Ralph Waldo. "Do what you"
*Green, John.
    "At the time"
    "Getting Harold's engine"
    "Maybe you are"
*Jen, Gish. "At this age"
*Kermit the Frog. "You are no"
*Kinney, Jeff. "Let me just"
*Livingston, Donovan. "Lift your voices"
*Lookouts, The. "What a man"

*Redgate, Riley. "Monday morning was"
*Rowling, J. K. "I look back"
 Silverberg, Amy. "The age is"
*Watson, Renée, and Ellen Hagan. "Be
  butterfly stroke"

HISTORY

 Caro, Robert. "I hope that"
*Hamer, Fannie Lou. "I'm sick and"
 Hardy, Thomas. "And as the"
*Kennedy, John F. "Ask not what"
*King, Martin Luther, Jr. "With this
  faith"
*Luce, Clare Booth. "No woman has"
*Malcolm X. "We didn't land"
 McCrae, John. "Take up our"
 Mendelsohn, Jane. "Much later, when"
*Peck, Richard. "But most of"
*Robeson, Paul. "To be free"
*Roosevelt, Franklin. "So first of"
*Steinbeck, John. "You can see"
*Tubman, Harriet. "If you are"
 Whitman, Walt. "And still a"
 Wilson, Woodrow. "If I am"

HUMOR

*Anonymous child. "I never asked"
*Baptist, Kelly J. "Then I put"
 Berman, Miranda, and Gaby
  Moskowitz. "Frankly, I didn't"
 Brookner, Anita. "She was a"
*"Dogs have masters"
 Ephron, Nora. "Your adolescent's
  weekly"
 Frazier, Ian. "Casting for steelhead"
*Goldman, William. "I had a"
*Harrison, Jim. "Keep an eye"
 Hemon, Aleksander. "Among the
  Hemons"

 Lamb, Charles. "A [pun] is"
 Lardner, Ring. "A couple yrs"
 Leon, Donna. "I have long"
*Marx, Groucho. "I don't care"
*McDaniel, Hattie. "There is only"
*Mowatt, Farley. "That mood remained"
 Orwell, George. "A not unblack"
 Parker, Dorothy. "Every time the"
*Peck, Richard. "Her tongue's attached"
*Rizzuto, Phil. "When I was"
*Rowling, J. K. "Why should the"
 Schulz, Kathryn. "Wraiths only scare"
 Seinfeld. "I mean if"
 Sheridan, Richard Brinsley. "Sir, they
  [newspapers] are"
*Smith, Red. "Here were two"
*Stengel, Casey. "I've made up"
 Strachey, Lytton. "Discretion is not"
*Trillin, Calvin. "Blackstone declined to"
*Tucker, Sophie. "Keep breathing"
*Twain, Mark. "Your skull was"
*Uecker, Bob. "We tried to"
 Vowell, Sarah. "Our good ship"
 West, Mae. "I always say"
 Wilde, Oscar.
    "Every great man"
    "Some cause happiness"
 Wilson, Woodrow. "If I am"
 Yoachim, Caroline M. "You
  run down"

IDENTITY

*Adele. "To earn my"
*Alcott, Louisa May. "Does genius
  burn"
 Aurelius, Marcus. "Even while a"
*Austen, Jane. "I think I"
 Bauer, Gerard. "The voice is"
*Binchy, Maeve. "I don't have"
 Brookner, Anita. "She was a"

Buckley, Christopher. "Call me whatever"
Chekhov, Anton. "A carrot is"
Chin, Frank. "The music's run"
Choi, Yoon. "Every morning he"
*Clements, Andrew. "If you asked"
Crisp, Quentin. "If you describe"
*Cummings, E. E. "An artist is"
Didion, Joan. "the act of"
*Dunbar, Paul Laurence. "What dreams we"
Elliott, Alicia. "Even though she'd"
Glaspell, Susan. "A new town"
*Green, John. "Maybe you are"
*Hamer, Fannie Lou. "I'm sick and"
*Imagine Dragons. "Don't you tell"
*James, P. D. "When I heard"
Johnson, Georgia Douglas. "The heart of"
Kincaid, Jamaica. "Wash the white"
*King, Martin Luther, Jr. "With this faith"
Kingsolver, Barbara. "You jump out"
*Kinney, Jeff. "Let me just"
*Lookouts, The. "What a man"
*Lipsyte, Robert. "But he wasn't"
*Malcolm X. "We didn't land"
*Martí, José. "I have two"
McLaughlin, Mignon. "The young are"
McMurtry, Larry. "I have known"
Morales, Rosario, and Aurora Levins Morales. "I am a"
Oliver, Mary. "I had to"
*Platten, Rachel. "I have only"
*Redgate, Riley. "Monday morning was"
*Robeson, Paul. "To be free"
Rogers, Elizabeth Lindsay. "I was not"
*Satrapi, Marjane. "The harder I"
*Schmidt, Gary D. "The terrified eye"
Shakespeare, William. "Who's there?"
Smith, Zadie. "I am the"

Thomas, Dylan. "I'm a freak"
*Tolkien, J. R. R. "I sit beside"
*Tubman, Harriet. "If you are"
Tyson, Neil deGrasse. "We are all"
*Uecker, Bob. "We tried to"
*Watson, Renée, and Ellen Hagan. "Be butterfly stroke"
*Woodson, Jacqueline. "Your *only* ended"

LOVE

*Austen, Jane. "I only entreat"
Donne, John. "Our two souls"
Glaspell, Susan. "A new town"
Eilish, Billie. "Up all night"
*Hurston, Zora Neale. "I did not"
Johnson, Georgia Douglas. "The heart of"
Joyce, James. "Love loves to"
*Saint-Exupéry, Antoine de. "It is the"
Shakespeare, William. "That time of"
*Swift, Taylor. "My heart's been"

POLITICS/LEADERSHIP/LEADERS

*Barnhill, Kelly. "It's a terrible"
*Belafonte, Harry. "You can cage"
Burney, Fanny. "If you have"
Caro, Robert. "I hope that"
Colin, Chris. "I thought that"
*Davis, Ossie. "It's not the"
*Kennedy, John F. "Ask not what"
*Kierkegaard, Søren. "The tyrant dies"
*Macmillan, Harold. "Jaw-jaw is"
*Madariaga, Salvador de. "Nations don't distrust"
McLaughlin, Mignon. "The young are"
*Roosevelt, Franklin. "So first of"
Shakespeare, William. "I come to"

Vowell, Sarah. "Our good ship"
*Wheat, Clayton. "Make us to"
Wilde, Oscar. "Every great man"
Wilson, Woodrow. "If I am"
Wotton, Henry. "An ambassador is"

SCIENCE, NATURE, ENVIRONMENT

Bailey, Elisabeth Tova. "But when I"
Buhler, Brendan.
    "Think of your"
    "You are mostly"
Carson, Rachel.
    "Hard upon the"
    "It is also"
*Cudmore, Becca. "It's not that"
Dickinson, Emily. "Some things that"
*Dovey, Ceridwen. "The visual models"
Frazier, Ian. "Casting for steelhead"
Hemingway, Ernest. "You could ride"
*Hunt, Will. "I hesitated before"
Jones, Chris. "Studying the data"
Kingsolver, Barbara. "When the lump"
*Kingsolver, Barbara, and Steven Hopp.
    "Picture a scarlet"
*Kolbert, Elizabeth.
    "Today Greenland has"
    "This is 400"
Konnikova, Maria.
    "A plate was"
    "Consider what you"
Macfarlane, Robert. "This is the"
*Montgomery, Sy. "Many times I"
Powers, Richard. "There are no"
*Schmidt, Gary. D. "The terrified eye"
Tyson, Neil deGrasse. "We are all"

SCI-FI/FANTASY

Atwood, Margaret. "There's no doubt"
*Auxier, Jonathan. "Nan would count"

*Barrie, J. M. "Liza was in"
*Bond, Michael. "Without waiting for"
*De la Peña, Matt. "But over time"
*_Frozen_. "Some people are"
Game of Thrones. "The only time"
*Goldman, William.
    "But in the"
    "I had a"
    "I'm gonna heave"
*Juster, Norton. "Milo nibbled
    carefully"
*Lowry, Lois. "Yet he felt"
*Milne, A. A.
    "I am Sir"
    "I sometimes call"
*Riggs, Ransome. "Fireplaces were
    throttled"
*Rowling, J. K.
    "And then the"
    "I look back"
    "Little could be"
    "Why should the"
*Saint-Exupéry, Antoine de. "It is the"
Schulz, Kathryn. "Wraiths only scare"
*_Star Trek_. "Make it so"
*Thurber, James. "Somewhere a
    ponderous"
*Tolkien, J. R. R. "In a hole"
*Van Allsburg, Chris. "I was listening"
Vonnegut, Kurt. "So it goes"
*White, E. B. "So every morning"
*White, T.H. "There were several"
*Williams, Margery. "When a child"
*Wolven, Nick. "You got to"
Yoachim, Caroline M. "You run down"
Zusak, Markus. "A billion or"

SPORTS

*Bambara, Toni Cade. "So I'm strolling"
Frazier, Ian. "Casting for steelhead"

Friday Night Lights. "Clear eyes, full"
*Goldman, William. "I'm gonna heave"
 Kepner, Tyler. "Players across the"
*Larmer, Brook. "Now Li, the"
 Lardner, Ring. "A couple yrs"
*Lipsyte, Robert. "But he wasn't"
 Plimpton, George. "One heard the"
*Rizzuto, Phil. "When I was"
*Smith, Red. "Here were two"
*Stengel, Casey. "I've made up"
*Uecker, Bob. "We tried to"
*Ursu, Anne. "I'm the pitcher"

TRAVEL/LOCATION

Buckley, Christopher. "Call me
 whatever"
Carson, Rachel.
  "Hard upon the"

 "It is also"
 Glaspell, Susan. "A new town"
 Hemingway, Ernest. "You could ride"
 Hemon, Aleksander. "Even if I"
*Hunt, Will. "We go down"
*Kolbert, Elizabeth.
  "This is 400"
  "Today Greenland has"
 Li, Leslie. "The grizzled vendor"
 Macfarlane, Robert. "This is the"
 Morris, Jan. "Sometimes Sydney
  seems"
 Reed, Stanley. "The earth is"
 Rogers, Elizabeth Lindsay. "I was not"
 Simeti, Mary Taylor. "Strong and
  harsh"
*Steinbeck, John. "You can see"
*Yeats, William Butler "I will arise"

APPENDIX B

GENRE

I've sorted the sentences according to the work they are drawn from: long-form prose fiction, short stories, drama, poetry, religious texts, and nonfiction. The last category includes essays, articles, speeches, biography, autobiography, interviews, and letters. I've also listed sentences drawn from music lyrics, films, television, and comics separately. An asterisk indicates those works I've found suitable for younger students (middle-schoolers, for example). Search the index by author name to locate the sentence in the text.

FULL-LENGTH PROSE FICTION

This category includes adult and young-adult novels, as well as illustrated children's books.

*Acevedo, Elizabeth. "The whole meal?"
*Ahmed, Samira. "Can nature be"
*Alcott, Louisa May. "Does genius burn"
*Austen, Jane.
  Mansfield Park "I only entreat
  Northanger Abbey "I cannot speak"
  Sense and Sensibility "Seven years would"
*Auxier, Jonathan. "Nan would count"
*Barnhill, Kelly. "It's a terrible"
*Barrie, J. M. "Liza was in"

Beckett, Samuel.
  Murphy "The sun shone"
  Worstward Ho "Fail better"
*Bond, Michael. "Without waiting for"
*Boyne, John. "What kind of"
Brookner, Anita.
  "An autumn sun"
  "A cold coming"
  "She was a"
Cervantes, Miguel de. "Until death, it"
Chandler, Raymond. "I killed my"
*Childress, Alice. "I am lonesome"
*Clements, Andrew. "If you asked"
*Cline-Ransome, Lesa. "Every day I"
Crisp, Quentin. "If you describe"
*Danziger, Paula, and Ann M. Martin.
  "IF I DIDN'T"

345

FULL-LENGTH PROSE FICTION *cont.*

De Vries, Peter.
  Let Me Count the Ways "We're not primarily"
  The Tunnel of Love "The value of"
Dickens, Charles. "I recollect Peggotty"
Ferris, Joshua. "Some of us"
Fitzgerald, F. Scott. "So we beat"
Forster, E. M. "Only connect"
Godden, Rumer. "As she [Madame]"
*Goldman, William.
  "But in the"
  "I had a"
  "I'm gonna heave"
*Green, John.
  "At the time"
  "Getting Harold's engine"
  "Maybe you are"
*Haddon, Mark. "I know all"
*Harrison, Jim. "Keep an eye"
Heller, Joseph. "If he flew"
*Hiaasen, Carl.
  "His mother caught"
  "As the brakes"
*Jen, Gish. "At this age"
Joyce, James.
  Finnegans Wake "They lived and"
  Ulysses "Love loves to"
*Juster, Norton. "Milo nibbled carefully"
King, Stephen. "And somewhere in"
*Kinney, Jeff. "Let me just"
*Lipsyte, Robert. "But he wasn't"
*Lowry, Lois. "Yet he felt"
McCarthy, Cormac. "You forget what"
Mendelsohn, Jane. "Much later, when"
Morrison, Toni. "Her imagination is"
*Na, An.
  "It sits in"
  "This drink bites"
Nguyen, Viet Thanh.
  "An X-ray of"
  "She had been"

Obreht, Téa. "As my grandfather"
Orange, Tommy.
  "Except sometimes. When"
  "We'd been over"
Powers, Richard.
  "In summer, water"
  "There are no"
*Redgate, Riley. "Monday morning was"
*Riggs, Ransom. "Fireplaces were throttled"
*Rowling, J. K.
  Fantastic Beasts and Where to Find Them
    "I look back"
    "Little could be"
  Harry Potter and the Prisoner of Azkaban "And then the"
  Quidditch Through the Ages "Why should the"
*Saint-Exupéry, Antoine de. "It is the"
*Salinger, J. D. "If you really"
*Schmidt, Gary D. "The terrified eye"
*Sugiura, Misa. "I wish I"
*Smith, Alexander McCall "She nodded, and"
Smith, Zadie. "I am the"
Tan, Amy. "I went to"
*Taylor, Mildred D. "If that's what"
*Thurber, James. "Somewhere a ponderous"
*Tolkien, J. R. R.
  The Hobbit "In a hole"
  The Lord of the Rings "I sit beside"
*Van Allsburg, Chris. "I was listening"
*Watson, Renée, and Ellen Hagan.
  "Be butterfly stroke"
*White, E. B. "So every morning"
*White, T. H. "There were several"
*Williams, Margery. "When a child"
Woolf, Virginia. "What brought her"
Zusak, Markus. "A billion or"

SHORT STORIES

Atwood, Margaret. "There's no doubt"
*Bambara, Toni Cade. "So I'm strolling"
*Baptist, Kelly J. "Then I put"
Brinkley, Jamel. "But his life"
Chin, Frank. "The music's run"
Choi, Yoon. "Every morning he"
Danticat, Edwidge. "My Madonna cried"
*De la Peña, Matt. "But over time"
Elliott, Alicia. "Even though she'd"
*Federle, Tim. "The mall is"
Glaspell, Susan. "A new town"
*Henderson, Leah. "As I balloon"
Jackson, Shirley. "The people of"
Joyce, James. "His soul swooned"
Kincaid, Jamaica. "Wash the white"
*Magoon, Kekla. "To be close"
Melville, Herman. "I would prefer"
Parker, Dorothy. "Every time the"
*Peck, Richard.
    "The Electric Summer" "But most of"
    "Shotgun Cheatham's Last Night Above Ground" "Her tongue's attached"
Silverberg, Amy. "The age is"
*Ursu, Anne.
    "'I'm the pitcher'"
    "'So?' Logan asked"
Vonnegut, Kurt. "So it goes"
*Watson, Renée.
    "As soon as"
    "The dining hall"
*Wolven, Nick. "You've got to"
*Woodson, Jacqueline. "Your *only* ended"
Yoachim, Caroline M. "You run down"

DRAMA

*Bennett, Alan. "I'm all in"
Harwood, Ronald. "To carry on"
Howe, Tina. "You then proceeded"
Hudes, Quiara Alegría. "A boy enters"
*Myers, Walter Dean. "But my daddy"
Shakespeare, William.
    Hamlet
        "More matter with"
        "Tis true, 'tis"
        "Who's there?"
    Julius Caesar "I come to"
    King Lear
        "A sovereign shame"
        "Let him fly"
    Macbeth "Fair is foul"
    Richard II "I wasted time"
    The Tempest "Full fathom five"
Sheridan, Richard Brinsley. "Sir, they [newspapers] are"

POETRY

*Blake, William.
    "The bird a"
    "The road of"
*Cummings, E. E. "1(a"
Dickinson, Emily. "Some things that"
Donne, John. "Our two souls"
Doolittle, Hilda. "Can the spice"
*Dunbar, Paul Laurence. "What dreams we"
*Frost, Robert.
    "Fire and Ice" "Some say the"
    "Mending Wall" "To each the"
Hardy, Thomas. "And as the"
Johnson, Georgia Douglas. "The heart of"
*Martí, José. "I have two"
McCrae, John. "Take up our"

POETRY *cont.*

*Milne, A. A.
   "I am Sir"
   "I sometimes call"
Morales, Rosario, and Aurora Levins
   Morales. *"I am a"*
Sassoon, Siegfried. "You love us"
Shakespeare. "That time of"
*Yeats, William Butler. "I will arise"

FILM, TELEVISION, MUSIC, COMICS, INTERNET

*Adele. "To earn my"
*Doomtree. "Broken bones are"
Eilish, Billie.
   "I Love You" "Up all night"
   "My Strange Addiction" "Don't ask
   questions"
Flake, Emily. "But what is"
Friday Night Lights. "Clear eyes, full"
Frozen. "Some people are"
Game of Thrones. "The only time"
*Imagine Dragons. "Don't you tell"
Jaws. "You're gonna need"
Lookouts, The. "What a man"
Maude. "I want it"
*Meme: "Dogs have masters"
Mendes, Shawn. "Does it ever?"
*Platten, Rachel. "I have only"
Project Runway. "Make it work"
Seinfeld. "I mean, if"
Star Trek. "Make it so"
*Swift, Taylor. "My heart's been"
Top Gun. "I feel the"
Tyson, Neil deGrasse. "We are all"
West, Mae. "I always say"
*Ylvis. "Ducks say 'quack'"

RELIGIOUS TEXTS

*Papyrus of Sobekmose. "O Heart that"
Psalm 55, King James Bible. "The
   words of"
Second Corinthians 4:8, King James
   Bible. "We are troubled"
*Wheat, Clayton. "Make us to"

NONFICTION

Adler, Mortimer. "In the case"
Alcott, A. Bronson. "To be ignorant"
*Alter, Alexandra. "Jim Kay's favorite"
*Angelou, Maya. "The minister's wife"
*Anonymous child. "I never asked"
Aurelius, Marcus. "Even while a"
*Austen, Jane. "I think I"
Bailey, Elizabeth Tova. "But when I"
*Baker, Russell. "Life seemed to"
Barzun, Jacques. "Teaching is not"
Bauer, George. "The voice is"
*Belafonte, Harry. "You can cage"
Berman, Miranda, and Gaby
   Moskowitz. "Frankly, I didn't"
*Binchy, Maeve. "I don't have"
Buckley, Christopher. "Call me
   whatever"
Buhler, Brendan.
   "Think of your"
   "You are mostly"
Burney, Fanny. "If you have"
Caesar, Julius. "I came, I"
*Calvino, Italo. "A classic is"
Caro, Robert. "I hope that"
Carson, Rachel.
   "Hard upon the"
   "It is also"
Chandler, Raymond. "In spite of"
Characters and Observations. "As
   cowardly as"
Chekhov, Anton. "A carrot is"

NONFICTION *cont.*

Leon, Donna. "I have long"

Li, Leslie. "The grizzled vendor"

*Livingston, Donovan. "Lift your voices"

*Luce, Clare Booth. "No woman has"

Macfarlane, Robert. "This is the"

*Macmillan, Harold. "Jaw-jaw is"

*Madariaga, Salvador de. "Nations don't distrust"

*Malcolm X. "We didn't land"

*Marx, Groucho. "I don't care"

*McDaniel, Hattie. "There is only"

*McLuhan, Marshall. "The medium is"

McLaughlin, Mignon. "The young are"

McMurtry, Larry. "I have known"

McPhee, John. "[Christian] Menn was"

*Montgomery, Sy. "Many times I"

Morris, Jan. "Sometimes Sydney seems"

*Mowatt, Farley. "That mood remained"

Obama, Michelle. "I see now"

O'Gieblyn, Meghan. "Once she returned"

Oliver, Mary.
  "I had to"
  "Would one tell"

Orwell, George. "A not unblack"

Percy, Walker.
  "But for writers"
  "The total freedom"

Plimpton, George. "One heard the"

Reed, Stanley. "The earth is"

Renkl, Margaret. "If you are"

Resnik, Sarah. "You want to"

*Rizzuto, Phil. "When I was"

*Robeson, Paul. "To be free"

Robles, Frances. "It's everything I"

Rogers, Elizabeth Lindsay. "I was not"

*Roosevelt, Franklin. "So first of"

*Satrapi, Marjane. "The harder I"

Schulz, Kathryn. "Wraiths only scare"

Sexton, Anne. "It doesn't matter"

Simeti, Mary Taylor. "Strong and harsh"

Slater, Dashka. "'That boardroom,' says"

*Smith, Red. "Here were two"

*Soloski, Alexis. "Nancy Drew, the"

Southey, Robert. "The arts babblative"

*Steffens, Lincoln. "Morality is moral"

*Steinbeck, John. "You can see"

*Stengel, Casey. "I've made up"

*Stewart, Potter. "Swift justice demands"

Strachey, Lytton. "Discretion is not"

Thomas, Dylan. "I'm a freak"

Thoreau, Henry David. "I have a"

*Trillin, Calvin. "Blackstone declined to"

*Tubman, Harriet. "If you are"

*Tucker, Sophie. "Keep breathing"

*Twain, Mark. "Your skull was"

*Uecker, Bob. "We tried to"

*Van Gogh, Vincent. "First I dream"

Vowell, Sarah. "Our good ship"

Weiner, Jonah. "The sole decorations"

*White, E. B. "The time not"

Whitman, Walt. "And still a"

Wilde, Oscar.
  "Every great man"
  "Some cause happiness"

Wilson, Woodrow. "If I am"

*Woolf, Virginia. "Thinking is my"

Wotton, Henry. "An ambassador is"

Wright, Charles. "Nothing's so beautiful"

INDEX

ABOUT THE AUTHOR

Geraldine Woods has taught every level of English, from fifth grade through AP, most recently at the Horace Mann School. An award-winning teacher, she's created dozens of curricular units on writing and close reading. Woods is the author of more than 50 books, all nonfiction and many about grammar, style, and usage. Her most recent book is *25 Great Sentences and How They Got That Way* (Norton, 2020). She posts wry commentary on language on her blog, grammarianinthecity.com.